RALPH FRIEDMAN SAYS: *"Tales Out of Oregon* is different. The best description of the material I can come up with is 'historical' but it is not a history book. Rather, it is off-beat history, and if I could be more precise, I would be. But the city of history has many avenues, and if I am content to roam more than one street it does not mean that I have left the city."

Ralph Friedman shows
the pioneers and the citizens of
The Promised Land
in a collection of stories and interviews
with real Oregonians
from the first expedition in 1805
to today.

TALES OUT OF OREGON

Ralph Friedman

BALLANTINE BOOKS • NEW YORK
An Intext Publisher

Ballantine Books, Inc.
101 Fifth Avenue, New York, N.Y. 10003

Contents

Briefly . . .

Neither of the books my wife and I have published are "standard" works. (My conventional book writings have been paid for by other publishers.) Our first venture, *Oregon for the Curious,* is an off-beat travel guide; it has been called "different" by so many reviewers that we have come to take that judgment in stride. From the hundreds of letters we have received, it is evident that readers—at least a significant number—also accept with approval the uniqueness of the book.

TALES OUT OF OREGON is also different. The best description of the material I can come up with is "historical" but it is not a history book. Rather, it is off-beat history, and if I could be more precise I would be. But the city of History has many avenues and if I am content to roam more than one street it does not mean that I have left the city.

TALES OUT OF OREGON is comprised of four sections. Each is different in mood and form and style from the three others. Twelve people read the manuscript prior to its entering the print shop and, as fate worked out, the vote for the "best" section was equally divided—three each. I cannot tell you my favorite, I am too close to the book, but I would be glad to know which you like most.

The first section, In My Beginning, is autobiographical, but it tells more about Oregon, especially Oregon of the 1930s, than it does about the author. Some time back the eminent Western writer, the late Mari Sandoz, urged me to write a book about my wandering days during the depression years. I did not take her strong suggestion seriously until the tone and form of this book began to emerge in my mind. So I fragmented her proposal and put into the first section my driftings through the state. You will find me in the Springfield jail, on a mad ride with men fleeing from the state police, singing operatic arias in the pit of a cannery, mounted on the storm deck of a wild horse, watching stick games inside a tepee during an Indian festival, sharing a prune dryer with a girl and her collie, being tossed out of a country dance, discovering the Coast, climbing mountains, tramping over Central Oregon, tumbling with a bed when a freight train roared by, and much, much more.

The second section of TALES OUT OF OREGON is Birth Of A Book, the zany history of our basement publishing firm. Despite the many handicaps it faced, *Oregon for the Curious* became quite successful, so successful that we received at least 500 inquiries, most of them verbal, as to how we published the book. The details of our publishing venture are in this section, and of this part of TALES OUT OF OREGON the well-known *Oregonian* columnist, Francis Murphy wrote: "The success of the book is an absolutely fascinating story."

The third section, Leaves Of The Past, comes closest to being traditional historical popular writing, but there is an off-beat quality in the selection of topics and the way they are presented. In his phase of the book you will read of the first great cattle drive in the United States, the legend of the Blue Bucket Mine, the only Negro with the Lewis and Clark Expedition, the short saga of Pete French, the incredible run of Chief Bigfoot, a dramatic day at Copperfield, and the poignant words of Chief Joseph.

The fourth section, A Gallery Of Moderns, received the greatest publicity prior to the issuance of the book, simply because some of the 30 vignettes in this section appeared as feature articles in the *Oregon Journal*.

Here you will meet a man who as a boy lived two seasons with the great Chief Joseph; the grandson and the great-grand-daughter of the two men who, legend has it, "crossed the line" at the 1843 "divide meeting" at Champoeg to give the Americans a 52 to 50 triumph for provisional government; a man who seven decades ago attended the trial of Pete French's killer, Ed Oliver; an old-time Basque sheepherder; an octogenarian who describes stagecoach stations in Southeastern Oregon; men and women who remember the homestead rush early in the century; men who were punching cattle years before the coming of the automobile; and a ferry-boat operator of a half-a-century ago.

And there is also—well, look through this section and see for yourself.

And now—good reading!

Tales Out Of Oregon

In My Beginning

The morning fire in the eastern sky warmed every hill it lighted. The tawny fuzz gleamed brightly; the harvest had taken the long braids of the grain, leaving the stubble to August's sun. The amber hair of reaping crested the maiden-breasted hillocks and curled down the fruitful belly and thighs of the undulating hills. A slip of wind stole up a slope, puffed loose a spray of dust, and dodged into a draw as a bird scolded. When the dust had settled the bird wheeled above the slope, swooped to the lip of the draw, then spiraled with wings flapping feverishly, and flew away, singing. The boy turned from the bird to the hills again, looked long at the catharsis of the season, wrote it a poem in his mind, and waited for a ride.

From time to time the boy paced down the road, away from town, or back toward it, but he always returned to his knapsack. It was not as big as the pack he had owned a week ago, but it would do him until he reached home, now more than three thousand miles off, the way he was traveling.

He would never see the big pack again, he was certain of that. It belonged now, probably, to someone as poor or poorer than himself, someone who could surely use the shirts and trousers and socks and other things that bulged the canvas body and strained its flap.

Still, he was glad, eternally glad, he had had the presence

1

of mind to have shucked off the big, heavy pack. If he hadn't, he wouldn't be here now, warmed by the morning fire in the eastern sky, tingling with the excitement of a new land.

A week ago, more or less. The railroad yard at Sidney, Nebraska. He shuddered in the remembrance. Tell it once and forget it, he said aloud.

The bulls had been active, routing the bindlestiffs from the jungle. Every hobo the railroad detectives had been able to root out was roughed up and warned not to return. The boy had hidden in the wild grass, protected more by night than the bending blades, with only the lower rim of the moon visible through the blotched clouds and the geysers of smoke spawned by the yard donkeys that clanged dolefully, matching the eeriness of the nocturnal montage.

The bulls protected the sitting freight train as though it were Fort Knox. You couldn't board it or even get near it. You had to wait until it started. Then you'd scramble out and run for it, hoping you could hop it before some sneaky bull, staking himself out near the tracks, would collar you and come down hard on your noggin with his club or whatever else he carried.

Finally the train started. "Yip-ee!" cried a yard bull as he triumphantly waved his Stetson in circles above his head. He had won; not a hobo on deck.

The boy sensed something was wrong, had been wrong from the beginning. Freight trains start slow, he muttered, standing up. Even if you have ridden only a dozen freights you know something about them, you know that they pull out of the yards nice and easy, ambling along like the last thing they want to do is be hurried.

But this train was already moving quickly, gathering momentum in big gulps. The boy rushed for the train, reaching it halfway between the engine and the caboose. He thrust his hands forward to grab the rungs of a flat car, running alongside it. But it was rolling too swiftly. He felt he was being sucked under the wheels. There was only one way out: to push off and fling himself away. But as this determination gripped him he saw coming down the next track another train, advancing toward him. If he threw himself from the flat car it would be into the next track, into the path of the oncoming locomotive, as big and frightening as death.

It was then that the boy did something he could not now account for, because it was such a wise action and one which he was sure he was unprepared by any training to do.

With incredible quickness he slipped off his pack, thrust it away from him, and hurled himself upon the flatcar.

From Sidney to Sterling, Colorado he cursed his decision to leave the tall grass and try for the train and from Sterling to Denver he rejoiced in his being alive. In Denver he withdrew the few dollars from the money belt wrapped around his waist and purchased at a second-hand shop a knapsack, a shirt, a sweater and a pair of socks. At a hole-in-the-wall bookstore he paid a dime for a battered book of poetry. Then, before heading west again, he marched down to Skid Road and shelled out 25 cents for a hearty meal. In the year of 1933, a quarter at the right restaurant could put a lot of food on the table and when one is innocent of luxuries, food has only one purpose, to fill the stomach.

The sky fire spread, scorching the hirsute mounds, consuming the shadows in the hollows, gnawing at the purplish rims of distant hills. Noon came and went by. So did dozens of automobiles, their drivers ignoring the pleading thumb and the beseeching eyes of the thin, blonde boy at the side of the road.

He took from his knapsack two sweet rolls, which had been a day old when he had purchased them for a cent each the afternoon before, in Spokane, and ate them quickly, so as to be free for a ride if one came along. It had taken less than the summer to learn that stale sweet rolls could deaden hunger.

After a while a long black touring car, probing cautiously out of town, eased past him, the driver looking more at the hitchhiker than the road. A hundred yards down the road the car stopped. It had taken the driver a moment to make up his mind.

The boy sprinted for the car, grabbing his knapsack on the run. He opened the door, said hello to a big, solid, elderly man dressed in a light suit and a Panama hat, and made himself a passenger.

"Where you going?" the man asked, the automobile still motionless.

"Portland."

The man shifted into first and the car rolled forward.

"You live in Portland?"

"Chicago," the boy said.

"That your home?"

"Yes."

"You going away from home?"

"Away and toward."

The man cast a long sideways look at his odd passenger. "What does that mean?"

"I'm going to Portland on the way back to Chicago. You see, I want to touch every state. I've been all over the East already."

"You're pretty young to be doing it alone," the man said flatly. There was no emotion in his words. It was the voice of a man who had lived beyond the boundary of emotion; he had seen too many things and people come and go to raise a fever on essentials and events that would soon join the storehouse of past experiences, most of them infinitely more important than what he would find now and hereafter.

"Joseph Conrad," the boy said pedantically, "once observed that the best time to go to sea is when you're young. Since I couldn't go to sea I thought I'd see the land."

"Who's this Conrad?" the man asked.

"A very great writer."

"Oh."

They passed through Ritzville. "Not much of a place," the man said. "But all the farmer needs is a grain elevator, a bank and a good store."

He studied the wheatlands closely. "Good country. A fella could make it here. Take some work, but a fella could make it."

The boy asked: "Are you a farmer?"

"Was. All my life. Still got some land, but it's rented out."

"You have an Iowa license. You farmed there?"

"All my life. I'm seventy-five now. All through, but I still got some land. Never took a long trip before. First chance I've had. Wife passed away last year." He touched the brim of his Panama with the blunt fingers of a broad hand that had been a work tool almost all his life. "Nothing to hold me down now. All alone." He sounded lost. "Got these folks in Portland. Cousins of some kind. Spent a summer with us nine years ago."

They entered Lind and almost as soon left it.

"Think I'll go to Los Angeles after Portland," the man said. "Got a niece there."

"And after that?"

The man shrugged. "It's a big country. Got a lot to see."

At Pasco the man stopped the car. "Let's eat."

"Go ahead," the boy said. "I'm not hungry."

"That's a lie," the old man replied slowly and without malice. "Come on."

When they passed the great gap of the Columbia, at Wallula, the boy gasped audibly.

"What's the matter?" the man asked.

The boy exclaimed: "It's beautiful! Dramatic! Isn't it tremendous?"

The man leaned a bit to the right for a better view. "A lot of water," he appraised. "They could use some of that water back there, in those dry lands up there."

So they rounded the bend and found Umatilla and followed the mighty stream to Arlington and Biggs. The old man drove steadily, pausing occasionally for gas. He set no speed records and it was past sundown when they reached The Dalles, where they ate again.

At Hood River it was twilight. The Iowan paused for a rest stop. "Well," he sighed, stretching out his arms and producing a small smile, "Portland isn't far off. We're almost there."

But they were not almost there. Darkness quickly covered the rift of narrow road. Its shoulders seemed to have been effaced in the first fleeces of fog. The man drove slower but erratically now, intent on maintaining his lane and wheeling desperately to do so. When a truck bore down from the opposite direction he stiffened and braked and swung to his right.

Then, out of the maw of night, lights flickered, electric lights, patches of them, strings of them, promenades, looking like a hymn-singing convention of fundamentalist fireflies. This was the dam under construction the newcomers had been told about at The Dalles—Bonneville Dam, the first dam on the Lower Columbia, the second on all the Great River of the West.

Unfortunately, the ecstasy upon association with the lights was too soon adjourned. Darkness was total again, save for the meekly stabbing lights of the automobile. The road was even narrower and now wound with the frenzy of a snake gone mad. There were cliffs—the lights showed you that much at curves—and they were terrifying to behold, each seeming about to crash down on the road. The shoulders appeared to drop off into bottomless pits. "I wonder maybe if we didn't turn off on a country road," the Iowan muttered. And his shoulders stiffened.

The boy didn't know. He was scared. The terror of fog and wind and pitch darkness was upon him. His fingers lurked close to the door handle, ready to jump if the car was going to crash. He wanted to cry "Stop and let me out!" but the words would not form. He felt a sense of doom for both of them.

The man cut his speed to 15 miles an hour, then to ten. A car they had not heard raced around them and the boy yelled: "Follow his lights!"

"All right," the man groaned wearily, but there were too many curves and when the speedometer showed 20 the man chose to revert to isolation and caution.

But then a few lights pinpricked the moist curtain of darkness and after an interval of complete darkness there was a canopy of lights. And then more lights and more lights and Sandy Boulevard.

Somewhere in Portland the man let the boy off, in front of a large grocery, fruit and vegetable stand that did not have any doors. This made an impression upon the boy because he had never seen a food store without doors or a food store open at 11 p.m.

Somehow the boy found his way to Burnside Street. The beds in the missions were full so he slept on a bench. He had gone about as far as Lewis and Clark, almost to the end of the Oregon Trail. The exhilaration of discovery overcame his fatigue. He had traveled beyond books; he had come on his own. It was a moment of glory.

The boy was I. It is pitiful how much I have forgotten; it is incredible how much I have remembered. I find if ofttimes difficult to recall the names and faces of people I met last month—even last week—but I can recount clearly the appearance and speech and mannerisms and walks of hundreds of persons I knew, even briefly, when I was a boy. For as a youth I was highly impressionable; life was a series of indelible impacts; my mind was raw film and tape. With Emily Dickinson I could proclaim: "I find ecstasy in living; the mere sense of living is joy enough." And living was feeling, relating, recording.

The next morning I rejoiced again at my triumph: I had reached the fabled Oregon. And I quoted to myself the motto on the coat of arms of Captain John Smith: *Vincere est vivere*—To overcome is to live. It took me some time to realize that it is easier for the young to overcome—that those who do so when they are older, and in the thralldom of habit, and burdened with deadening responsibilities, are the real heroes. If the young object, I apologize. Perhaps I am too old to see all sides now. I would merely like to have it reported that I, too, was once young.

So I hiked across a bridge and caught a ride to Oregon City, thus establishing a pattern that lasted for years. I do not recall ever getting a ride out of Portland on US 99E that took me past Oregon City. There I legged it through the tunnel and waited for some kind soul to carry me further.

That day, as was the general rule thereafter, the rides were short: Canby, Aurora, Hubbard, Woodburn, Salem (where I spent an hour or two looking at the outside and inside of the state capitol), Albany, Tangent, Shedd, Halsey, Harrisburg, Junction City, Eugene. It took an awful lot of rides to reach Eugene. The people who picked me up were generally farmers or salesmen or merchants, going from one town to the next.

Though I saw these little towns only briefly they impressed me, in one summing up of my senses, as settlements but a stride beyond the day of the dray horse. They were all sturdy and slow-paced, picture market hamlets, and none seemed to have been scabrously afflicted, or to have had the guts sucked out of them, by the depression. The contrast with the maimed and wounded towns I had seen across the country was striking.

It was almost night when I reached Eugene, but I could not resist visiting the campus of the University of Oregon, little dreaming I would spend so much time there two decades later.

For some reason, when I was young, a college or university was always a magnet. I approached each campus as though it were a shrine and I a pilgrim in search of the fountainheads of faith. In my youthful mind, each college and university epitomized the holy grail of scholarship. I know better now, of course.

It was with the same reverence that I entered each library, no matter how dismal and impoverished. My thirst for knowledge was unquenchable and my respect for it unequivocal. Every library, however decrepit, has more great thinkers present than are found in the grandest of universities. Still, I have little respect for libraries which genuflect or bow in fear to the censorship of barbarians, whatever the titles of these idiots or the shape of their collars. A community without an open-idea library lives in intellectual feudalism.

Continuing on from Eugene that evening I hiked to Springfield, thus rooting another precedent. Try as I would, I could seldom secure a lift beyond Eugene, and when that was the farthest I could reach in one day, I moseyed on to Springfield.

It was not a difficult trek, perhaps four miles. Time to unwind and reflect in the pleasantness of the early night. There was always a touch of silk in the air and the breeze seemed to be strumming a guitar.

Springfield then was a small town, about 600 population, with one business street, dimly lit. Every time I saw the street, until it changed, I thought it belonged in a Western movie. There was to the street a homey, leathery feel; the tang of the plain; the stillness of open country. The street seemed a hundred miles removed from cosmopolitan Eugene.

So on that first night I found the jail and stayed there, as I did several times thereafter. The jail was easy to locate; the only people on the street were sitting on wooden boxes and straight-back chairs outside the little building.

"Can I sleep here?" I asked.

"Sure," said one of the men. "Soon as the marshall comes. Sit down a spell and take the load off your feet."

It was a most unusual reception—and I think that on later visits I returned to the Springfield jail, instead of trying the Eugene jail, because of the cordial casualness I always met in Springfield.

I sat down and the men continued their palavering. By and by the town marshall arrived and also seated himself. The crackerbarrel conversation continued. Wondering if I had been overlooked, I advised the marshall, whom I could identify by the badge pinned to his shirt pocket, that I would like to sleep in his jail. "I reckon," he said. And the talking went on.

What did "I reckon" mean, I wondered. After a few pondering moments I repeated my request. "Sure," grunted the marshall, a middle-aged man with a strong, friendly face. "Sure," he added. "But it's kind of warm inside. Set out awhile and enjoy the cool."

I was the jail's only occupant. The marshall said: "If you need anything, just step outside and wait. I'll be around shortly."

What could I need? The cot had a mattress and a clean blanket. There weren't any bed bugs or spiders. There was even toilet paper. It was the cleanest, coziest jail I was ever to call home in Oregon. I have paid good, hard-earned money for motel and hotel rooms that have been far less comfortable.

The next morning, after a breakfast of stale pastry, I departed for new discoveries and experiences. By the time the day ended I was not so sure that so many experiences in 12 hours were so good.

Firstly, I caught a ride with an elderly man driving a sedan. About 15 miles down the line the car hit a slick spot and was thrown into a spin. As it seemed to be toppling on its left side, I thought: At least I'll be alive. Then the car straightened but before I could sigh with relief it spun again, now to the right. My heart rammed into my throat. Once more, at least for a fleeting second, it seemed to be on four wheels and then it was off-balance, tilted leftward. Through gritted teeth I heard myself sobbing: I'm safe. And then the car careened to the right and I could see blacktop rushing at me. But somehow the driver brought the car under control and we made it safely to Cottage Grove.

"Well, far as I go," the driver announced, and we both left the car. I followed him by half-a-step and observed that he was quite stiff-legged. With the insufferability of youth I asked, "Do you have rheumatism in your legs? You walk pretty lame."

"No," he replied evenly. "I've got artificial legs. Got my legs cut off in a logging accident."

I was certain that he was speaking the truth and I shuddered—for him and for me and for both of us. And thankful indeed that when we were spinning, lurching from one lane to the other, no cars were oncoming.

My next ride was with a very handsome young fellow, a traveling salesman in his late twenties or early thirties. I sat in his new coupe and told him of my most recent hitch-hiking experience.

"I guess you never know what to expect," he philosophized. "But he shouldn't have given you a ride, risking your neck. He was just thoughtless!"

About then we had come to Drain. At the south edge of town we spied two voluptuous females, in their late teens or early twenties, standing alongside two pulchritudinous suitcases.

"Wow!" the traveling salesman cried. "Wow!" and jammed on the brakes. He backed his car with an ostensibly adroit manner and asked a needless question: "You girls looking for a lift?"

But now there were four of us and the coupe could only hold three. The decision was obvious: if I wanted to continue I was to stand on the running board. Which I did, anxious to put miles behind me. The gay, grinning blade drove with relish and with a carefully subdued air of suavity, but he drove slowly. Still, my knapsack, which I had slung over my shoulder, either was pulling me away from the door or pushing me through the open window and into the upper torso of the ample young woman on that side of the seat. The sudden bursts of intimate collision were not comfortable to either of us; otherwise it was not an unpleasant ride.

At Roseburg the dapper salesman pulled alongside a restaurant. "I guess you girls must be hungry." Since I was not a girl the message was not difficult to translate. I headed for the edge of town.

About half an hour later a mill worker, dressed in grimy denims, gave me a haul to Winston. As he drove he opened a paper sack, took out a sandwich, and bit into it. In an instant he spat the contents out onto the road and cursed his bloody wife.

"Damn that woman!" he growled. "She knows I hate cheese. I oughta take back this stuff and push it down her throat!"

"What's wrong with cheese?" I asked.

"You like it?" he demanded.

"Sure," I said.

He thrust the remainder of the sandwich and the bag at me. "Here! You take it! You'll be doing me a favor."

"There's an apple inside," I said. "And a piece of cake."

"Hate 'em both," he grumbled.

So then I knew for sure that he could see that I was hungry but did not want me to feel that the food was a handout.

How often had things like this happened to me in my summer travel across the country—and how often were they to happen again and again in the times thereafter when I was on the road. When the poor, the working people, the small farmer on the edge of despair, when these gave, they gave gently, without ostentation, sometimes almost in apology, and when they gave gruffly it was because they wanted to avoid the show of philanthropy or charity. But the middle class—and these included college professors and doctors and clergymen—they gave as though they were vastly superior to the takers, as though they either expected the profoundest gratitude or a quick disappearance, preferably both. They made of taking an act of painful humility and often I would go hungry rather than chance the contempt that came with a piece of middle class bread or meat.

The mill worker's lunch, which I finished afoot at Winston, was a feast for body and soul. I was patting my lean belly when the shrieking of brakes threw my nerves into alarm.

"Hop on!" someone shouted.

I grabbed my knapsack and jumped on the running board of a dark grey coupe. The car sped off in a backfire of pebbles.

"See any cops?" a voice inside asked. It was the passenger, a man with a scowling, tense face.

"No," I gasped.

"State cops."

"No. Why?"

"They're chasing us."

I did not ask why. At that moment—and for many moments to come—my only concern was to keep from being thrown off the running board. The situation was particularly precarious because I was hanging on with one hand, the other grasping my knapsack, which was being batttered by the wind.

"My knapsack," I uttered hoarsely, hoping the passenger would offer to hold it for me.

"Hang on to it!"

"Let me off!" I demanded.

"Hang on!"

If you remember US 99 in 1933 you will recall how crooked and hilly it was. The coupe bolted up hills and flew down them, gyrated around curves, spiraled, whirled, coiled, with the driver accelerating and braking furiously. Sometimes he decided not to brake and it seemed to me we turned curves on two wheels. And all this time, by some miracle, I hung on with one hand, and with the other kept my knapsack from flying away, as we raced through towns, passing everything we came upon and startling cows, horses and farmers.

It is amazing how dual our senses are, how much we operate on different levels at the same time. While I was being swept in peril on this wild, careening flight, and desperately gripping the window frame for dear life, I was simultaneously struck by the beauty of the region. Everything was green—so green; moist, spongy, brilliant, paint-splashed, fresh, exciting; greener than any green I had ever seen. So close together are life and death; so twined were the torrent of surging color and my uncertain hold.

At Grants Pass city traffic forced the driver to slow down. I leaped off the running board, momentum sending me staggering down the street. When I looked up, the dark grey coupe was gone.

All in one piece, I pointed my path toward Medford and reached it through the courtesy of a young missionary, just back from Africa. Learning that I was Jewish, he sought to convert me. I did not mind his zeal but I was apprehensive by his opening a Bible and reading it instead of looking at the road.

An aged man, his face a mass of gentle wrinkles, came bopping along in a small open farm truck and carried me to Ashland. He drove as though he were handling a team of horses and we had to shout to hear each other, because there wasn't any roof or doors or windshield to the cab, but at least it was a safe journey.

At Ashland the old man took me to a cafe where he bought me a piece of pie and a glass of milk and told me about himself and his family. He was past 80, he said, and he had come across the country on the Oregon Trail, when he was ten years old. So intrigued was I with this voice of history that I plied him with questions for two hours. He bought me another piece of pie and another glass of milk and wove a story so rich in detail that I could see the wagons, the campfires, the tiny settlements; I could hear the singing of the emigrants; I could sense the spirit of exhilaration at the trail's end; and I was there when the house and barn were built.

He was the first of scores of old-time Oregonians I was to meet. In the next few years I was to hear many tales of men and women, now long, long gone, who themselves crossed the Oregon Trail—a few were close to being centenarians when I met them—or whose fathers and mothers, as young people, had come West. I could trace the second generation pioneer stories I heard back to the 1840s.

The bright sun was arching deep westward, blinding drivers who had to confront it, when at last I left Ashland, the parting words of the old timer still warm in my ear and heart: "Come back and stay with us—long as you like."

A flashy new roadster halted near me; the driver, a middle-aged man with a nail file mustache, critically examined me, and as I approached he drove on. I remember him quite well and it is possible that I may have been the last person to have seen him for more that a split second before his sudden end.

About 20 minutes after he sped off, leaving me angry and frustrated, a quiet, affable, elderly traveling salesman, bound for Yreka, gave me a lift. As we climbed the Siskiyou grade we observed cars parked along the roadside. Up ahead stood a state police vehicle. We, too, halted and came out to see what had happened. Down the slope we saw two cars, both wrecked. One was the flashy roadster. The drivers of both cars were dead.

And that was how I left Oregon—on a note of violence, a wondering about fate, and a question of whether I would ever return.

More than a year was to pass before I entered Oregon the second time, again from the north, and again down US 99.

It was October and though I had but a few dollars in my jeans I had $100 in a postal savings account, my prize for a season of Wenatchee apple knocking.

What was Portland to a young migratory worker but Burnside Street, the skid road of town? For 35 cents a night I bedded down on an army cot, that must already have been salvage at the start of the Civil War, in a hotel whose name I have forgotten. The working stiffs on Skid Road rarely said: "I'm staying at X Hotel." It was almost always "A flea bag on Third" or "A flop house on Second," or some such realistic cataloging. For after a while, most hotels —to be charitable in nomenclature—looked alike. The dreary cots under the starveling bulbs dangling from peeled calcimine ceilings in the stifling chicken wire coops; the dark and dank corridors, reeking of some strong and cheap antiseptic poured on to purge the floors of urine, sweat and vomit; the hacking coughs of sick and dying men; the anemic glow of lit cigarets; the acrid odor of cheap tobacco and unwashed garments—the sights and sounds and smells were universal.

I have spent hundreds of nights in flophouses, bunkhouses, boxcars, under bridges; always there was at least one working stiff, generally a thin, middle-aged man, lying still on his back, eyes open, and slowly puffing a cigaret.

"What are you thinking about?" I once asked. The man turned by inches and when he had locked eyes with mine he said: "Nothing."

The skid road working stiff was, for the most part, a man who lived within himself. He did not tell anyone his troubles; he knew everyone else had his own. He did not engage in trivial conversation, except what was necessary: he knew what the other fellow would reply. You had to have a sympathetic heart and a respect for yourself and others to know these men.

If one word can be used to summarize the entire milieu of Skid Road it has to be, I believe, anonymity. Anonymity in the deepest meaning of life. As Skid Road was isolated geographically from the bone and marrow of the city's resident populace, so were its denizens alienated from almost every meaningful social content. That to which they could most adhere and identify, though they might not always realize what was motivating them, could also be stated in a single word: protest. Every significant action, however destructive these acts might be to themselves, was a protest against a scheme of things which had made them less than human. Those who were conscious of their place in the labor market sometimes joined together in radical organizations, where they felt a sense of manhood. It is difficult for most middle class people to believe, but the migratory worker engaged in a strike, which could cost him an arm or an eye or his life or could have him imprisoned for months or years, found more dignity in the battle he waged in union with his rootless brothers than he had ever known in solitary existence. The strike—or the radical organization—even gave him a name, his own. On Skid Road he was "Heavy" or "Swede" or "Dakota" or whatever appellation might be stuck to him.

The working stiffs came to Portland from all parts of the state and the Northwest; they trundled in with their tin or cardboard suitcases or bindles from logging camps, railroad sidings (where they had been gandy dancers), the apple orchards of Wenatchee and Yakima, the wheatfields of the Palouse, the Big Bend and the east of Oregon. They came with their slim winter grubstakes, watching each penny, hoarding their grubstakes until winter was done and work opened up again.

Some of the men sought jobs in Portland but after a while most of them gave up. The "locals" or "home guard" had everything; who needed an outside man when so many taxpayers were unemployed?

A few of the working stiffs drank heavily; every winter an agonizing number disintegrated and dissolved into winos or alcoholics.

You couldn't walk down Burnside or its tributaries without seeing the flotsam and jetsam of Skid Road. They drank everything alcoholic they could get their hands on, including the most potent of canned heat—stuff which could easily blind you or scramble your brains.

There is a single scene that haunts me: I saw it a score of times on Burnside and a thousand times elsewhere. A glassy-eyed, rag bundle of a man, neurally frozen against a wall, his empty hands fixed rigidly, fingers apart, catatonic, with a smashed bottle of wine or alcohol splintered and murky at his feet.

Once, as I suddenly came upon this scene and was nailed to a halt by anguish and horror, two giddy winos tottered by, observed the wine curling down the sidewalk in a dusty, spit-bubbled stream, and shook their heads with acute displeasure: "All that good stuff going to waste."

Contrary to white collar legend, most of the men of Skid Road had no affection for alcohol. Some of them might go off on a Saturday night binge now and then, when they were working and had Sunday to rest up, but on Skid Road the great majority regarded firewater with as much contempt as did the Salvation Army.

I am talking about Skid Road during the depression days, when it was largely a community of migratory workers. With the coming of World War II it changed its character, because the young entered the armed forces or merchant marine and the older and able-bodied could find steady jobs.

The Skid Road after World War II was of men who had disintegrated too badly to leave it or who were decomposed onto it. Skid Road today, almost anywhere, is hardly worth the symbolism. Geographically it has suffered from attrition brought on by urban renewal. Socially, all the vices attributed to Skid Road are common in the suburbs.

Another fallacy nourished by the middle class, which seeks to absolve itself of awareness by contending that the downfall of men lies in their own defects, is that a high percentage of the Skid Road habitants are former professionals —doctors, lawyers, teachers, musicians and the like. You hear it said: "Some of the brainiest people in the country are bums on Skid Road. It's full of intellectuals—a lot of college graduates are there."

It is not so now and it was not so when I knew intimately the Skid Roads of America, including Portland. From time to time you came across a man who had once been someone of importance, generally in a minor way, or who had had a profession. But these men were rare. The formal intellectuals, that is, men with the proper academic background, were about as scant as rich men posing as beggars (another fallacy).

Few of the working stiffs or winos had ever been past two years of high school. A good many hadn't even gone beyond the eighth grade. Most of the men came from poor families. A significant portion were from other lands. particularly Scandinavia, and they had gone to work too soon back there and come to this country too late to receive any appreciable schoolroom education.

There were some men who could fluently discuss ideas. I have heard more stimulating discussions and incisive appraisals on Skid Road than in graduate school seminars, but the men on Skid Road who could talk intelligently of Aristotle, Voltaire, Mill, Ricardo, Veblen and Marx were few.

Still, what few there were I later blessed, for they provoked me to abandon a defense of my biases and to search for truth.

When I came to Skid Road, in Spokane and Seattle

and then Portland, in 1934, I had read widely by the standards applied to an 18-year-old, but I was still ridden by cliches and conventional assumptions. One evening I chanced upon an informal four-sided streetcorner debate between Wobblies, Communists, Socialists and Free Enterprisers. The radicals did not shock me for what they were—they, too, were migratory workers—but for their ideas. Soon I was challenging them. I argued that they did not understand economic theory, that they did not know the first thing about American history. They flung at me lists of questions, statistics, gists of philosophies. Determined to prove them wrong I hiked down to the library to find ammunition for my support. When I returned the next night, to begin the contest anew, more arguments were ignited. Back to the library I marched and soon realized that in order to effectively demolish anyone I first had to read that person and in order to understand what the writer was saying I had to start with an open mind. It was very difficult, but it was an adventure in learning from which I have never retreated.

I stayed around Portland about a week or two. I found a few one-day jobs: washing dishes, chopping wood for fire, carting garbage. But it was evident that I could spend the winter here going downhill, financially, and I couldn't afford that. My eye was on attending college, any college that would take me, and since I had no counseling on the matter I didn't know that any college would accept a fellow who had only one hundred dollars.

So I lit out for the orange groves of California. This time I hitch-hiked down US 99W. Oregon was still green and the emerald meadows wore a sheen of rain brightness and a mystic air of wonder. Any moment I expected a leprechaun to slip out from behind a tree and take me by the hand, to where to I did not know and would not guess.

The little towns were but islands in these faerie vales. And when I reached the hills south of Monmouth, those bosomy uplifts that tumble like waterfalls into a scintillating basin, I wanted to go no farther. But then arrived a cold, stinging wind and I knew I could not stay. So that evening I reached Eugene and strolled to Springfield and slept in my cozy little jail.

Out of Springfield the next morning a truck driver said he was bound for Marshfield, now Coos Bay. So I said, Fine, let's go.

It took a long time for him to get there, but we did, and late in the afternoon I stood on the wondrous Oregon Coast.

The next day I saw the Pacific, at Bandon, and would have felt like John Keats says Cortez felt when he first spied the Pacific, except that I viewed nothing but a wall of fog.

Later, however, the sun seared the fog into little patches which the wind puffed away, as gently as one blows in a whisper upon a blade of grass, and the great waters lay before me, an illimitable universe of mystery, violence and beauty. The best I could do was recite Lord Byron. It wasn't good enough but it was all I knew.

The Coast in those days was a good deal more interesting than it is now—at least for me. There was a salty, palm-calloused, canvas sail character to the little towns, each huddled unto itself. There were few motels, as we think of motels now. Tourism was pretty small potatoes then. The money came from the sea—through cargo vessels or fishing boats—and from the forests and the ranches, the latter having a rude, frontier exterior that seemed to belong elsewhere.

Ten hours after leaving Marshfield, where I spent the night in a boxcar, I wound up in Brookings. The next morning I crossed into California for the second time in two years.

A slope of grass faced a rise of weeds and both looked detached and superior. And I was a stranger and rootless.

June, 1936. Somewhere along the Columbia River. I had come up from California to seek work in the fields and orchards but there seemed to be a dozen hands for every job.

I backtracked to Hood River and The Dalles, finding a few days' work there in the cherries and apples. The only opening The Dalles employment office offered was scrubbing pots and pans in the kitchen of a leading hotel. I took it sight unseen.

The usual frantic kitchen, with crises-psyched cooks gyrating in the normal mad tumult of sweaty havoc. I was home to Hades.

In the kitchens I knew as a young man none of the cooks or waitresses knew or cared to know my name. I was "Hey you!" or "Boy," or "Hey dishwasher!" Nowhere have I met such unbridled arrogance as in kitchens, nowhere greater contempt for fellow employees. There are many places I have worked where the human being was regarded as a nothing; I can't think of anyplace where I have been more of a nothing, and this includes cotton and hop picking—which is about as low as you could get fruit tramping—than where I slaved as a land scullion.

Well, I started in this place with a sink full of pots and pans and it seemed I never got ahead. Everytime I was about to reach for a deep breath somebody was throwing more stuff into the sinks or piling it up around me. When it came time to eat I was too tired and at the end of the day, which seemed like a week, the dollar a day I was supposed to get didn't look very impressive. So about half-way through the third day I walked out, not asking for my pay or telling the cooks to go to hell.

What now? It was Sunday and I was once again unemployed. As I was pondering my immediate future a bull-necked man with a reddish face and shoulders four ax-handles broad squeezed himself out of a car and grinned at me. "Howdy," he said. "Howdy," I said. "Fine day," he grunted, swabbing his forehead with a big bandanna, and rumbled down the street.

An hour later, when he returned, I was still on the same corner, still debating which way to go. "Lookin' fer work?" he asked. "That's right," I replied. He bore in with more questions, all the time staring me square in the eyes. Finally: did I want to join the Civilian Conservation Corps? Was I eligible, I asked. "You are if I say so," he replied. So I tossed my suitcase into his car and we tore off for Simnasho and the Warm Springs Indian Reservation. There, in the CCC, I worked first as a clerk and then on crews maintaining barbed wire fences.

The reservation was my first deep look at central Oregon. It was exhilarating, as much for its first-glance dry drabness as for its pastel flecked buttes, open pine woods, tumbled

hills and the snowcones of the Cascades. Several of us 3-C
youths climbed some of the peaks. None of them were too
arduous for me. I was young and strong and afire with
purpose. And I was wise enough to know that if you do
not climb a mountain the first time you have a chance,
you may be unfit when you return.

The views from the top would have driven my soul to
heaven and my knees to earth if I had not, the previous
year, climbed in the High Sierra. Still, no two mountain tops
afford the same panoramas and the sights from the Cascade
peaks were at times almost overpowering. On a clear day
one could see so far—a mist ocean of mountains and their
geometry of spires, vermilion plains creased against the roll
of amber horizons, the green haze of fecund valleys, steel
blue sheets of lakes, grotesque lava formations, darkling
masses of trees plunging down one slope and striding up
another. It was a world to awe the innocent voyager, and I
often thought: this is how it must have been for those who
came when there was yet no name for Oregon.

Three or four times I went with the supply truck or one of
the rangers to Bend and Madras. Bend had its belt hitched
tight to weather the depression but Madras lay shattered and
shriveled, wearing the face of a "blowed-out" Oklahoma
dust bowl town.

In front of an empty store lean men squatted, the sun
beating upon them, and spoke in vacant voices of roads
leading nowhere while behind them the door, which had not
been locked, creaked to the pull and push of a scrawly
breeze.

One night a week—I think it was Saturday—movies were
shown in the recreation hall. The Indians were not welcome,
as they once had been. Until a couple of months back, I was
told, only Westerns had been shown. Evidently the Indians
had gotten fed up with the exasperating dramatics of the
U.S. cavalry thundering through a canyon each week to rescue a beleaguered wagon train. One Saturday, so the story
went, the Warm Springs' wrath exploded and whatever ob-
jects lay near reach were hurled at the screen, the projector,
the windows and the walls. The brave paleface CCC lads,
most of whom came from the industrial East, dived under

tables until the carnage was complete. As I suggest, I don't know if the story is true. But I hope it is.

In the time I was there the Indians held a festival, whose name and function I have long forgotten, and their kinsmen and friends came from many miles around, in jalopies and buckwagons, to join in the ceremonies. They set up their tepees, complete with soft drinks, and commenced their rounds of visiting. No convention I have ever seen—and as a reporter I have covered my share—had more blackslapping, hugging, handshaking and laughter. Never talk to me of stoic Indians.

Inside the long house the traditionally garbed elders, sitting cross-legged on the floor, chanted or mumbled or played some game I could not understand or watched the stick games and the dancing. Most of the dancing was done by the young men, who seemed to have the beat and the movements but not the spirit. The spirit lay in the hearts of the elders, whose parched, deeply wrinkled faces reminded me so much of the ancient Hebrew patriarchs. When they departed from this earth they would take the culture of their fathers with them. Their sons were turning—were forced to turn—wanted to turn—to the ways of the conquerors.

Almost everyone gambled—the old men craftily and the young men with naked zest. Inside our barracks the CCC lads were rolling dice; inside a tepee the Indian young men were pursuing their own games of luck. It was hard to tell where the climate was more feverish.

The changing culture was very evident during the festival. Most of the Indians had never known a tepee as a permanent abode; the young ones thought it romantic, quaint or uncomfortable. Several of the young men dancing wore hose held up by garters. One of the dancers wore practically nothing but a loin covering and sunglasses. A beautiful girl, traipsing unsteadily on high heels down a washboard field, was attired in a smart dress and silk stockings. Of course I looked at her legs—and I did a double take! For beneath her silk stockings her long underwear showed.

We in the CCC ate well—but not so with the Indians. Not as much as we did they have to put on the table. Butter, for instance, was quite common to us but to the Indians it was a luxury. Their daily poverty was conspicuous and a few were reduced to the role of beggars and a few got stinking drunk but most were determined to be proud and independent.

Judged by the white man's standard, Indian health was poor, illiteracy high and ambition almost nil. But the very society which expected the Indian to conform to middle class mores and rise to its theoretical goals rejected the Indians from entering the mainstream of that society. What else could develop but cancerous frustration?

On Sundays, for their own amusement, the Indians would stage a rodeo. Mostly it was bronc-busting, the broncs being wild horses rounded up in the hills a day or two earlier. The horses were wiry, tough, shrewd, high-spirited, tricky and justifiably nasty. They wanted no more to be ridden by a man than you or I would. At the very first opportunity they made their intentions clear.

The canny Indians were as clever as their horses. They stood at the chute and breezed about how easy and sporting it was to ride these outlaws. Being excellent horse breakers, the Indians could stay with every thrust and gyration. Well, at least they had good batting averages. The listening CCC lads, whose experiences wouldn't have qualified them to ride a broken down mare on a milk route, sometimes took the bait. Then an electric verve of anticipation tremored through the Indians, followed by uninhibited jubilation when the paleface bit the dust.

Why the CCC fellows continued to be hooked by the Indians was beyond me. But who am I to be critical, for the fever of conquest gripped me, too, and before I knew it I had said: "Let me try."

Ere I could pull back my words I was in the saddle. Oh, the helping hands. And then, before I could really see the horse's mane, there was a convulsion of motion, a blaze of sky, a moment of being dumb alone in wild space, the fulgurous stab of avenging hooves and then the shock of impact. I didn't know where the horse was but I was sprawled among some sickly bunchgrass or weeds or sage, with a piercing pain shooting up from my wrist. And then came the laughing Indians, helping me to my feet and patting my back and assuring me that I had made a "good try" and next time would "stay all the way."

There were those precious days when I hiked into the juniper hills, mauve-flecked and ocher-streaked, rippling with rushes of tawny grass and breathing sage and thorn brush, and etched, where eyes from the plain could not see, with bands of seaweed green.

And one day a ranger took me with him to Sherars Bridge where, above the untamed Deschutes, I saw the fishing platforms of the Indians—not nearly as spectacular as at Celilo Falls, where Indians speared and netted for salmon in the boiling pools of the Columbia from steep basaltic cliffs, but impressive enough to remember to this day.

And then there was Simnasho, at the edge of camp—a wooden sidewalk leading to a small frame church and a house or two. It seemed so whimsical and without substance, shut off from the world of the reservation, and yet, somehow, in the odd web of this milieu, to be a part of the frontier mood.

After about six weeks on the reservation I received a letter from a friend, offering me a better-paying job. Unfortunately, it did not materialize but it drew me from the state and, except for two transitory visits, I did not set foot on Oregon soil again until the following summer.

For several weeks in 1937 I drifted about the eastern part of the state, sometimes looking for work and sometimes just looking. I put my hand to a miscellany of chores on farms, ranches, at homesteader shacks, in small towns and at sagging gas stations halfway between nowhere and neverwas. Sleep came in jails, barns, abandoned churches and storefronts and out in the open, wherever night might catch me.

If a rancher said, "You can stay at my place but it's seventeen miles off the road," I said, "Fine, let's go," even though I knew I might have to walk every step back. But I saw an awful lot of interesting country that way, some of which I did not see again for a quarter of a century, and some, I would guess, which I have never set eyes on again.

Basque sheepherders, bowlegged cowpokes, desert hermits, flint-eyed goldpanners, potbellied sheriffs and their swaggering deputies, cattlemen working their heads off to stay one step ahead of foreclosure, widow women who ran back-country general stores without asking favors or giving any, raggedy migratory families bouncing along on scrapheap jalopies held together by baling wire and whose tire tubes needed patching at least twice a day, circuit-riding preachers who could lasso a heifer as easily as exhorting sinners, big city drummers who rolled through the sparsely settled land in search of orders, rarely home and rarely hearing from or writing to their families—this was the stuff a young man who wanted to be a storyteller could put in his pouch for a good smoke when the time came.

Tell me, have you ever really looked at the sky of Eastern Oregon, ever really studied its cloud formations? Do you remember them, salmon pink, blue grey masses with pastel fringes, bristling howitzers charged with gunpowder, armadas of dirigibles, great hawks fixed in a swoop over the silent plateau? Fat fleecy clouds that strutted like gossipy geese across a barnyard sky? Tiny furry clouds that leaped along the rim of the hills like kittens at play?

The clouds, the draws, the wadies, the sage, the ghostly rimrock hills, the gritty pines, the far off slopes speckled by cattle, the nervous deer, the doomsday buzzards, the loping coyotes, the crouched bobcats, the traces across land that looked bleak as the Sahara—these impressions and a thousand others piled up that summer. But mostly I recall a brief nocturnal incident.

This night I was tramping a lonely dusty road when sounds that seemed to be music reached my ears. Was it my imagination, or some strange birds in concert, or a flapdoodling wind skipping up and down some draw? As I rounded a bend the answer became clear. There, on a slight knoll, was a schoolhouse, cheerful light pouring through the open door and revealing, inside, a dance.

At a time like this, how can you feel but good? The night was velvet soft, the moon bright-full and gay. I hummed: Buffalo girl, won't you come out tonight, come out tonight, come out tonight—though I couldn't dance for love or money.

So I approached. The men were tall and the girls were fair. The three-piece orchestra was in a happy lather. The sideline sitters and standers clapped and beat time with their feet. Platters of food, which instantly alerted my appetite, were crowded rim-to-rim on an oilcloth-covered table. I entered. A young lady beckoned with a smile. I took another step. A young lady said hello with the turn of her chin. I put my suitcase down. Before I could stand straight again three of the tall men were at my side, ordering me to leave. "But I haven't done anything," I protested. "It's not what you've done, it's what you're thinking," came the grim reply. One of them tossed my suitcase out and the other two made sure I followed.

The night was young and the girls were fair, but sometimes you can't win for losing.

Back again I came to Oregon in the late spring of 1938, this time up US 97 from California, and during the summer cut in and out of the state. There was even less work than usual. Times in those years never seemed to improve. I did just about everything legitimate I could think of to rustle up victuals. For a spell, it seemed, the only way to get a meal was to mow lawns. It got so that I associated lawn mowing with being broke and hungry, which perhaps explains why I don't like to mow lawns now.

Some work did turn up—pitching hay, binding hay, joining hordes of suitcase farmers in the grain fields around Pendleton. None of it lasted long.

The summer of 1939, when I came from the north this time, was a bit better. After hanging around a pea cannery at Freewater, I finally got on. It was hard work, dumping boxes of peas on the conveyor belt, 12 hours a day, seven days a week, with lunch on a hit-and-run basis, but the worst part was the layoff and the uncertainty. I would gladly have worked 84 hours a week instead of waiting around six or seven hours to go to work or to be told there was no work that day because there weren't any peas.

To ease the frustration, especially when we were told there would be no peas for two days in a row, I hitchhiked to the Wallowas. The vistas of the Alpine range were relaxing for they seemed to be saying that there was in life a grandeur and a glory far greater than my own problems, that there loomed for all of us horizons to outstrip and resolve our discontentments.

When the cannery at Freewater closed—it shut down

with a whimper instead of a bang—I moved to Walla Walla, where luckily I found work in another cannery. This lasted only a week, but it was a week of solid work. I burned my hands on hot cans and once another fellow trucking cans tripped and the load fell against and on me and I sweated like the inside of a tort and my cheap shoes rotted in the puddles of water, but never for a moment did I gripe. The exhilaration of working instead of waiting, the beauty of being assured that tomorrow the doors would be open instead of being forewarned not to expect anything, the joy of making an honest buck more than compensated for all the little annoyances.

With the close of the Walla Walla cannery I started thumbing my way to California. As I was passing through Newberg a short, round man in overalls asked if I wanted some work in his prune dryer. "Sure," I said, and we piled into his middle-aged Chevvie.

A couple of mornings I was sent out to knock plums. But most of the week or ten days was spent in the dryer. In fact, I slept more hours in the dryer than in the house and probably ate as many meals in the dryer as in the farmer's kitchen.

There isn't much about the dryer I remember. My work was very simple: putting trays of plums into the ovens and removing trays of prunes. At least that's what I think it was. I am sure that anything much more complicated would have been beyond my resources.

Although not difficult or heavy, the chores were tiring, simply because the hours were so long. Several nights I did not take my clothes off. Instead, I napped on the floor for a few minutes now and then.

This brings up the most interesting aspect of my dryer experience. Working with me much of the time was the farmer's daughter, about my age, and always nearby was her five-year-old collie.

When it came time for napping, the girl would sit against the wall and close her eyes. The collie would lie across her knees. And I used the collie as a pillow. Neither the girl nor the collie, both of whom were very sweet and everlastingly patient, ever complained.

Because I had read a few books the girl set me up as a

personal oracle, and night after night she would pose the question: should she marry her insistent boy friend or should she go to college? Three years before she had graduated from high school and had since been bound to the farm, but now she felt free, and what should she do?

Few people take advice, and none from me. So I do not know what course she followed. But whichever, although I never saw her again, my best wishes were always with her.

• • •

The late spring of 1940 saw me again in Oregon. Once more I beat a path to Freewater. Once more there was the long and tedious wait for work.

I had a few days in the fields pitching peas but I was always nervous there, afraid that my opportunity for cannery employment would be lost. So, in company with scores of others, I waited in the shade outside the office for the call that took so long in coming.

The applicants consisted chiefly of three groups: college students, dispossessed farmers from the midwest, and seasoned fruit tramps. The college men kept to themselves and put on superior airs; the ex-farmers were jumpy and eager to please the foremen (they would have taken jobs for half the hourly wage), and you never knew what moods you would strike them in, as small businessmen or laborers, because they were mixed up by memories of the past, the realities of the present and dreams of the future; the hoboes, because that's what the seasoned fruit tramps really were, took daily defeats with patience and humor. They were the true individualists, the men of the long view, though none of them would ever amount status-wise to a hill of beans.

One of the college students, a prune-faced, horn-rimmed English major from Washington State, was quite a snob. Day after day he showed up with a thick book, always the same tome. When one of the ex-farmers or hoboes asked him what he was reading (the other collegians never cared to know), our academic friend would cast a curt and contemptuous reproach with a slight movement of his head and return in that split second to his consummate dedication.

This had been going on for about a week when a hobo, who had been steadily watching the intellectual, arose, sauntered to the book reader, and drawled: "Well, has he got her in bed yet?"

The young man was so shocked that he jumped up, slammed his book shut, and hastened off to sanctuary on the other side of the office building. The fruit tramp hunched his shoulders resignedly and rolled a Bull Durham. And I stored that incident in my mind as more grist for the mill.

Finally I was hired, to work nights, the same as the year before. It was a trick, which I never mastered, to sleep in the heat of day, especially on a porch, but others fared no better. My job this time was down in the pit, a deep concrete stall where I wore hip boots and a rubber apron to keep from being soaked as I hosed down slopped-over peas.

Down in the pit no one could hear me. (Even on the floor you had to shout to make yourself heard above the roar of the machinery.) So, to pass the otherwise boring hours away, I entertained myself. I went through operas and light operas and musical comedies, singing every role I knew. I recited Shakespeare with all the open bellows of my lungs. I made speeches such as might have been heard in the Roman Senate or on Boston Commons on the eve of the American Revolution or in front of the Bastille during the French Revolution. Poetry—from *Paradise Lost* to *Casey at the Bat*. Long rolling poems, which I made up, spun out hour after hour and forgot when dawn pecked at the skylight. I drew up the lineups of football teams and announced games play by play. And I was an instant chronicler of history: riding with Watt Tyler as he led his ragtail peasants on London town, crying: "When Adam delved and Eve span, Who was then the gentleman"; with Francis Marion as the Swamp Fox raided the Redcoats; at Thermopylae with Leonidas; slashing a road to freedom with Spartacus and his unchained gladiators; at the side of Odysseus as he faced the boiling horror that lunged between Scylla and Charybdis; with the hungry-eyed Mountain Men at their wild rendezvous on the Green River; climbing the icy Chilkoot with the Klondikers—and more and more.

After a couple of weeks the twelve hours were cut to eight and then to six and then to four and then to two. The peas were running out. It was time to leave.

Thumbing my way toward California I had a premonition

that it might be some years before my flesh would again touch the body of Oregon. So I traveled slower, depositing each nuance of nature, each encounter, each reaching out and each receiving in the vault of memory.

More than ever I wanted to record, to interpret, to reveal this land, as I wanted to express all the rhythm and tumult of this country into whose bosom I had been born.

In the cool blue slant of dawn, when I arose, breathing the musk of the prairie, it was with lips probing for words; in the night, between patches of moonglow, in the coolness of the cordial breezes, I ached for words. The contralto voices of the living streams called, but I was muted by their clarity. Here was a world and its people whom I could not describe as I felt them. It was painful, frustrating, exasperating, depressing and terrifying to yearn to be a master designer and to be no more than a hapless smithy straining at the forge of language.

When I left Oregon in the fall of 1940 it was the end of my fruit-tramping in the Pacific Northwest. I never returned as a migratory worker.

Looking back upon those days, that era of my life, it seems to me that I have not the ledger perfectly straight. In what year did I pick hops near Independence? In what year, on a rainslick twisty road near Canyonville, was I nearly run over by a truck? Outside what town did a Negro youth and I huddle around a cheerless camp fire one night because the town boasted that no Negro ever stayed there past sundown?

Where have the streams of memory gone? Where has the wind carried off our bits of living? Under what stones do our experiences lie? I am sorry I cannot recall more except that which needs no place in a book such as this.

During World War II I was in Oregon briefly, stationed at Camp Adair, which the troops called Swamp Adair. I would up in a hospital and after a while had a girl friend, a librarian. She was transferred to Alaska and soon forgot me.

After she left I was taken by ambulance to Barnes General Hospital in Vancouver. If you had to be sick, it was as good a place as any. One of its assets was a lovely Red Cross girl. But, as my luck would have it, she was sent to France and soon forgot me.

In 1950 I had two companions: a wife and an automobile. In early May they saw Oregon for the first time. Neither seemed delighted.

The Oregon Coast road was not the highway it is today. This was particularly true of the southern part, which had so many hairpin curves that a straight stretch of pavement was looked upon either as a reprieve or with suspicion.

There was a particularly demoralizing pattern: the road sliding downhill at an angle until it ran into a mountain wall and then climbing at an angle until a "V" was completed. In dry weather this design, or even the sometimes interminable serpentining, would be merely tedious, but in the rain and fog it was nerve-straining and tortuous. We did well to drive 200 miles in a single day.

The fog was opaque and porous: you couldn't see ten feet ahead and the swirling, soggy, grey mass absorbed and negated the effectiveness of your headlights. It was ridiculous to look for a line down the center of the road; you were smarter to go by the shoulders; there, at least, some daylight struggled against the fog.

There were times when I absolutely did not know where I was going, and had I been wiser I would have called it quits at the first motel. But there was always the eternal and foolish hope that a mile up the road, perhaps, the fog would lift. I was sure that if I gave Old Man, our faithful 1942 Plymouth, the reins, it would do as well as I could.

The most chilling moment came at one of those places where the road literally adhered to the head of the cliffs tumbling down to the ocean. We had been curving for miles and when the spongy fog suddenly gathered into a wall we could not see a thing, ahead, left or right or behind, but I knew we had to turn. "Which way?" I cried. "Left!" my wife shouted. But instinct, for lack of a better word, directed me to swing right. As I did I glanced leftward and a hole through the fog showed what would have awaited us if we had gone left: a precipitous drop to the rock-studded sea.

It takes only a few of such instances to convince you that you are quite mortal and frail: that you are living on borrowed time, and who knows when you have made the last loan?

But even with the fog there was an occasion for bliss. Late in the afternoon of our second day on the Oregon Coast we scanned oceanward a massive form, a bulky mystique in the grayness, and as we passed it we wearily wheeled into a tiny sea village. A motel of comfortable design, looking more like a true and weathered hostelry than another dash of modern blandness, stood just off to the side of the road. We halted there and inquired about accommodations.

As it turned out, we were the only tenants that day or night. So at a price we could afford we were given one of the roomier units. Best of all, it had a fireplace—a luxury hitherto unknown to us on personal terms.

That night we sat before the companionable, chattering fire, my wife and I declaring with childish awe, "Isn't this wonderful? Aren't you glad we stopped here? Have you ever seen anything so nice?" And the fire replied with crackling gusto, cheerfully welcoming us to its fold.

The next day we did not leave until mid-morning. The fog had broken up soon after we arrived and from the picture window of the unit we could witness the sea in motion.

It was really the first ample view of the Pacific afforded my wife and she watched enraptured, murmuring and gasping at the play and rhythm and structure of the tides: the crouching feline tide, springing at the shore with claws of spray; the ripsaw tides cutting a path to land; the steam-roller tides, leaving even surfaces behind them; the tides that advanced in perfect semiarcs or arose suddenly in an untwining of hooded cobras or reached for the sky in blue steel spires. Where the tides had coalesced with the foreshore in passion and silently drawn away, there remained a thousand patterns, each with its own legibility, and together forming a mosaic. With the withdrawal of the next wave came new individual configurations and total compositions. The rapid changes of the magic etchings were more than the subtle beauty of the beach; they were the processes of life, in every philosophical meaning, at work in an open laboratory.

Before we left we strolled to Haystack Rock, the only persons on the sand. Half-shrouded by eerie swirls of fog wraithing around the monolith, the rock seemed unreal, and when a seagull swished out of a gray cavern into a scratch of light, and cried when it wheeled above the weaving, moaning seapools pressed against the nether base of the offshore apparition, I thought I heard a seawitch laugh. My wife shivered, too, but she assured me it was only the damp hand of the wind.

As we turned to look for the last time, the wind had paused for breath, rendering calmness to the slate blue surface. Then a stealthy breeze, stalking from behind a headland, ripped the membrane of the great ocean body and churned the water to pulp.

We returned to Cannon Beach many times, in the wake of the first romantic experience, but eventually, as the realities of tourism manifested themselves, our enchantment waned.

It was also in 1950, in late August, that the three of us—wife, car and myself—saw Central Oregon for the first time together. "Have a good look at it," I advised my wife. "We may never see it again." My prophecy would not have made me a good fortune teller. We have returned a score of times.

In September of 1952 we moved to Eugene, where I enrolled at the University of Oregon as a graduate student. I stayed on until 1955. Why I remained so long has always been a mystery to me. It makes logic only when one realizes how much of what we do is really illogical. We Americans are probably the most mobile people on the face of the earth, yet most of us stay too long at too many things and places. Chained from one day to the next, we do not have the courage to break our chains, and our tears only rust them and ourselves.

These years were the most stifling and barren of my life. It was the time of the toad, the days of the locust. I saw the brightest graduate students I know leave and wondered why I did not go with them. It was an agonizing period, yet this I have believed since childhood: that nothing is ever completely lost, that out of every painful, even catastrophic experience, there is a lesson to be learned which may prove useful in the future. Perhaps I am wrong. But out of these University of Oregon years came many lessons, each often considered in detail and often put to practice. The tragedy is that it took me so long to learn them.

There was one compensation, however: I acquired an education on how to use the facilities of a library.

You may think this very fatuous, but how many people really know how to fully exploit the resources of a library? Every writer should, and by this time I had been free-lancing for several years.

Through the University librarians, and particularly one, a magnificent woman to whom I was often a bother, I learned the detective work that goes into fruitful research. The chase can be as exciting as anything you have ever done.

I did not realize how involved and joyous—though often exasperating—library research could be until my librarian friend showed me how to start with an obscure footnote and track it, through other footnotes and through every kind of printed (and sometimes unpublished) material available, until the prime source is reached.

Researching thusly, I found much material that had not appeared in the literature I had read on many subjects.

The trouble, of course, is all the time consumed. This is the high, generally insurmountable hurdle facing almost all struggling free-lancers. Oh, the lucky people who get grants!

In the summers my wife and I, carried by our stout-hearted car, poked inquiring noses into as many parts of Oregon as we could reach. Before long such names as Burns, Cottage Grove, Florence, Hermiston, Ontario and Willamina became as familiar to her as the names of streets in her native New York City.

In the late spring of 1955, having finally cast off from the university, I was free to spend all my time writing. Since my wife and I had no jobs then, we started without a cent of guaranteed income.

We had, by this time, developed a few "accounts," meaning that we were stringers, or space-rate correspondents for some publications, all of which were trade journals.

One of these was a drug store publication and it printed just about all the prose and photos we submitted. An affluent free-lancer would have looked at the rates we received with a jaundiced eye but we were quite satisfied. This single account paid our rent and bought our food for five years.

Came July in 1955, we loaded the car, strapped our sleeping bags and tarps inside the rack that rode the top, and took off. It was to be the first of our extensive expeditions throughout the West.

Our bread and housing account, as I have suggested, was the drug store periodical. Over the years we visited about half the drug stores in the eleven western states, and in some states covered almost all of them. After a while my wife could converse with pharmacists in their own esoteric language and I could gauge, after a few minutes, how much of total volume was accounted for by the prescription or cosmetic department or the soda fountain, if there was one.

For the free-lancer, time is raw material that cannot be treated lightly. We sought to make every moment count. In a city that had several drug stores we found it expedient for us to work in a trail pattern, my wife one drug store behind me. I would gather information for articles and when she caught up with me I would tell her what photos should be taken; she had now become the photographer of the team. At evening we searched for a motel with kitchen facilities—rarely spending more than five dollars—and while she was preparing supper I would visit the stores, making notes. Sometimes, if the stores would close early, and we wanted an early start out of town the next morning, I would also take the camera. If the stores were open late, we would return after supper for photographs. Many days, we were in front of drug stores when they opened and we were in drug stores when they closed, long, long after dark. Not the same ones, of course. Some days we visited as many as 35 pharmacies. When we wanted to make time on the road, we paused in a town that had only one drug store, and while the tank was given a gulp of gasoline I would dash to the pharmacy, practically run around the inside of it, asking questions and scribbling notes, and sprint back to the car. The entire operation took only about ten minutes and paid for the gas.

Sometimes we picked up hitchhikers. We asked where they lived, and then I proceeded to tell them where the drug stores in their town were located, who owned them, and a mass of details about each pharmacy. One day I realized how much really useless information I had accumulated, and it frightened me. It took years before this data slipped away, to my relief, from the front cells of my memory bank.

But while the drug stores were important to us we were constantly on the lookout for other stories: trade, travel, hobby, personality, political, sociological, historical, ethnological—anything that showed up.

We began our journey in 1955, as we did every long trip, without anything planned. We had only the most general of ideas where we might be going. Any promising lead could send us off in another direction. On each trip we gathered material that has since been used by at least 100 markets. (I include a syndicate, which services dozens of newspapers, as a single market.)

In Prineville, one afternoon, while strolling past the office of the Oregon Cattlemen's Association, I stepped inside and heard myself saying that we were anxious to do a story on a pioneer cattleman. Until that moment I had not even thought of it and was almost startled by what I had said. The official took me seriously and after a couple of long distance calls it was arranged that we were to go to John Day.

Frankly, I had no heart for the trip. I was sure it would not turn out well. Too much time would be expended for a story I knew I could not sell. To prove my point, I telephoned the editor of a west coast magazine and asked him if he would be interested in an article on the Old West of Oregon as personified by a legendary cattleman. "Of course," he replied happily. "Sounds fine. Put a lot of meat in it." With that pun our fate was sealed; we drove to John Day.

The cattleman put us up at his home and he and I talked for two days. By the close of the second day he was convinced that I knew nothing of the cattle industry and hadn't the ghost of a chance of learning. He would have felt better if we had packed our things and left.

You don't have to be a mind reader to sense a man's fears. Not when he is almost shouting it to the mountain tops. Clearly, there was a mood of trouble. So on the morning of the third day I suggested: "Look, let me alone in your study for a few hours. Let's see what I can do. If it doesn't please you we'll forget it." He agreed, and I went to work.

By mid-afternoon I had a rough draft of several thousand words. He sighed, took the sheets and sat down in his recliner. I went out for a walk.

When I returned I heard him saying to my wife, in a voice agitated with confusion and delight, "I don't know how Ralph did it. I just don't know. He didn't seem to be getting anything I was telling him. He asked the craziest questions. He didn't seem to be listening half the time. How did he do it? This is great, this is the real story!"

"It's an old tale," my wife replied. "I've seen it happen often before. Some people have been about ready to throw him out because they felt they were wasting their time on him. Then, when they see the story, they're very pleased. After the first time they never question his methods."

Well, the cattleman fed us T-bone steak about twice a day. It had been years since we had been able to afford anything so expensive. I hadn't thought I'd ever get tired of T-bone steak but the day we left I was glad to have halibut for supper.

The story, by the way, made the cover of the magazine. As by-products of our visit we sold articles on the cattleman and the John Day valley to about half a dozen other publications. Before we left town we visited the drug stores and found them little gold mines, making about thirty dollars in two hours work. (Of course, it took us another two hours to put the material into article form and we spent money for film, developing and enlarging, but still, we considered thirty dollars for four hours work, which was really eight hours work, quite rewarding. In later years we would have thought we were doing a bad job if we had spent a combined total of three hours for the same money.)

We were hungry then, not only for money, however little we received, but to lodge a foothold in the writing business. Once my wife made a trip from Eugene to Pendleton to cover a convention, and while she was there she worked some drug stores. She traveled by bus the 650 roundtrip miles, spent two nights at a hotel, paid for eight meals, spent at least ten dollars for photographic supplies and services, took almost a day to write the articles, and for all of this received no more than sixty dollars. You could do better on relief.

When we returned to Eugene after our safari in the summer of 1955 we rented a house at a price we could afford. It was old, leaky, creaky and drafty. When the wind sought entry it did not have long to wait. The winter was cold (the pipes in the laundry room froze) and try as we could, we never did get the interior warmed up to above 60 degrees until spring came.

The house sat (or sagged) across the street from the railroad yards. If I had wanted to leave home I wouldn't have had far to go to hop a box car.

As in all places we had lived in, this came furnished. The bedroom was on the second floor facing the yards and the first night we slept there the first train knocked the bed down. It really did. The vibration dislodged the bedboards and we landed on the floor. After it happened twice again we simply laid the mattress on the floor.

The next night we moved the bed into the room on the other side of the second story. This was better, but now we found that the second we touched the bed it commenced to squeak. It twanged like a tomcat that had got itself caught in a clothes wringer and was blaming the world. If we lay in bed and held our breath everything was fine, but as soon as one of us breathed the squeaking would start again. So the next day we went down to a brickyard, got some bricks, dissembled the bed frame, propped the bedsprings on the bricks, and then it was only a matter of adjusting ourselves to a lumpy mattress.

There were other problems with the trains. When they passed, the switch on the oil stove was knocked from "on" to "off." In the beginning we weren't aware of it and wondered why the house was growing colder. The chill settled slowly, of course, and was in our bones before we realized that maybe the stove wasn't functioning. After we got wise to the mechanism, we always checked the lever after a train passed.

The noise was something else. We more or less became accustomed to it but our friends never did. It was disconcerting for seven or eight people to be sitting around, talking, and then everyone had to sit quiet and look at each other until the train passed.

After a while we could tell, just by the sound, what kind of a train was passing and how long it was. At first, when a long train passed while we were having company, we'd get up and pour coffee. But after the vibrations rattled a few cups and saucers and spilled some coffee, we gave it up as too hazardous.

There is an element of the gypsy in the free-lance writer who lives by large output of articles. Every lead tinged with the faintest flush of promise sent us on the road. We slushed up the hills above Willamina to find an old hermit; where the driving ended we were given a lift by horse and wagon to a remote cabin. We went hunting for old mines and forts. The state was our beat: Lowell to a pepperoni maker; Wamic to explore the Barlow Trail; Dallas to simulate a bloodhound search for a lost man; Frenchglen for the story of Pete French; the rangelands around Post for bands of wild horses. And many others.

Came the summer of 1956 and it was time for another tour of the West. Once again we loaded the car, stored what we could not carry, and took off. Two months later, when we returned, we could not find, within the condition of our pocketbook, a decent place to live. So we wrote our way down to California, making expenses and a few dollars to boot.

In 1958 I came through Oregon alone, gathering material for political, travel, trade and economic articles. As always, the state was green and refreshing, but the hand of urban growth had been laid upon city, township and prairie. From Ashland to Portland and from Portland to Ontario there was a metropolitan stirring; if the masonry of metropolitanism could not be seen, the spirit of striving for bigness could be felt. The Oregon of my boyhood heart was passing into the realm of nostalgia.

There were five of us when we came to Portland in the late summer of 1959: my wife, a child now, a dog, a new car (a 1953 Packard), and myself.

For the first time since 1950, when I was for the last

time a merchant seaman, I had a job: correspondent for a chain of international business newspapers.

In the years following, each opportunity that availed itself was spent in further exploration of Oregon. We snaked up and down every backroad we could find, my wife with three cameras and I with a stack of notebooks. When people asked me how many of the 36 counties I had seen, I replied, with a bit of a snort: "Hell, my dog's been in every one!" My child became such a callous traveler that she could not understand why her Portland playmates had never been to Sumpter, Hart Mountain, Butte Falls, Arock, Condon and Buckhorn Springs.

Out of our wanderings, out of the hundreds of travel articles I had written, out of my boyhood migrations, there came our *Oregon for the Curious*.

I have often been asked how long it took me to write the book. When I reply that it is a difficult question to answer I am greeted with quizzical expressions of eyes and words. But now maybe you know. For the book is not an ordinary travel guide. Intertwined with the prosaic information on covered bridges, Indian battles and old inns is the story of a love affair with Oregon that began when a boy of seventeen flung himself on the waves of his romanticism.

A Book Is Born

The first edition of *Oregon for the Curious*, published in March, 1965, numbered 134 pages. It seems to me I could easily write a book of 500 pages about *Oregon for the Curious*, most of it devoted to our experiences as a one-book publishing firm.

Two years after the book first came off the press, it (the first and second editions combined) had sold more than 20,000 books. All things considered—unknown writer, unknown and inexperienced publishing firm, no advertising budget, no organized distribution system, and other negative factors—the sale of the book constituted a minor miracle. Many persons sensed this, for when I was invited to speak to various groups—and the invitations mounted as sales climbed—almost everyone was far more interested in how the book was published than in the off-the-beaten-path places of Oregon (they had the book for that).

Of course, those most interested were people who either had a book of their own in mind to publish or knew someone who did. These groups combined, I came to suspect, account for at least half of Oregon's adult population.

The problem in telling about the book, as implied, is not lack of sufficient material but keeping the material from running over into a book of its own. It will be a difficult job, but I will try. This is what happened in 1965.

We (my wife and I) felt that no major publisher would

be interested in our book, for several reasons which we need not enter into here. At the best, we believed, an approach to "name" publishing firms would delay the book by a year.

Nevertheless, several persons sought to persuade us to contact a national publisher. The most compelling argument was advanced by James Quick, then book department manager of J. K. Gill. "Do you have $5,000 to gamble?" he asked pointedly. It was a good question. It had taken us many years to save that amount—savings that came by dimes and quarters and single dollars, money earned by grinding out copy 16 hours a day, seven days a week. And now, all these savings, all these years, staked on a single throw of the dice. But we concluded that we should publish the book and we resolved that if we lost our bet we would not weep. It seemed to us that the very act of daring, after a rather cautious life, was worth the money.

We have often been told, not asked, that the toughest part of our venture was in the writing of the book. Actually, this came most easily. I had been writing for many years but neither my wife nor I knew anything about putting out and selling a book.

While building a manuscript I discussed the book and its marketing possibilities with a good many people whom I considered wise in these matters. The only individuals who expressed any optimism were those who saw, to the exclusion of everything else, easy and handsome revenues for themselves. One suggested alliance could have led us to disaster. Had we accepted another proposal it would have meant agonizing procrastination, culminating in no book at all being printed that year. But once we had made a fact of the $5,000 gamble—it turned out to be at least a $10,000 wager —we did not permit ourselves to be delayed by the grey flannel siren calls of local Madison Avenue types.

For those who are dreaming of financing publication of your own book, let me wag a cautionary finger in your eager faces. If you seek advice, you will receive miles of it, tons of it. It is incumbent upon only one person (and we can here regard the family as a person) to accept or reject the advice. That person is you. No one else should be entrusted with decision-making responsibility. No one else will really want to be. If you accept bad advice, the people who give it will not want to be burdened by the consequences or with the blame. More likely than not, they will deny having offered their views. At best, many will shrug their shoulders, smile with ill-concealed contempt, and stroll away.

As my manuscript was fattening, I informed various souls of our project. At least 90 per cent immediately volunteered to purchase at least a single copy. Some persons said they would buy five or ten! These heady promises almost intoxicated me. My sobering period, which I have sometimes called my withdrawal pains from the narcotics of illusion, began the day the book came off the press. Seventy-five per cent of the people who said they would buy the book now requested free copies. (In some cases, request is a weak word.)

I did not realize how many people I knew—or was supposed to know—until the book appeared. Persons to whom I had never said more than hello—and sometimes not received a reply—suddenly reminded me how close was our friendship. Individuals who had done no more than given me the time of day presented me with a bill for services, the price being a free book.

As the first part of the manuscript neared completion, I started looking about for a printer. Representatives of at least half-a-dozen firms came to see me. All were fluent. Each suggested a style that was the "only one." Each guaranteed to "relieve you of all your worries." Each warned me that if we wanted "quality work" there was but one direction we could go. And I was given at least half-a-dozen addresses.

The multitude of choices and arguments led a tenderfoot such as I was then to confusion; confusion tipped me into frustration; frustration rocked me into despair. Even my wife, who has better perspective in such things, began to show battle shock. Finally, however, we made a decision and breathed easier. At least, we told ourselves, the printing part is accounted for; no more worries on that score. It turned out that getting the book through the printer was the most exasperating of all tasks.

If you have printers for friends, as I told anyone who cared to listen, you don't need enemies. I am not speaking of the wage workers at the machines, who are as good and as bad as craftsmen elsewhere. I could live with these work-ers, whose faces I never saw. Our problem was with the representatives of the firm, whose ostensible purpose in life seemed to be to drive sober men to drink and sane men to asylums.

Eventually, after many unsettling experiences, we found the reasonable understanding we sought. Even thereafter things were not perfect but at least we were never too far removed from reality. The days of the crazy house had for-tunately come to an end.

Sanity in our relationship with the printer came with the entrance onto the scene of Dick Mort, a young, clear-thinking fellow who knew layout and production and who at no time attempted to overpower us with his knowledge, double-talk us into untenable positions, or move faster than we were prepared to go.

The great improvement in the second edition was partly due to Dick Mort. It was also partly due to our realization that we could not expect to have the printer make the de-cisions for us.

Henry Lee, a straight-tongued man with a rugged, relaxed face, did the cover. He and I discussed the contents of the book at length before he drew his design. Henry Lee under-stood what the appeal of the book would be—the off-the-beaten-path places—and his cover reflected the purpose of the manuscript.

All sorts of lovely little things happened before the book came into being. For instance, there was the time when I left the completed manuscript on a bus. Hastily I phoned the transit company dispatcher, who informed me when the bus would be returning. I met it at the corner of Fourth and Morrison, after a painful, fidgety wait that seemed to span hours. Not until the bus driver handed me my plastic portfolio and I found the manuscript safe inside did I—could I—halt my spinning mind.

And then there were the constant changes that had to be made even while the galley sheets were being corrected. Al-most every day some place I had mentioned burned down or was torn down or was going out of business. For a while I thought of issuing the book in loose-leaf form, so that it could be kept current on a daily, if not hourly, basis.

Being an old journalist, the value of publicity was plain enough. But I knew few people in the media. Actually, and perhaps ironically, the only persons I felt I could approach with confidence were two of the most critical journalists in the state: Francis Murphy, columnist of *The Oregonian*, and Ed O'Meara, city editor of the Oregon *Journal*.

Ed O'Meara I had known from the days when he edited the Sunday *Journal's* "Northwest Living Magazine." Occasionally he had purchased an article of mine. Since coming to Portland I had seen him several times; the exchange of conversation was never more than a few casual words.

Francis Murphy I had approached two or three times before. He was always cordial and neutral, two marks of a decent and tough journalist.

I had no importance to confer on Ed O'Meara or Francis Murphy. Even if I had favors to grant I would not have done so, and they would not have accepted my gratuities. The book would have to stand on its own, which was the way it should be.

Ed O'Meara is hale, witty and girthed with sentimentalism. The idea of a modest-income journalist investing many years of hard-earned savings in a book appealed to him. He spoke with an admixture of sympathy and awe on the courage it required to launch such a scheme. "I'll tell you what," he said. "When the book comes out I'll buy a copy and I'll review it in my column in the *Catholic Sentinel*."

He was true to both promises. Several times in 1965— and several times thereafter—he told me how much he was enjoying the book. Each time I was grateful that the book had not betrayed his confidence in me or soured his generous nature.

Francis Murphy was the first person outside our family to see the completed manuscript and photo material. I left a copy of the text with him for a few days. When I returned for the manuscript I found he had made a small sheaf of notes and had some questions to ask about how I had researched the material. He was consistently pleasant, somewhat enthusiastic and abundantly impersonal. As I walked out of his office I had no idea what and how much he would say. Thousands of persons read his review, which occupied most of a column, before I did.

A family should make arrangements for a new child. The book was our baby—the first of its kind we had ever anticipated—and we had to prepare it for life. Many tasks were involved. One was the procurement of a business license, made out to Pars Publishing Company.

For weeks I had played around with a name that would be representative of our entire family. Pars was the answer: P for Phoebe, my wife; A for Amy, our daughter; R for Ralph; and S for Shmateh, our dog.

The business began with a very small filing box, a few envelopes, a dollar's worth of postage, no rubber stamps, no letterheads and scarcely an idea as to what was going to happen. My wife, whom I named Director of Sales, set up bookkeeping headquarters in a corner of a basement room, which on Wednesday afternoons was the meeting place of a Blue Birds group, and selected a bench near the furnace as the shipping department. The administrative base traveled with her, for there was still washing, cleaning, ironing, cooking and other chores to carry on.

As we gathered accounts we acquired equipment. Some of it was tinged with sentiment. For our wedding anniversary I gave my wife two reams of company letterheads; for her birthday I presented her with a deep filing cabinet, which in time also became choked with purchase orders and invoices.

The book was supposed to have come out the last week in February, then March 1, then March 5, then March 9. The delays were agonizing and costly. On March 8, for example, I was interviewed on KPTV. There was immediate viewer interest but no books were available—and so the value of the TV publicity was greatly diminished. Television, as I learned, creates instant demand but has a short-selling life span.

Between Monday, March 8 and Friday, March 12, 1965, there were anxious moments and stunning disappointments. The first time we saw the map in print was three days before the book was off the press. It had, in condensation, come out so small that it was practically worthless and when Robert Frazier, of the Eugene *Register-Guard*, in reviewing the book, stated that the map was of no value, I quickly noted my agreement. It was too late to change the map size short of chancing another long delay; had I been shown it two weeks earlier I would have spread it over four pages, instead of two.

Right then we vowed to ourselves that no book we thereafter published would be ready for the press without our having approved it in detail and in due time.

Finally, on Thursday afternoon, March 11, we were notified that a thousand books would be ready at ten o'clock the next morning.

Now the full weight of our gamble began to bear upon us, and for the first time, really, we took a cold, unromantic look at the long haul ahead.

We had ordered 7,000 copies. At one time I had considered a press run of 10,000. Why I had chosen 7,000 instead of 10,000 I cannot remember, but now, in retrospect, I wonder what insanity had possessed me to order as many as 7,000.

Have you ever looked at 7,000 books? I mean, really looked at them, as though they were your own, to sell? It is a shuddering experience. And when the books are in your basement, cartons and cartons of them, you can weep at the monstrous spectacle.

Have you ever gone into a bookshop and looked at all the volumes on display? I mean, looked at them from the standpoint of competition? And you, with your little book, up against a thousand giants and ten times as many betterknown pygmies. It is a depressing sight. (You see, I am speaking as a publisher now, instead of as a writer and booklover.)

With a great show of optimism, I reckoned that if we could average the sale of 10 books a day, we could sell out the 7,000 copies in two years. But after I had spoken to James Quick I had little faith to go on.

"What makes you think you'll do so well?" he asked, in response to one of my more exuberant moments. "Why," I exclaimed, "at least two hundred people have promised to buy copies! How's that for a start?" "Don't be so sure," he remarked wryly. "And," he added, with a piercing casualness, "that still leaves some thousands to go, doesn't it?"

Seven thousand books were coming and we had pre-sold only about 100, through postal cards sent to persons we had interviewed while bumping around the state. Advance orders numbered only 400. Only one bookseller had faith in *Oregon for the Curious:* James Quick. He ordered 250 copies, as a purchase, and made plans for a window display. The few other dealers who consented to carry the book insisted on a consignment arrangement, which we were then too weak to deny them.

Finally Friday arrived. Early in the morning a friend and I drove to KGW-TV, where I was interviewed. Then we dashed to Gill's, to leave a dozen 11 x 14 prints, which Al Monner, the well-known *Journal* photographer, had blown up from my wife's negatives. And then, O Land of Promise and Despair, we raced to the printer. Some cartons were ready; I had almost not expected them. We loaded them and headed downtown, giving the first copies to Francis Murphy and Ed O'Meara.

"Well," Ed O'Meara greeted me jovially, "I see you finally made it. We'll see what we can do for you. Maybe we'll get you a few beans so the book won't be a total loss. I hate to see a man work so hard and go broke so soon.

"Of course," he added, with a broad smile that was underlined by the iron of editorial responsibility, "it all depends on how good the book is."

He assigned Al Monner to take my photo and Travel Editor John McWilliams to review the book.

"Well, young fellow," Ed O'Meara called with a genial wave as I was leaving, "if you lose your shirt, I think I've got an extra one at home."

Then began the rounds of the bookstores. They were completed in less than an hour, we had so few orders.

The great day had ended almost as suddenly as it had begun. I returned to work. That evening I told my wife: "Now we have to settle down to the slow sell. A few books here and a few books there."

"Or a single book here and a single book there," she replied stoically. At that point, she was less prepared than I to enter a contest for ebullience.

On Saturday the entire family—man, woman, child and dog—journeyed downtown to see the window display at Gill's. It looked mighty pretty.

We ventured inside and asked a clerk if anyone had

bought a book yet. "Oh yes," she bubbled. "Why, we must have sold 20 yesterday." I felt as though the Ninth Wave had washed me onto Cloud Nine.

Television had sold books Friday and Saturday and its impact carried over into Monday. Meier and Frank, which had taken 50 books Friday, on a consignment basis, phoned for 100 books, this time on a regular purchase order. A restaurant owner in Lakeview phoned for two dozen copies.

On Monday I was interviewed on another TV station, KATU, and this was the day Francis Murphy's column on the book appeared.

I had long thought that Francis Murphy was the most widely read newspaperman in the state but I had not really realized how great was his credibility. On Tuesday we had an inkling. First thing in the morning, a phone call from the Oregon State University bookstore, 50 copies; a call from Lincoln City, 50; a call from Bend, 25; a call from North Bend, 10.

In the afternoon the phone continued to ring—orders from stores in almost every part of the state. My wife had a discount percentage schedule—made up for us by James Quick—broken down into quantity categories, but she hadn't yet computed net prices. So, while the callers placing orders were requesting net price quotations, my wife was feverishly figuring while trying to maintain a business composure. One dealer, who asked for a complete net price breakdown, closed his remarks with, "Have your secretary make it up and send it to me." My wife gulped, but evenly replied: "I am the secretary as well as everything else."

Later we received more phone calls as well as telegrams, special delivery letters and air mail letters in response to Francis Murphy's review.

That Tuesday we placed an order with Fred Meyer for 750 books—and now we were on the way. The next day, Meier and Frank phoned to request a second shipment of 100 and Gill's asked for another 250.

On Friday a photo of myself and a long article by John McWilliams appeared in the Oregon *Journal*, arousing more reader interest. Other reviews, in other publications, kept our camp fires burning.

By the end of March almost 3,000 books had been delivered to dealers, but only a few had sent checks. We wondered about the others. My wife phoned James Quick. "Am I supposed to send out statements to all these stores?" "You'd better, if you want to get paid," he replied dryly.

In the initial wave of enthusiasm, letters from in and out of the state were sent to "Oregon For The Curious," or Pars Publishing Co. When the letters were returned because of insufficient address, the writers sometimes queried Francis Murphy or one of the other reviewers. Later, through the intervention of someone I slightly knew at the Post Office in Portland, a letter dispatched to Pars Publishing Co., Portland, Ore., would reach us.

For the first few weeks we received at least a dozen phone calls a day from persons asking where they could purchase the book. And people we had never before seen came to the house to buy copies. Some came from as far as 50 miles away. One man roused us out of bed at 6 a.m. There was excitement and tumult in our lives; either the phone or the doorbell was ringing.

While we were seeking to enlarge the circulation areas in Oregon, word of the book spread nationally. Orders began to arrive from New York, Texas, Pennsylvania, California, Idaho, Washington, Alaska, Nevada, Ohio, Indiana, Colorado, Michigan, Virginia, Illinois and Florida. How many books Oregonians sent to people elsewhere we do not know, but there must have been some, for we received laudatory letters from every sector of the country but the deep South. Somehow, with what was going on down there and the way we felt, we were just as happy about the omission.

One of the by-products of the book was the therapeutic value I gained from it while in Providence Hospital.

Not too long after the manuscript was completed I had a freak accident, severing an artery and a tendon in my left hand. Early in April I entered Providence for an operation. It is doubtful that the hospital had ever known a less indomitable patient.

That first night in the hospital I was nervous enough to climb walls, as my wardmates sympathetically described later. Fortunately, I had a few books with me, and by trying to sell them I could take my mind off the awful event that was soon to confront me.

An anesthetist arrived to see me after supper and very frankly I told him I was scared of the operation, however minor it was. Happily donning a clinical look, he inquired with the detachment and tone of a scalpel wherein lay my fears. "Unravel your mind to me," he counseled. "Tell me about your childhood. Perhaps we can trace the fear and conquer it." This sounded like a bad Class B movie so I asked him if he had read my book. He had not. Now it was my turn to assume an acting role. "Don't you love Oregon?" I demanded. "Of course I do," he remonstrated with umbrage and pride. "I'm as patriotic as the next man." "Then you should get this book," I charged. "You'll discover the state through it." Perhaps he felt that I had gone mad and reasoned he would do best by humoring me; perhaps, I don't know, but he bought the book and bade me goodnight. And so I was spared an exercise in amateur psychoanalysis, without which, at that point, I could do very well.

I had taken four books to the hospital and sold them that evening. The next morning I was wheeled into the operating room. Everything was informal; nothing was as it is on television. I would say that the doctors were dressed as mechanics, or as butchers, except that they might not like this, and I have great respect and devotion for some doctors. The nurses weren't crisp and tense at all; they stood around slouchily talking about their children and where they were going to shop. Not that I minded the scene; it just seemed strange; nothing at all like TV drama or popular fiction. Everything was so casual; and in the middle of a joke I was plunged into a void which seemed but a moment when I awoke, though hours had passed.

Consciousness returned in the recovery room. "Nurse, I'm in pain," I groaned hoarsely. "Yes, Mr. Friedman." A form at my side. "Nurse, nurse." "Yes, Mr. Friedman." A shadow advancing. "Nurse, please." "Yes, Mr. Friedman." The brush of footsteps. My first thought: how patient they are. Then, I wondered numbly, how do they know my name? Someone said: "He looks like he might be ready to be taken out." A voice at my ear: "What's your name?" "Ben Casey," I drawled. "He's all right!" and I was wheeled out.

My wife was with me when I was returned to the ward. I was in deep discomfort and could scarcely speak, but as she left I whispered, at least I think I did: "Bring more books."

Well, I was in the hospital about five days and sold about 20 books. I could have sold many more but I was too weak and, also, I underestimated the potential. I sold books to my wardmates and to nurses and doctors and technicians and to visitors. Actually, at least eight people came into the ward just to purchase books from me. At least another dozen brought books, obtained elsewhere, to have autographed. My talking about the book and selling it took my mind off my physical troubles to an appreciable degree, and permitted time to pass more easily, for I found that I could not read. Before one injection of drugs had a chance to settle itself, I was needled again. There was no rest for the wretched.

All through April the book sold like it was redeemable in gold bonds. Not exactly, of course, but sometimes it seemed that way to us. In May it began to slow down, though we still averaged 150 books sold per week. And then I began to experience the manic-depressive minds of some book merchants.

When the book was moving well I was warmly welcomed. "Where have you been? How are you? You must come in more often!" Everything was peaches and cream. But when the book slowed down my presence was anathema. "Oh, it's you again. Can't you see I'm busy?" And sometimes I was so completely ignored that I felt I would be more conspicuous if I had been swept under the carpet.

By the end of June we were rationing books. The mountain of cartons had evaporated to a pimple on the floor. We sighed and ordered another 3,500 copies. They were promised for August 1 and arrived July 30. I bowed to the printers.

In the third week of July, exhausted from publishing and writing (I had continued my free-lance work throughout), we drove to the coast for a week's rest. When we returned, on a Sunday, we found a special delivery letter from a woman in Berkeley, requesting immediate mailing of a book.

The letter contained a review which had appeared in the San Francisco *Chronicle* of July 18, the day after we had left for the coast. Monday morning, as I prepared to leave for the neighborhood post office station, where our mail had been held, I remarked to my wife: "I'll bet there are ten orders as a result of that review." "Maybe," she commented doubtfully.

I dumped the mail into a shopping bag, drove home, and started emptying the contents. Within a moment it became evident that I had committed a massive understatement. The reaction to the *Chronicle* article was phenomenal: we counted orders from about 100 California communities. Months later—indeed, more than a year later—we were still receiving orders inspired by that review. All told, the *Chronicle* article accounted for the sale of more than 500 books.

Later, after we had received an almost appalling number of letters from Californians who wrote that because of the book they had purchased land in Oregon and were seeking to induce their friends to join them here, I began to acquire guilt feelings. The book wasn't meant to increase the population of the state but somehow the Californians—and others— couldn't understand this. I wrote a tongue-in-cheek article, which the Oregon *Journal* printed, advising out-of-staters to stay away. "Oregon is a lovely place to visit," I began, "but it is a mess to live in." Unfortunately, the only people who took these words seriously were a few Oregonians. "How can you tell such lies!" they demanded.

A number of the *Chronicle* readers who immediately wrote us wanted copies before the new run would be off the press, so my wife rushed around, buying up what she could find, at retail prices. It was an odd way to run a business, but our entire venture had been conducted in a not altogether conventional manner.

The second edition did even better than the first. It had its own excitement, too, but nothing can equal the first flush of adventure.

As stated at the beginning, the book (first and second editions combined) sold more than 20,000 copies in the first two years. This may not seem much, until you consider that the book is limited to a single state; that most travel books do not sell 10,000 copies nationally; that more than 90 per cent of privately published books do not sell as many as 500 copies; and that, as I must repeat and emphasize, the book was published and distributed by a pair of amateurs.

In the spring of 1965 we were often complimented upon the quality of the book. After that, much of the talk turned to money. "You're getting rich, aren't you?" "Making lots of money?" "You must be rolling in dough." "I think I'll write a book and get prosperous."

It took the sale of 20,000 copies for us to break even—not in out-of-pocket expense, which is all most people consider important, but in total time and effort, which is the way a professional writer looks at things. In other words, if I had written for magazines and newspapers instead of spending all that time and energy on the book—all phases of it, from research to distribution—I would have received as much money as we netted from the sale of 20,000 copies.

Still, in the summing up, while we are grateful that we did not lose money, the matter of profit became less a cardinal theme as the months went by. Our lives were charged with a new kind of electricity; something was always happening. We met hundreds of people we might never have known. Oregon became more intimate to us, through phone calls and letters and personal visits. The education we received was priceless.

"Fame" and "exposure" were not important; these are ephemeral things. But the confidence we gained in our ability to triumph in alien fields gave us a certain kind of strength, poise and sophistication we did not have before.

Maybe we could never do it again, but we had tasted the glory of triumph once, and we would not soon forget it.

Leaves of the Past

Over the years—since 1950—I have written scores of historical articles on Oregon. They have covered every period and every part of the state. A few of my favorites are included in this section. The others I wrote specially for this book.

One article has particular interest—"End of an Empire," the story of Pete French. It has significance here because there is more on Pete French in the section: A GALLERY OF MODERNS. These, vignettes of men who grew up in the Pete French country, are based on interviews made almost a decade after my research for "End of an Empire." If this proves anything, it is, it seems to me, that Pete French grows more virtuous as time passes.

The Great Cattle Drive*

Five years before Texas cowboys started driving herds of wiry Longhorns into Shreveport and New Orleans, 12 years before Jack Cureton began the arduous two-year operation of moving cattle overland to San Francisco from Texas to supply beef for the Gold Rush thousands, and a full 28 years before the Cherokee trader, Jesse Chisholm, marked the trail from Texas to Abilene, the West knew its first cattle drive.

The year was 1837, and Texas had nothing to do with it. The route lay from the Bay Area of California to Willamette Settlement in Oregon, 30 miles from the Great River of the West, the Columbia, and the hero had never been a cattle raiser or cow-puncher.

This trailblazer, an ex-cabinetmaker named Ewing Young, was a man of resourcefulness and courage, however, and years of rugged outdoor living had prepared him for this challenging assignment. The black-bearded giant had left his turning lathe in Tennessee to take up a life of trapping, and for 12 years was the central figure in the fur trade of the Far Southwest, where the Mexicans knew him as Joaquin Joon.

Young first came to California from New Mexico in the winter of 1828-29 with a trapping party, working the streams north to the Tuolumne. He returned to Taos in the spring to marry a Mexican woman, held with her a spell, and came back to California in 1831. He was a Mountain Man, too restless to stay put. For the next three years, until he met Hall J. Kelley, "The Apostle of Oregon," Young moved far and swiftly, leaving few traces.

Kelley was a Boston schoolteacher who had taken upon himself the task of being the chief propagandist of the "On to Oregon" movement. He was twenty-six when he began writing on Oregon and forty-three when he set out for the

*Reprinted from *Westways,* June 1955.

"promised land." Meeting Young in California, he sold him on Oregon, and the two, together with five other men and 98 horses, began the long trek north.

Along the way they were joined by nine men with 56 horses, and all went well, except for five desertions and some bolting steeds, until they reached Fort Vancouver. Governor Figueroa of California had sent a letter by schooner to Dr. John McLoughlin, Chief Factor of the Columbia District for the Hudson's Bay Company, accusing the Young-Kelley party of being horse thieves, and the stern "White Headed Eagle" refused to permit them into his compound.

Although the charge was false, Young, who turned to farming, lived under a cloud for two years, until the arrival of W. A. Slacum. Sent out by President Jackson to survey the Oregon country without arousing British suspicions, Slacum exonerated Young. More important, he assisted in organizing the Willamette Cattle Company, of which Young was made president. P. L. Edwards, whose diary gives us the keenest insights of the drive, was elected treasurer.

The company was the first community enterprise backed by all Oregon elements, and upon its success depended the fate of the handful of American settlers, new and cattle-poor. Without proper livestock they could neither expand nor raise their standard of living.

On January 17, 1837, Young, Edwards and nine other Oregon settlers left for California on the American brig *Loriot*, which Slacum had secured, to buy and bring back cattle. After pausing at Fort Ross, where the men were left off to work at Cooper's Mill until the drive was ready, the *Loriot* proceeded to Monterey, where Young and Edwards sought permission from General Vallejo to take cattle out of the country. Vallejo replied that it was the prerogative of the civil government at Santa Barbara, and so Young went there. Finally, with Vallejo's aid, approval was granted.

Edwards went north to recall the men while Young purchased horses near Santa Cruz and drove them to San Jose. The Spanish cattle, slim-flanked, "wild, snorting brutes," were obtained from the missions at San Jose and San Francisco. Altogether, Young bought 800 cattle at $3.00 a head and 40 horses at $12 a head, with the bill coming to $2,880, almost exhausting the company's funds.

The wildest cattle were starved and beaten to subdue them, but then they were too weak to travel, and many soon collapsed. By the time the first obstacle, the San Joaquin River, was reached, on June 25, 80 animals were missing.

Young looked upon the San Joaquin not only as a barrier but as a training ground for the numerous rivers ahead. A strong corral was built on the shore, and cattle driven into it. Three weeks later, on July 12, a few cows were "induced" to follow their calves, which were reluctantly towed across by drovers in a canoe.

The next day a mass crossing was attempted, but in mid-stream the herd panicked and thrashed back, leaving 17 cattle drowned.

What to do now? Young pondered broodily and came up with a last alternative. The animals would be lassoed and towed across singly. This nerve-wrecking chore took a week, leaving the men, who at night were busy with herding and guarding on both sides of the river, weary and irritable.

None was more exasperated than Edwards who, together with Young, had worked harder than anyone else. When the cattle had finally crossed the river, Edwards, riding to a new encampment, saw the horse he had been leading, loaded with the party's ammunition, jerk away and dash into a pond. All the powder was soaked, forcing Edwards to return to Yerba Buena for more ammunition. Little wonder he cried out in his diary: "The last month, what it has been! Little sleep, much fatigue, hardly time to eat, mosquitoes, cattle breaking like so many evil spirits, and scattering to the four winds, men ill-natured and quarreling, another month like the past, God Avert! Who can describe it?"

But there was progress. At least the distance was narrowed, one grimy, red-eyed mile after mile, and on August 20 the party successfully forded the Sacramento River not far from its source.

Now the country was mountainous, with each hill higher than the one climbed. Pointing to a yet steeper mountain that blocked their path, Young challenged Edwards, "Now, if you are a philosopher, show yourself one!"

Young himself retained the philosophical mien of the Mountain Man when some of his cattle escaped into the thick bushes, but he put his patience aside when rebellion threatened. Tired of eating dried meat, the drovers demanded a beef be killed. Young refused, stating that the meat would have to be carried over the range ahead, and the party was already overtired. "Then we'll give the order ourselves!" one of the men shouted. Young looked at him with the coldness of one accustomed to danger, and replied, "Kill at your peril." The men backed down and the drive continued.

On September 12 the cattle came off the Siskiyous into the Rogue River Valley, but the party's troubles were not over. In 1835 some Indians to the north had attacked a party which included several men now with Young, and these spoke privately of revenge. It was only after one of the men killed an Indian boy approaching the camp in friendly manner that Young learned what was up. He ordered the men to cease their attacks, and insubordination flared anew. With knife and gun pointed at him, the men threatened Young's life. But he faced them down again, and once more an uneasy peace was restored.

Word of the unwarranted slaying filtered north and several days later an ambush was attempted. Young, however, had prepared for such an eventuality, and the attack was quickly repulsed.

Now, nearing their destination, the men's spirits rose. The grass seemed lusher, the cattle tamer. In the middle of October, nine months after its departure, the party reached Willamette Settlement, to feverish rejoicing, and the great cattle drive was over. The 632 cattle which survived were sold at $7.67 a head, with drovers being paid one dollar a day wages in cattle.

For all who participated, the drive was an unforgettable experience. Yet, as P. L. Edwards later wrote: "Few of our party, perhaps none, would have ventured on the enterprise could they have foreseen all its difficulties. . . . Most of the party cursed the day on which they were engaged, and would hardly have exchanged a draught of cool water for their share of the profits."

Luck, Legend and a Liar*

A legend, a lucky millwright, and a liar . . .
Thus began the tale of Eastern Oregon gold.

The legend is made of that gossamer stuff of history floating in the air of romance; it has the tenuousness of myth, out of which storytellers weave fables, and the substance of possibility, from which hope is born.

The lucky millwright is real enough; his deed was very simple; as prosaic as any incredible feat.

And the liar—he is a combination of all things, an embodiment of the diverse elements that led to the wild period of roaring gold camps in the tranquil shade of Eastern Oregon's hazy Blue Mountains.

This is the legend:

One autumn day in 1845, a section of Meek's Cut-Off Party, desperately groping for a more direct route from Ft. Hall to the Willamette Valley, paused their grimy wagons by a rippling stream somewhere on the high desert of eastern or central Oregon.

(Was the river the Snake, Malheur, John Day, Crooked or Deschutes? A hundred expeditions later went broke guessing vainly.)

Camp was made. Women washed clothes and children splashed in the trapped pools of the stream. Men, eager to fatten the skinny larder, tried fishing, but the water ran too swift for their lines.

"Look at all the pretty yellow pebbles!" a child cried.

"There's lots of them!" another exclaimed. "See!" And pointed along the water's edge, where the butter-colored rocks lay as far up and down the stream as anyone could see.

"Let's pick them up," a boy suggested, reaching for a laundry bucket, painted blue: this blue bucket was to be the "hero" of the legend.

*Reprinted from *Cascades*, June 1962.

While the bucket was being filled, a girl pulling up grass shrilled, "More!" Her father looked at the roots and went for a shovel. Deep as he dug he found yellow pebbles. "Funny," he muttered, and put away the shovel.

The train's blacksmith, curious, pounded a pebble on a wagon tire. It was softer than lead, which someone thought it was. Others said it was copper. One man called it brass! "Toughest I ever seen," growled the blacksmith. Flattened thin, the pebble still hung together. "Hmmmm," mused the blacksmith. He tried it as a sinker on his fish line. It worked. More such sinkers were made. The emigrants had a batch of fresh fish for supper. It was the biggest, most delicious meal they had had in a long, long time.

When camp was broken the next morning, the children wanted to take along the blue bucket filled with yellow pebbles, but they were told the scrawny oxen had enough to pull. "You'll see even prettier rocks where we're going," their parents said.

By the time the emigrants who were to become part of a legend had reached the Willamette Valley, a gabby New Jersey carpenter had departed for Sacramento. "Reckon I wasn't cut out for farming life," said James Wilson Marshall, after several months of Oregon rain.

On January 24, 1848, as Marshall was inspecting the tailrace of a mill he was building for John Sutter on the American River, something glittering caught his eye.

You know the rest.

News of the great gold rush and samples of gold reached Oregon, thrilling thousands, particularly members of the Meek train, now busily building farmsteads. "There's a fortune east of the mountains," they excitedly informed attentive ears. The tale raced through the state like wildfire: the "Blue Bucket Mine" became an Eldorado which took on the glamour of Jason's quest for the Golden Fleece.

A fruitless decade followed. Scattered colors were washed from the Burnt River and traces were found on the John Day River. It was all bad guesswork until J. L. Adams, with blazing eyes and prophetic voice, appeared on the streets of Portland in 1861, exhibiting nuggets and dust and declaring with as much certainty as enthusiasm that he had located the fabulous wealth of the "lost emigrant" placer in a rugged defile of the Blue Mountains.

Adams had little trouble in recruiting a company of adventurers, 58 strong. Most were farmers, itching for quick money.

Over the Barlow Toll Road, down into Tygh Valley, up the Deschutes and Crooked Rivers, through the John Day country, and criss-crossing the creeks between the Malheur and Burnt Rivers, the grunting Argonauts plodded.

Fatigue turned to discouragement, discouragement scraped nerves raw, raw nerves flared into angry suspicion. Confronted, Adams confessed he had fibbed. He did not know the location of any Blue Mountain mine; he had never before been in the region. He had made up the story to enlist a force powerful enough to cope with hostile Indians while prospecting.

Tempers erupted. Some of the farmers, who had left crops unharvested, wanted Adams lynched. A jury was selected; witnesses were heard. The verdict was guilty. Adams was spared execution, but he was stripped of everything but the clothes he was wearing and driven from camp.

It was mid-October, the wild goose chase was over. Time to return home. The company divided into two parties. One, led by H. H. Griffin, struggled northeast to find the main emigrant trail. On a chill moonlit night in a rocky canyon of the Blue Mountains, he vowed: "No more crazy business for me." But anyway, out of force of habit, he toted his pick and shovel and sluice pan to a rushing stream nearby and started digging.

Sure enough, he found yellow metal. "It's here!" he shouted. "The Blue Bucket! Boys, there's bushels of it!"

It wasn't the Blue Bucket, everyone agreed later, but gold aplenty there was in Griffin's Gulch. Even J. L. Adams, who like a shunned and famished dog had trailed the party, living on food left at campfires by compassionate souls, was called in and allowed to stake a claim.

Gold discoveries are never well kept secrets. Spring saw thousands swarming into the hills. Griffin's party, done with the creek, moved ahead of the onrushing horde, locating four miles southward, on a gulch they named Auburn, Eastern Oregon's first gold town.

Ten weeks later Auburn numbered more than 1,000 houses and 60 stores and better than 5,000 persons. Gunmen, prostitutes, tinhorns and easy riders were in abundance—but who cared? Auburn was Oregon's second biggest town.

In every direction a host of camps overnight sprang up. Like Roman candles, they peaked quickly and sputtered out. Nobody now knows their exact location.

Six months after its founding, Auburn was chosen seat of newly organized Baker County. The next year it reached its zenith—6,000 population! But mining swiftly declined—and so did Auburn's fortunes. In 1864 the post office was discontinued, in 1868 the county seat was moved to Baker. Today, all that was Auburn has been obliterated.

The placer diggings, worked clean, gave way to lode mining. West of Auburn, south and north, hard rock towns developed: Sumpter, Granite, Bourne, McEwan, Whitney, Bonanza, Greenhorn, Lawton and Buffalo. All but Sumpter and Granite have either settled back to earth or are completely deserted, their dilapidated ruins staring blindly at grass-grown streets.

Granite and Sumpter were founded in 1862. Typically, the towns flourished, then waned, as gold was found, then depleted. Still incorporated, Granite's population today consists solely of colorful Otis Ford, who from his porch governs an intact but silent city.

The narrow gauge railroad out of Baker in 1896 boomed Sumpter. The town boasted three newspapers, twice as many churches, and four times as many saloons. It erected an opera house which, for some reason, barred sheepmen. Twelve miles of tunnel were simultaneously in operation. A paper ecstatically asked: "Sumpter, golden Sumpter, what glorious fortune awaits thee?" What indeed? The Masonic Hall sleeps on the hill, the brick vault of the old bank shelters pack rats.

Each new discovery recharged the legend of the Blue Bucket Mine. Its lure beckoned thousands, including some of the Meek party, who more than two decades after their overland trek went searching for the site they had fabled. But the desert sand had long ago blotted out the wagon tracks. Each stream they saw looked no different than any other that ran out of the pine timber into the high country. "Where, where?" they asked in agony.

Where could be anywhere. Seventy miles southwest of Auburn, in that feverish year of 1862, some tired prospectors stretched out on Whiskey Flat. Billy Aldred, spotting some interesting looking dirt across Canyon Creek, waded over. Having no sluice pan at hand, he stripped, knotted the sleeves and legs of his underwear, filled the longjohns with dirt, recrossed the creek, and fell to washing the dirt.

Within hours, Canyon City, first town in Grant County, was born.

The inevitable followed. A saloon was in business within three days, on the fourth the gamblers arrived. On the seventh day the shootings started, the most famous of which involved a dark, mustachioed card shark, Black Dan.

Mortally wounded, he called upon his errant camerados to lay him out on a saloon table. But Dan was not for packing his poke in shrouds of grey. To beguile the last moments of his earthly pilgrimage he had "the women of his acquaintance," as an early scribe put it, called in. They sang songs and toasted Dan with slugs of whiskey until "the spark of his unprofitable life was extinguished."

A grave was chipped out of the frozen ground, but when it was ready the body of another man, who had been drilled with finality while Dan lay perishing, was slipped into it. When Dan's pals arrived they found his grave had been jumped. Furious oaths whirled down Whiskey Flat. But another hole was dug, and Dan boarded the stage to the land where every hand is a royal flush.

In its prime Canyon City had 10,000 more people than its 500 today. Pack trains bulging with supplies choked its narrow streets. The Pony Express galloped into town from The Dalles. Unionist Oregon miners stormed up a hill on July 4, 1863, as the battle of Gettysburg was being decided across the continent, to tear down a Confederate flag hoisted by California Johnny Rebs.

Into this churning, zesty carnival rode young Cincinnatus Heiner (Joaquin) Miller, whose gusty ego was matched only by the grandeur of the Blue Mountains. A few weeks after he arrived, in 1866, he was elected the first judge of Grant County, serving until 1870, when he left the burly gold camp to blaze literary fame as the bard of a loftier mountain range—"Poet of the Sierra."

Altogether, about $30 million in gold was taken from the streams and hills west of Baker. A like amount was hauled out of Sparta and Cornucopia, northeast of Baker.

Sparta, also founded in the 1860s by men pursuing the myth, is a molten corpse now. Cornucopia, the most productive of all mining towns, was born in 1883 and worked full blast until October 31, 1941, when the Union Companion was abruptly closed. Mass exodus immediately followed. Only Chris Schneider remained. He is still there, watching Oregon's last ghost town erode to splinters and dust.

Cornucopia is the end of the saga that started in 1845, with weary emigrants halting their wagons by a rippling stream.

And where, after all, is the Blue Bucket, that started the quest for gold in Eastern Oregon?

Your guess is as good as the next.

End of an Empire*

Into the valley of the Blitzen young Pete French came riding on that sweet spring day of 1872, little knowing when he came to the river that before he crossed his last stream, 25 years later, the rimrock lore of Oregon would have been fattened on his name.

For 70 long, wild and wonderful miles the valley unrolled along the Blitzen River, north from the emerald foothills of the almost 10,000-foot-high Steens Mountain. Save for the blur of startled deer across the prairie and the rimrock barriers breaking the sea of marshland, grass and sage, the country was empty and endless. Almost 250 miles from a railroad, the valley—deep in Harney County—was a cattleman's paradise; exactly the place Pete French had been seeking since he started the drive from northern California.

*Reprinted from *Westward*, April, 1957.

Here in eastern Oregon he would establish the cattle domain of his dreams, a range empire similar to that of the Spanish grandees.

The dream was a big one for the short, wiry, dark-complexioned, energetic Peter French, who had started his work life riding for the wealthy California stockman, Dr. Glenn. But Pete was a far reacher. Everyone admitted that —friend and foe.

French marked off a spread of 160,000 acres and on the choicest spot built the headquarters of his fabled P-Ranch. A few years later, when he married Ella, daughter of Dr. Glenn, he erected a white mansion for his bride. But Ella's days on the range were few. She left Pete for San Francisco and city life, urging him to come along. Pete frowned and declined. The big dream was more meaningful to him than any woman, than life itself.

Fearless and inexhaustible, he rode the range with his cowboys under the burning sun and through bitter winter blizzards. On the long drives to railheads, usually Winnemucca in Nevada, Pete was longer in the saddle and ate more dust than any of his hands.

Until the country was opened to homesteaders, French was virtually undisputed baron of all he surveyed. Only the Indians challenged him, battling him for their ancient hunting grounds.

In a score of skirmishes, French led his men; always the swiftest and the most daring when danger struck. Twice the Indians almost slew him. Once, trapped in a rimrock canyon, he shot his way out. Several months later, again caught alone, he raced his mustang to the door of his ranch house, leaping from his horse and firing as he dashed for safety.

With the coming of the homesteaders, everything changed. Within a decade French became the most loved and most hated man in the range country. The hundred armed *vaqueros* who patrolled his P-Ranch, guarding his cattle and discouraging prospective settlers, adored him. Emigrants going through to the Willamette Valley blessed him for loading their wagons with food. Children in Burns, the county seat, pocketed silver dollars when Pete French came to town. Broken-down cowpunchers had ten dollar bills pressed into their palms by the black-eyed cattle king. Women walked out of their way to smile at him. But homesteaders cursed his name and carried on guerilla warfare against him, ambushing his riders and chopping down his gates.

Utilizing the high-handed methods of his epoch, French fought savagely to retain and extend his holdings. He financed his *vaqueros* to homestead land, which they turned over to him. He bought out settlers, and when they would not sell he stampeded their cattle, set fire to their barns, diverted water from their land, and threatened them with violence.

By the standards of "fair play," French might be regarded as a selfish and cruel man. But the old timers of Harney County see it otherwise. Eighty-three-year-old Jesse Welcome of Burns, who as a boy received many a silver dollar from French and whose father knew well the cattle king, says simply:

"French did what he had to do, because that was the way things were in those days. It was a war that couldn't be avoided and Pete French fought the best way he could. Any man in his shoes would have done the same. It isn't a matter of good or bad—it's what was."

The bitter range war of Pete French versus the homesteaders went on until December 27, 1897. Then, in one single moment, it came to an end.

On that day, as French and several of his *vaqueros* were getting a thousand head of cattle ready for the drive to Winnemucca, working the stock in the rain, a homesteader named Ed Oliver rode out of the sage toward Pete and his men.

French recognized the man immediately. Oliver had been in his pay as a rider before turning settler. The two men hated each other.

"Stay out of my field," French shouted, motioning Oliver away.

Oliver cursed under his breath and rode on until he was abreast the unarmed French. Angered, Pete struck Oliver's horse across the head with his whip to turn the stallion away.

Quickly Oliver reined his horse under control, and as the stallion wheeled toward French the homesteader drew a gun from his hip.

Startled, French yanked his horse around and spurred away. But Pete was always a curious man. He turned in his saddle to look back and, as he did, Oliver fired. The bullet struck French in the forehead. It spun him back to normal riding position and his head struck the rainsoaked mane of his pony before he fell off. He was dead when he hit the ground.

In their confusion and grief, none of the cowboys who hastened up thought of chasing down Oliver. Manuel Clark, one of the riders, and Bert French, Peter's brother, knelt for a moment beside the slain figure, then silently mounted and rode to the house for a tent. They did not want the boss to get wet while they fetched the coroner.

Ed Oliver fled the country but returned soon after to stand trial before a jury of homesteaders. They speedily acquitted him.

The range war ended in that jarring instant when Pete French was struck by Oliver's bullet. The strong man had fallen; no one else could carry on.

Upon Pete's death a large chunk of the P-Ranch was acquired by a livestock company. This land, and eventually all of the Blitzen Valley, was bought by the federal government for creation of the Malheur Wildlife Refuge. The marshes were returned to a primitive state, as they were before French came driving his cattle—when the solitude of the Blitzen was disturbed only by animals and wandering Indians.

The white mansion burned down long ago and all that is left of the fabled P-Ranch headquarters, now a refuge maintenance station, is the great round barn where Pete stored his hay.

A dreamy stillness hangs over the land of Pete French, broken only by sounds of the wilderness: the howl of a coyote in the brush or the chilling scream of a mountain cat prowling down from the hills.

From the marshes come the crackling chatter of the tule wrens, the plaintive cry of the killdeer, and the flight song of the jacksnipe. The guns have long been silenced, the Indians many years ago departed, and the shacks of homesteaders strung far apart along the lonely dirt road to Burns abandoned to rain, sun, snow and field mice.

Still, in all this emptiness, the sage and rimrock speak of Pete French and the wind calls his name, beckoning him to return. Stormy, hot-blooded, charitable, gentle and terrible—here was a man the elements could understand.

York of the Elkskin Trailblazers

In the gloomy autumn of 1805 a small party of explorers, who had begun voyage into the wilderness at St. Louis, reached the Pacific Ocean, blazing the first overland trail from the Missouri River to the far sea. In all the glorious annals of the way west, no single chapter is grander in its achievements than the epic tale of this intrepid band, known to history as the Lewis and Clark expedition.

For western trailblazing purposes, the actual starting date of expedition was April 7, 1805, when the party bade farewell to the Mandan villagers (60 miles above present Bismarck, North Dakota) and turned their eyes toward the Land of the Shining Mountains. The contingent consisted of Captains Meriwether Lewis and William Clark, three sergeants, 23 soldiers, three of whom spoke French, two French interpreters, a woman and her baby, and a slave.

The woman was Sacajawea Charbonneau, the "Bird Woman" wife of an interpreter. The slave was York, a young, large, handsome "intensely black" Negro, the bondservant of Clark.

Lewis and Clark have been immortalized in American history. Sacajawea is one of our most cherished Western legends. But if the Indians had conducted a popularity poll, York would have won hands down.

All of the men, and Sacajawea, were well liked. Speaking of the "Bird Woman," Clark once observed that the Indians looked upon a woman with a party of men as a token of peace. But none of the group was so royally welcomed and, to put it plainly, more adored by both sexes of all encountered Indian tribes as the smiling, affable, understanding, gay and extremely democratic York. In the West, where many of the Indians had never before seen a white man, a black man was still more of an oddity. But York was equal to the challenge: if he came as an oddity he departed as a friend.

Describing the impact the "Corps of Discovery" made upon the Indians, one writer declares: "The astonishment at the sound of the rifles, at quicksilver, at the air gun, at the burning glass, and even at Clark's Negro servant York are well known."

York's popularity was in some measure due to his pigmentation. With moistened fingers the Indians rubbed his skin, wondering if he was not painted. They yanked his hair, to see if it was really his own. And a few bold spirits asked him if he had really been born black!

On several occasions, both Lewis and Clark capitalized on the curiosity York held for the Indians in winning their support. The most conspicuous of these incidents took place the second week of August, 1805, after Lewis and three of his picked scouts had surmounted the Continental Divide, seeking desperately to make contact with the Shoshones, whose aid they urgently needed to reach the sea, and without whose horses the expedition might have failed. Lewis suspected the Indians were close by, but the frightened Shoshones, weak and fearful of aggressors, shied away.

Finally, after much persuasion, Lewis induced an old woman he had found to lead him to her people. There, after somewhat amicable relations were established, Lewis attempted to enlist the Indians into returning across the Divide with him and assisting in transporting the supplies of the main party through Lemhi Pass.

Noting the Shoshone reluctance, the captain told them of Sacajawea, the Shoshone maid who accompanied the explorers. (It turned out later she was sister to the tribal chief, Cameahwait.)

The Indians were somewhat impressed with the idea of a Shoshone woman traveling with a white man's party, but still they made no gesture of help. It was only after Lewis described to them York that they expressed willingness to aid the party. Most likely, they felt a price was attached to their curiosity, and they were willing to pay it. They had never even heard of a black man, and they were anxious to see what one looked like.

Still, there is more than York's color that must be taken into account to explain his enormous success with the Indians. It has been stated by some writers that York interpreted the culture of the Indians to the party. The diaries of the expedition are not explicit on this point, and it seems likely that York's contribution here has been overstressed, for the "Corps of Discovery" contained several frontiersmen who had spent half their lives among the Indians, while York had had no previous contact. But it is reasonable to assume that York, sensitive to the manner by which whites distorted the meanings of Negro ways, should genuinely feel—and project this feeling—that the patterns by which the Indians lived had vital significance to them, and ought not be trespassed by foreigners.

A free-and-easy diplomat, York had an off-hand knack of settling problems quickly and quietly, of appealing to the Indians as an equal, no more, no less, and of accepting their presents and compliments, whether from male or female, with rare tact and graciousness.

Historian George W. Fuller speaks of the expedition as the "dancing explorers." Another writer has called the party "a road show." One man carried a violin, an item faithfully packed along even when foodstuffs, medicine and guns had to be cached for lack of carrying power, and at camp after camp the fiddler struck up merry tunes while the men danced, sometimes entertaining the gathering Indians far into the night.

The star of the troupe was York, whose rich voice and lithe dancing never failed to please. An historian wrote: "The solo dances of Clark's Negro servant were always effective." From the Missouri to the Pacific, York entertained mightily, sometimes overdoing it. Once, among the Teton Sioux, he was so carried away by applause he started dancing on his hands, an action which drew stern frowns from the usually tolerant Captain Clark.

In the wilderness, York was without flaw. Powerfully built, he took as well as anyone to the rugged environment and the rigors of the journey. When things went wrong, he did not grumble; when danger approached, he did not shudder. He was an excellent shot, steady in the mountains, one of the strongest men when it came to pulling the boats by rope up the muddy Missouri or poling against the harsh tide, and, so it has been written, the best cook in the outfit.

York was often a member of a picked group accompanying the leaders of the expedition. For example, he was with Clark when that captain took six men to explore the mouth of the Willamette River, which the Indians called the Multnomah.

There is no indication that York suffered any abuse from the other members of the party. The very acts involved in living together, conquering the wilderness together, and depending upon each other for personal safety and survival created a cooperative atmosphere which sometimes carried over into policy-making decisions. Upon occasion the captains turned the party into a committee-of-the-whole, with everyone's opinion solemnly heard. Sacajawea and York had their say and their vote, the same as any other.

Not much is known of what happened to some of the Lewis and Clark band in their later years. Less is definitely known about York than any other participant. Journalists in the early nineteenth century had little interest in the accomplishments of a black man, and until very recently historians of the expedition have tended to treat York, which is all the name we know him by, as though he was an appendage who disappeared into thin air, to no one's concern, after the party returned to St. Louis. All we can say for sure is that York was the only man among the elkskin trailblazers not to receive any compensation from the government.

Later research indicates that York may have been with Clark when the captain married Julia Hancock. Shortly thereafter Clark is supposed to have given York his freedom, supplied him with wagons and mules, and set him up in the freight business, hauling goods between Nashville, Tennessee and Richmond, Virginia.

How long York stayed with the freight route is not known, but it is believed that he left it after a few years. Some writers conjecture that he probably rejoined Clark and died in Missouri. But there is another supposition, and one to which men of sentiment will subscribe. This, a rumor brought back to the settlements along the lower Missouri by fur trappers, has it that York was seen on the Great Plains, having the time of his life as chief of a Commanche tribe.

The rumor is not as implausible as it may at first glance appear. York had the qualities of a frontiersman and was competently qualified to penetrate the wilderness. He loved life in the open. The comforts of "civilization," however they were measured for a black man, had no lure for him compared to the untethered ways he had found in outdoor living. And we cannot forget the magnificence of brotherhood he must have felt among the Indians. Here was a people among whom he was judged, once the curiosity wore off, as a human being, without regard to prior status, and in whose ranks he could rise, by strength of leadership, to the most coveted position. The fact that he was a slave meant nothing to the Indians; his color, in later years, could have served as a real advantage, setting him apart from predatory, expropriating whites.

However York ended his days, it would be fitting that somewhere in the West a monument be built to this "intensely black" man, whom the Indians affectionately regarded as the Great White Father's finest ambassador.

The Long Run of Bigfoot*

He was seven feet tall, weighed 300 pounds, and was so fleet he spurned the use of a horse. His footprints measured 18 inches long and 6 inches wide, and he had the stride of a giant, which he was. He could cover 50 to 80 miles a day, sprawl on the earth for a few hours, then rise to travel another 50 to 80 miles. His name brought terror to stagecoach passengers and lonely homesteaders, to hardy miners and armed teamsters for more than ten years in the frontier settlements between the Grande Ronde Valley of Oregon and the Great Salt Desert of Utah. In the Snake River country he was known as the "Scourge of Idaho."

*Reprinted from *Westward*, April-May 1958.

This is the story of that giant, Chief Bigfoot. It is not a pretty tale, but it is a page of the Old West never before fully recorded.

Following the Civil War the grand march westward increased its tempo. From the Missouri River to the Land of the Shining Mountains and beyond, caravans of covered wagons filled the plains and hills. Standing on a butte, one could see a line of prairie schooners stretching to the far horizon, where the canvas of blue sky was nailed to the brown wheel ruts.

As the emigrants surged westward, expropriating ancient Indian lands, the Indians protested; then fought back in mass; then, when their organized resistance was shattered, carried on erratic guerilla operations. Some Indians, splintering into outlaw bands, took to thievery and murder. The most desperate of these badmen was Chief Bigfoot.

Leading a small group of picked Snake River warriors, Bigfoot ranged freely through eastern Oregon and southern Idaho, leaving in his wake a trail of riddled bodies and slit throats. Whole trains of emigrants were slaughtered, their bones left bleaching on the banks of the Burnt, Boise and Snake Rivers.

For several years after Bigfoot reached Idaho Territory he confined his lawlessness to stealing horses and supplies, killing only when his escape was blocked. But after his wife was killed and his small son carried off by a force of men sent out after him, he discarded whatever ethics had kept him in relative rein, and killed those whom he robbed, evidently determined not to leave any witnesses. But his feet gave him away every time; his large moccasin tracks were found at countless scenes of depredation.

Rarely traveling with more than five confederates, he moved so stealthily few ever saw more of him than his footprints. Those who did meet him on peaceful terms, as did Enoch Fruit, the noted horse thief who kept a ferry at Farewell Bend on the Snake, found him to have a complexion which once had been rather fair but had become deeply tanned, a fine-looking face with a full and handsome set of teeth, a heavy shock of long, black hair, somewhat inclined to be kinky, and large, black, wicked-looking eyes.

Numerous posses were organized to catch the mountainous marauder, but Bigfoot eluded every trap with a speed and skill that astonished his pursuers. One day his tracks would be seen on the Weiser, and the next day he would appear on the Owyhee, 80 miles away. Though his warriors rode sturdy ponies, Bigfoot was never mounted. No ordinary horse could carry him and his fleetness on foot was so phenomenal that once, when tracked by three men riding swift steeds, he outdistanced them.

This chase, on a hot August day in 1866, began near the head of the Malheur River, when J. F. Wheeler, Frank Johnson and Ben Cook awoke one morning to find three sets of moccasin prints near their camp, one set well known throughout the area for its size. Swallowing a hasty breakfast, the three took to the trail, Johnson remarking, "Well boys, we'll make it hot for old Bigfoot today."

The odds against Bigfoot seeing the noonday sun were ten to one, conservatively speaking. Wheeler, Johnson and Cook were crack shots, veteran Indian fighters, three of the finest horsemen in the Territory, and their steeds were rested. Cool and resolute the men rode forward, whipped on by a thousand dollar reward on Bigfoot's head.

After two hours of hot pursuit the Indians were sighted, trotting rapidly toward the Snake River. "Let's git 'em!" cried Johnson, and the men applied their big Spanish spurs without mercy to the already bleeding flanks of their spirited mounts. Within another hour the two smaller Indians were caught up with and shot down, their arrows and old-style guns no match for the high-powered Henry rifles of the whites.

By the time the brief fighting was over, Bigfoot was a mile away, leaping the sagebrush like a deer and covering the open ground with amazing strides.

"He's a dead one now!" Cook shouted, as the three took after the Indian. And it began to look for certain that the noonday sun was a sight Bigfoot would never again see. But for every yard he lost on level ground he gained a yard on rough terrain and rocky gullies, keeping the distance between him and the horses.

For 30 miles, over sagebrush and naked hillock, through startled cottonwood clumps and gaping clay ravines, swirling clouds of acrid alkali dust as they panted toward the

Snake, the chase continued. From time to time a horse plunged into a badger hole, falling and pitching its reckless rider over its head. But no horse was harmed, and the stubborn, frenzied men rejoined the hunt as soon as they could mount up again. Bigfoot saw the noonday sun come and go through bloodshot eyes, cracked a grin through his parched lips, and resolved to taste the soft wind of twilight.

Frothing, bleeding, thirsty, the horses lunged on, wincing under the stab of the Spanish spurs. Then the broad Snake River came into view, and the riders made one last desperate attempt to hurry their mounts on. But Bigfoot reached the river first. Plunging into the water without pausing, he struck out swimming for the opposite shore, carrying his gun and ammunition above his head.

"Git 'em, boys!" screamed Johnson in wild frustration. "Git 'em before he crosses!" But by the time the frazzled horses climbed the humped bank of the Snake, their riders saw Bigfoot clambering up the other side.

For a long dramatic moment Bigfoot stood erect and silent in clear vision of his pursuers before he let loose a blood-curdling yell that shook each rider to the core and almost bolted the horses. Then he hollered: "Come over, come over, you damn coward." But without waiting for a reply he dove into the thick willows and was gone beyond hope of capture.

"Well," said Wheeler, "you have to admit: that was the most amazing chase in the history of Idaho Territory." He paused, then added quietly, as though speaking to himself, "But I'll get him some day—if it's the last thing I ever do." And Wheeler did, two years later, according to the one man who claimed to be an eyewitness to the encounter.

Wheeler, so the story goes, had armed himself with a .44 calibre Henry, the first successful repeating rifle marketed in this country and the deadliest weapon of its day on the frontier, and had lain in ambush for Chief Bigfoot for four days at the entrance to the canyon where the Indian staged most of his depredations. When Bigfoot and two cohorts dashed up to intercept a stagecoach, Wheeler shot one Indian, the other fled.

And then stepping out into the open, Wheeler coolly traded bullets with the enraged giant, finally dropping Chief

Bigfoot with a barrage of shots only a few yards from his feet. So elusive he couldn't be tracked, the outlaw was doomed by the ambush technique and by his pride—his Achilles heel. For it was Wheeler's taunts that had lured Chief Bigfoot into a fatal duel where his speed was of no advantage and his rifle no match for his adversary's.

Wheeler himself met a violent end a dozen years later. After two interludes in Western penitentiaries, he was sentenced to be hanged for his connection with a holdup murder in Ukiah, California. While the sheriff's back was turned, Wheeler gulped a vial of poison. And so, like a Greek tragedy, the two principals in the West's mightiest duel were undone by their vices and left the frontier clear for other —and more conventional—settlers.

Naughty Copperfield

"Thar she comes!" The rock-fisted blaster threw his cap into the air as the waggly Union Pacific steam engine, sending out cheerful whistles and bright puffs of smoke, bellied into Copperfield.

"Yippee!" the blaster shouted. "Ain't we gonna have fun?"

And he started for the train, which had shivered to a halt. But the gambler and the bartender at his sides, grabbed his shirt tail and yanked him back.

"Now remember," cautioned the gambler, winking at the bartender and nudging the blaster, "we're gonna be sweet as jam today." "And right proper, too," agreed the bartender.

"S'gonna be a dandy!" roared the blaster. "The whole town 'n half'n the county's out. Sure gonna be a drunk tonight!"

As the first of the train's passengers stepped down, onto the gristled earth of Copperfield, the crowd pelted the gawky, youngish man in military uniform with good-natured barbs. "Hey Shorty, wanta try your luck?" "Come clear 'cross the state for a good drink?" "This climate beats the rain in Salem any old time, don't it?"

The jests continued as one after another of the men in uniform disembarked. Then, as a woman made her appearance, a barrage of cries thundered from the crowd, echoed against the basaltic hills across the Snake River, and bounced back into Copperfield.

The woman, "not too young and not too old but surefire too wise," as the shrewd gambler put it, coldly surveyed the merry cynics, piloting her intense eyes over the enthusiastic, festive assemblage. Then she pulled her coat together, tilted up the broad brim of her hat, lifted a corner of her long, dark skirt to step over some slush, and marched down the street, the heels of her high button shoes crunching snow.

Ahead of her the streets were decorated with flags and bunting; bunting and ribbons were draped over saloon windows. She gritted her teeth and continued marching toward the city hall.

"This is more fun than a payday fight," laughed the blaster, and he whistled appreciatively through some half-broken teeth. The gambler, fondling the expensive fob of his gold watch, shook his head. "I don't like it," he muttered. "She walks like hell on wheels."

If the lady was strange to Copperfield, not so with the blaster, the bartender and the gambler. The town, on the Oxbow of the Snake, had led a muck-handed, whiskey-drinking, gambling life since the day it was born. Settled around the turn of the century as a ramshackle collection of prospector's rude cabins, it would have suffered the silent and deathly fate of hundreds of other such ephemeral settlements had not the Union Pacific decided to build two railroad tunnels near the site of the Oxbow power plant.

Having finagled advance word of the proposed construction, four promoters from Baker, the county seat 65 miles away, bought up a quarter section along the banks of the Snake in 1908, laid out the town, sold the lots for a huge profit, and within six months had retired from the scene.

By 1910 Copperfield was booming. A small army of muckers, powder monkeys and mechanics made the canyon of the Snake ring with dynamite and steel. Gaming clubs and saloons mushroomed all over the town, drawing customers from as far as 50 miles away. Before the year was over

Copperfield was widely known as the liquor and gaming resort for the surrounding country.

With protean zest and wild-spirited gusto, Copperfield set out to surpass the purplish, roaring mining camps of the 1860s. Dancing girls strutted wickedly, liquor flowed freely as the Snake, and at least once a week there was a maiming free-for-all.

The most classic brawl—at least the one that is best remembered today—was smashed and pounded out to the tinny tunes of the mechanical piano in Barney Goldberg's saloon. Later, the combatants bandaged each other's wounds and drank from the same bottle.

When the more moderate elements of Copperfield requested the City Fathers to subdue some of the more licentious individuals and activities, the town officials replied with scowling eyes of suspicion. A plea to the county authorities at Baker provoked the same reaction. Finally, as a last resort, the champions of decency carried their appeal to Oregon's governor, Oswald West.

The governor, a tough executive fitted out with high morals, ordered Baker County to put the lid on Copperfield's man-made volcano. Arrogantly turned down, he chose a show of strength and announced that he personally would lead a contingent of the State Militia to Copperfield. Back came word that a bullet awaited the governor. So, placing his bets on discretion instead of valor, as the boys in the back room say, he delegated authority to his dutiful secretary, Miss Fern Hobbs.

Armed with a declaration of martial law, Miss Hobbs departed on January 1, 1914 for Sodom on the Snake. Her "invasion force" consisted of a State Militia colonel, who was also warden of the state penitentiary at Salem, two pen guards, and five Militia privates. Accompanying the "invaders" was an even larger array of "war" correspondents.

As soon as the mayor of Copperfield heard that the governor's secretary had been dispatched to clean up the community, he declared a holiday, ordered the town decorated, and sent out a call for every manjack on both sides of the Snake to "attend the reception." Some of those who showed up, a few unwillingly, were grizzled prospectors who otherwise kept to their lonesome, regarding the gathering of more than three persons in one place as contrary to the laws of nature.

When Miss Hobbs reached the city hall she mounted a platform and read the governor's decree, demanding the resignation of all city officials. "If you turn down this order," she warned, "I will turn over to the commander of the State Militia the governor's declaration of martial law."

Concluding, she raised her head and awaited a reply. None came. There wasn't even a chuckle. But a few men smiled slyly, little aware of the storm that was soon to overtake them. "Then," declared Miss Hobbs, "I'll be more specific." She called each official by name. None responded. Ashen-faced, Miss Hobbs ordered the troops to collect all firearms, which the citizenry good-naturedly surrendered. "Now," said Miss Hobbs, "the State Militia has its orders to proceed." And she strode back to the train.

Within moments of her departure from the suddenly stricken scene, the troops began their day long job of bolting the saloons, destroying the gambling equipment, and carting all liquor bottles and bar fixtures out of town, where they were smashed and burned.

Copperfield never recovered from the shock. Several months later, after a fire, supposedly set by a frustrated saloonkeeper, burned the town to ashes, only a feeble effort was made to rebuild it. By then the tunnels were nearing completion and many of the men had left. After still another fire, one more gesture to start the settlement up again was made but this, too, ended in a sea of flames, leaving Copperfield to the legends of history.

Joseph of the Nez Perce

By now everyone should know the saga of Chief Joseph and the Nez Perces of the Wallowa Valley: how they were robbed of their land and then driven from it; the many battles they were forced to wage against far more numerous and better equipped soldiers as they sought to reach Canada and asylum; the surrender of Joseph at the Bear Paw Mountains in Montana; the exile of the Nez Perces to the treeless plains of Kansas and Oklahoma; and finally the return of Joseph and his people to the Northwest, not to the green vales of their Valley-of-the-Winding-Waters but to the coulees of Washington, on the barren Colville Reservation.

What kind of a man was Chief Joseph, also known as Young Joseph? He has been romanticized and deprecated. Is it not time to let him speak fully for himself?

Actually, he once did, and his translated account, a remarkable document by any measurement, literary or historic, appeared many years ago, in the April 1879 issue of the now extinct *North American Review*.

The long and dramatic statement—constructed like a lawyer's closing summation to a jury—provides a dramatic Nez Perce explanation of the background of the armed conflict, the uneven war, and the aftermath, even more tragic than the fighting.

It would be burdensome, perhaps, and perhaps impertinent to reprint the entire article, which the *North American Review* editor titled: "An Indian's View of Indian Affairs."

My purpose is to show Joseph as the sage, patriot, humanitarian and moral teacher that he was. What comes hereafter are passages I have extracted from the article. From this point on, it is Joseph who speaks:

Some of you think an Indian is like a wild animal. This is a great mistake. I will tell you all about our people, and then you can judge whether an Indian is a man or not. I believe much trouble and blood will be saved if we opened our hearts more. I will tell you in my own way how the Indian sees things. The white man has more words to tell you how they look to him, but it does not require many words to speak the truth.

Our fathers gave us many laws, which they had learned from their fathers. These laws were good. They told us to treat all men as they treated us; that we should never be the first to break a bargain; that it was a disgrace to tell a lie; that we should speak only the truth.

We did not know there were other people beside the Indian until about one hundred winters ago, when some men with white faces came to our country.

It has always been the pride of the Nez Perces that they were the friends of the white men. But we soon found that the white men were growing rich very fast, and were greedy to possess everything the Indians had. My father was the first to see through the schemes of the white men, and he warned his tribe to be careful about trading with them. He had suspicion of men who seemed so anxious to make money.

I buried my father in that beautiful valley of winding waters. I love that land more than all the rest of the world. A man who would not love his father's grave is worse than a wild animal.

When the white men were few and we were strong we could have killed them all off, but the Nez Perces wished to live at peace.

Suppose a white man should come to me and say, "Joseph, I like your horses, and I want to buy them." I say to him, "No, my horses suit me, I will not sell them." Then he goes to my neighbor, and says to him: "Joseph has some good horses. I want to buy them, but he refuses to sell." My neighbor answers, "Pay me the money, and I will sell you Joseph's horses." The white man returns to me, and says, "Joseph, I have bought your horses, and you must let me have them." If we sold our lands to the Government, this is the way they were bought.

I have carried a heavy load on my back ever since I was a boy. I learned then that we were but a few, while the white men were many, and that we could not hold our own with them. We were like deer. They were like grizzly bears. We had a small country. Their country was large. We were contented to let things remain as the Great Spirit Chief made them. They were not; and would change the rivers and mountains if it did not suit them.

We are all sprung from a woman, although we are unlike in many things. You can not be made over again. You [the white man] are as you were made and as you were made you can remain. We are just as we were made by the Great Spirit, and you can not change us; then why should children of one mother and one father quarrel—why should one try to cheat the other? I do not believe that the Great Spirit Chief gave one kind of men the right to tell another kind of men what they must do.

I have no right to take (the) homes (of others). I have never taken what did not belong to me.

I know that my young men did a great wrong, but I ask, Who was first to blame? They had been insulted a thousand times; their fathers and brothers had been killed; their mothers and wives had been disgraced; they had been driven to madness by whiskey sold to them by white men; they had been told by General Howard that all their horses and cattle which they had been unable to drive out of the Wallowas were to fall into the hands of white men; and, added to all this, they were homeless and desperate.

I have no right to take (the) homes (of others). I never could have killed a great many women and children while the war lasted, but we would feel ashamed to do so cowardly an act.

On the way we captured one white man and two white women. We released them at the end of three days. They were treated kindly. The women were not insulted. Can the white soldiers tell me of one time when Indian women were taken prisoners, and held three days and then released without being insulted?

I went to General Miles and gave up my gun, and said, "From where the sun now stands I will fight no more."

The white people have too many chiefs. They do not understand each other. They do not all talk alike.

I can not understand how the Government sends a man out to fight us, as it did General Miles, and then breaks his word. Such a Government has something wrong about it. I can not understand why so many chiefs are allowed to talk so many different ways, and promise so many different things. I have seen the Great Father Chief [the president], the next Great Chief [Secretary of the Interior], the Commissioner Chief, the Law Chief, and many other law chiefs [Congressmen], and they all say they are my friends, and that I shall have justice, but while their mouths all talk right I do not understand why nothing is done for my people. I have heard talk and talk, but nothing is done. Good words do not last long unless they amount to something. Words do not pay for my dead people. They do not pay for my country, now overrun by white men. They do not protect my father's grave. Good words will not give me back my children. Good words will not give my people good health and stop them from dying. Good words will not get my people a home where they can live in peace and take care of themselves. I am tired of talk that comes to nothing. It makes my heart sick when I remember all the good words and all the broken promises. There has been too much talking by men who had no right to talk. If the white man wants to live in peace with the Indian he can live in peace. There need be no trouble. Treat all men alike. Give them all the same law. Give them all an even chance to live and grow. All men were made by the same Great Spirit Chief. They are all brothers. The earth is the mother of all people, and all people should have equal rights upon it. You might as well expect the rivers to run backward as that any man who was born a free man should be contented when penned up and denied liberty to go where he pleases. If you tie a horse to a stake, do you expect he will grow fat? If you pen an Indian up on a small spot of earth, and compel him to stay there, he will not be contented, nor will he grow and prosper. I have asked some of the great white chiefs where they get their authority to say to the Indian that he shall stay in one place, while he sees white men going where they please. They can not tell me.

Let me be a free man—free to travel, free to stop, free to work, free to trade where I choose, free to choose my own teachers, free to follow the religion of my fathers, free to think and talk and act for myself—and I will obey every law, or submit to the penalty.

Whenever the white man treats the Indian as they treat each other, then we will have no more wars. We shall all be alike—brothers of one father and one mother, with one sky above us and one country around us, and one government for all. Then the Great Spirit Chief who rules above will smile upon this land, and send rain to wash out the bloody spot made by brothers' hands from the face of the earth. For this time the Indian race are waiting and praying. I hope that no more groans of wounded men and women will ever go to the ear of the Great Spirit Chief above, and that all people may be one people.

A Gallery of Moderns

There are many interesting people in Oregon. A few of them appear in this section.

The vignettes here are not of the conventionally heroic type. I approach people as people. I am too old to be bewitched by halos and to be blind to feet of clay. My subjects breathe, wiggle, dream, curse, have doubts, stub their toes, burst into passion, are sometimes very lonely and once in a while laugh at the wrong things.

Each person in this section is someone for whom I have affection. This does not at all mean that I agree with all their views. Some were pretty stuffy, irascible or self-centered. But each had—or has—some endearing qualities which evoked fondness.

These vignettes go back some years. A few people were met as long ago as 1955; a few were interviewed for the first time after parts of this book had already gone to the printer. Some of the people in this section are dead, I know for sure; some others might be. A few old-timers I inquired about as I was writing this book; in the case of several others I did not want to know—perhaps was afraid to know. I think the vignette of Jonas Mosser indicates my feelings on this matter.

It is the practice of some writers to turn "crude English" into "good English." Or, to protect their own image of erudition, they insert (*sic*) after every ungrammatical word or phrase. This method, I believe, is not only cruel, it is dishonest. It is tantamount to draining the lifeblood out of a person and mummifying the remains.

My people appear in print as they speak. I did not find them illiterate because of their "rough" language and to me their words, as they spoke them, had a richness, color, rhythm and poetry which are too frequently absent in our white collar sanitized speech.

What I am saying is this: I give you my people as I knew and know them. I hope you enjoy them as much as I did and do.

Joe Fine

The Cattleman

Joe Fine was the prototype of the literary image of an old time cattleman: tall, lean, grey, clear-eyed, soft-voiced, unemotional, holding everything in perspective, sentimental about the past, and cost accounting to the core. With his firm gaze, cheeks scoured by the winds, and lithe movement, which conveyed an impression of great self-confidence and authority, he reminded me of the movies and photos of William S. Hart, the greatest of all cowboy actors.

He talked a little like Hart, too; sometimes a cutting twang, sometimes a rambling drawl, sometimes tersely, with a formality that ran through words as a chill breeze stalks through the bunchgrass.

Joe Fine was one of the big cattlemen in Harney County. For 30 years he had been with the Roaring Springs Ranch, one of the largest cattle spreads in the state. When Mr. Fine was superintendent, a post he held for many years, Roaring Springs ran about 6,000 cattle. For a period of 10 years the ranch had also run about 35,000 sheep.

Still, though he had held an executive position, and on occasion had mixed with bankers, businessmen and meat company powers, Joe Fine retained his cowpoke brand of speech. For instance, he pronounced overalls as overhalls, and he clung to many of the idioms he had learned in his youth.

His father was one of the early homesteaders in the area, coming to Happy Valley, east and south of Burns, sometime in the 1880s. Joe Fine had lived in Harney County all his life. After he retired from the Roaring Springs Ranch, he and his wife moved into an apartment at the side of the leading hotel in Burns. It wasn't a big apartment but it was comfortable, with some of the latest conveniences, including television.

Joe Fine was moving on toward 75 but he was still mighty active. Early every morning, at least five days a week, he'd take off on his long, powerful automobile to inspect and supervise his holdings, which were in several parts of the county. He'd try to be home by suppertime, but sometimes he was a little late. He thought nothing of logging 200 miles a day over choppy, dusty dirt roads, rocky traces, humped fields and hill trails so narrow and slithery that even the snakes had to crawl around them single file.

In 1904, when Joe Fine was 12, he got his first job, wrangling for the old Island Ranch outfit, which was part of the Miller and Lux operations. For many years, Miller and Lux was the largest cattle company in all the West.

Life as a wrangler—"bringin' the saddle horses in an' out"—was very good, Joe Fine recalled. "It was the thing that I liked, and that's why I would make that statement. I really enjoyed it. We all had wagons, we was out in the wagons, we had no buildings, we just camped with the wagons in the summer. Of course, in the winter they had buildings to camp in. But I never worked in the winter then."

Joe Fine, with his perceptive eye of memory, was, I thought, the one man who could carefully describe what the Harney County cowpokes of the pre-automobile era wore.

"Well," he explained, "they wore boots and overhalls, levis, and at least overhalls of that type, and, overhall jacket, and just a decent kind of hat, but you never see these big hats much them days. You might see one fella with a big hat but you see four or five with just a decent size hat."

How about kerchiefs? "No, very little. Once in a while you'd see a fella with one, maybe if his neck would sunburn you'd see a fella have that. There was nothing fancy about them, the fellas. They just knew their job and they did it and they didn't care if anybody looked at them or not."

What kind of a fellow was the average cowboy?

"Very decent chaps," replied Mr. Fine. "You'd run onto

a kind of overbearing fellow once in a while, get to do a little dickering, you have the same thing now. Lots of people gets the wrong impression of what it used to be as compared to what it is now; you had less laws and they were less enforced during that time because they didn't have the facilities to enforce them, but your people wasn't any worse than they were now. I don't believe that. I don't think they were that."

Joe Fine was too young to know Pete French but Fine's father worked for French and "liked him very much." Joe Fine himself looked at Pete French from the viewpoint of one professional evaluating another. This was his judgment:

"French had a lot of things working in his favor, and they were all legitimate. There was laws that protected him and he was within the law at all times. He was reclaiming a lot of this land by draining it, draining these swamps, and there was provision in the law that protected that interest. But they would come in, these foolish homesteaders, would come in and squat on these acres, a certain area. Of course, these things were in his scope of reclaiming and naturally he wanted 'em to get out. That's where he was gettin' in trouble with those people. French didn't invite trouble at all. They invited it themselves. The fella that killed him had a homestead right off a place I have. There might have been times when French might have went a little too far. He was a hot-headed individual. But most of the time he was right. He had to be or he wouldn't have been able to go as long as he did."

Joe Fine didn't remember any "Indian trouble." He shook his head vigorously. "No, no. We was raised out here *with* the Indians. Y'know the Paiutes, raised right around here. They're not bad people, the Indians."

Harney County folks in his younger days "considered one another more, quite a lot more than they do now," Mr. Fine said. "Lot of people has the wrong impression of what happened here in the early time, you know. Especially in *my* time. People weren't any worse. *I* don't believe they were as *bad* as now. Lots of things happens to people *now,* mysteriously, but then it was open and above board. Everybody knew about it. Didn't pull no punches then. But they weren't troublesome or trying to do something that hadn't oughta be done."

Looking back, what did he miss most about the old days?

He shrugged, as though the answer was obvious. "Well, I used to buy a fair pair of boots for anywhere from two-and-a-half dollars, they cost you fifty now; that's quite a change in that. And buy your Bull Dur'm for seventy-five cents a pack and I guess they charge you three dollars now. Pair of overhalls cost sixty-five cents and now they charge you *four* dollars.

"Of course, as you go along you accumulate during your lifetime, but what I mean is, from month to month. You could buy more with thirty-five dollars than you can buy with $300 now.

"I had more money in my pocket when I worked for thirty-five dollars a month than I ever had since."

Norman Wilson

A Record is Broken

There are some men who trudge through life doing things any one of which might bring them fame. When the headlines do come they are caught unaware and often react confused and bitter. After the smoke of noonday glory drifts away they plod on again, this time doing more mundane things. When they are remembered, which is not often, it is for a particular situation. The name is seldom recalled.

Such a man is Norman Wilson, of Dallas. I met him when fame had been thrust upon his unwilling person. We became friends and through the years our paths have crossed, so that I can speak of him with some degree of accuracy.

Norman Wilson was 30 years old when I first saw him, in 1955, at a State forestry station three miles out of Dallas. Not long before, the bloodhounds he owned had reputedly broken the world record for following a cold scent, in a spectacular hunt which occupied the front pages of Oregon newspapers for at least several days.

I found him a burly, narrow-eyed man with a cold gaze, a teutonic head, powerful hands and a surly, icy drawl. There seemed to be such mayhem and anger in him that I almost physically recoiled. Yet I sensed, and rightly so, as I came to learn, that he was intrinsically a shy, lonely, proud man, caught in his own inner struggle: preserving as near a total concept of self-sufficiency as possible by remaining aloof and, opposed to this form of nihilism, a desperate reaching out for someone who would comprehend him. He was never an easy person to understand.

Wilson wanted nothing to do with reporters. Caustically he charged, and I believed him, that he had been quoted when he had said not a word, that he had frequently been misquoted, that many "on-the-spot" stories were written by journalists who were far away at the time, that reporters "twisted the facts just to get a good story." His voice was vitriolic when he said "good."

I recognized in Wilson someone something like myself: a wanderer who had tripped over bad luck every time he lighted; one who had seen rivers of sacrifice answered by pebbles of appreciation; a soul who grated at snobbery and believed, with Burns, "A Man's A Man For A' That."

Wilson had come a long road of toil and trouble in the 30 years of bruised living that had brought him to Polk Station, outside Dallas, where our initial meeting took place. Sometimes it seemed to him as though his life had been spent in only war and hunts.

At 16 he joined the Navy and spent 42 months in the Pacific flying off aircraft carriers as an aviation radioman first class and aerial gunner. Upon his discharge he enlisted in the Air Force. A year later he married Phyllis Grunwald of Los Gatos, Calif., his home.

The marriage was fortunate for Norman. It gave him an anchor: an intensely devoted woman without a shred of humbug who could live his hard life and yet soften his anger. A woman who failed him might have driven him so deep into disillusionment as to sour him on the whole human race.

In 1946 Wilson discovered what bloodhounds could do.

He explained, after he had taken me home that first day: "A buddy was lost in the Florida Everglades. Search parties looked three days. Then we got hold of an old swamp rat who had a bloodhound. They found him in a day. That's when I got the urge. I got my first dog in 1948 and two more three years later. I've never been sorry. Once the bug hits you, you've had it."

He was eventually to become immune to the bug but the way he talked that day you would have thought that never in his life would he be without bloodhounds.

His first bloodhound, Queen Guinevere of Laurel Oaks, whom Norman called Bernice, cost him $150. Five years later he bred her to a pedigreed bloodhound. The happy result was three pups: Doc Holliday, the largest of the lot; Big Nose Kate, perhaps the most affectionate; and Tombstone Tillie, the dourest. He addressed them as Doc, Kate and Till. On several occasions I was with the dogs but I never really knew them well enough for my presence to be accepted without skepticism. Generally, they either shied away from my touch or imperiously set their eyes in another direction. On the hunt they could look ferocious but were really so gentle that my wife, who photographed a simulated hunt in the brush, often joked about the bloodhounds not knowing what teeth were for.

Legend has it, or had it, that when bloodhounds reach their quarry, they encircle or pin down the pursued. There are such dogs, Wilson admitted, "the ones used by Southern prisons and Dixie cops." But he had no respect for them. When his dogs reached a lost person the scene was comic opera.

Visualize if you can this scene: the quarry has been lost five or six days, is half out of mind, hungry, cold, clothes and shoes ripped almost to shreds. The dogs dance around, yelp like babes, stand on their hind legs and plead with their eyes, saliva oozing down their flews. They expect dog biscuits or some other canine delicacies. The lost person, who seldom has a morsel of food, is then given a sad shake of the snout. The hounds seem to ask: Was this trip really worth it?

But Wilson, right on the spot, petted each dog and fed

it biscuits. The reward stimulated an equally good performance next time.

Wilson's career of searching with bloodhounds for lost persons began in California. Before he came to Oregon it had taken him as far as Alaska. By the time I approached him his dogs had traveled in cars, trucks, boats, helicopters, planes and in baskets tied to the sides of horses and mules.

In more than 60 hunts he had known but two failures and each time, he said, it was because he did not have enough faith in his bloodhounds.

Any one of his hunts might have made him nationally famous, but none did until Oregon. As scant as glory were the thanks he received. Men and women who beseeched him to find their children or brothers or husbands or mothers, promising "everything" if he succeeded, often forgot his existence the moment they threw their arms around their found loved ones. Few people paid him anything for his troubles; many did not even send him a thank you note.

There were times when Norman and Phyllis talked earnestly of selling the bloodhounds, which they eventually did, but there was always in their minds the thought that Norman and his dogs might be, as they certainly sometimes had been, the difference between the life and death of an individual. So they stayed with it, keeping themselves poor to meet canine expenses. It was vastly tougher to manage when Norman was unemployed, as he sometimes was—he is a proud man who will not back down when he thinks he is right, regardless of consequences. "But we somehow squeezed by," recalled Phyllis, with a wry smile. "At least the dogs kept on eating."

The search which blew a brief gale of fame upon Norm Wilson began without his knowledge. He entered in its closing phase and emerged as the principal actor. For him it was just another difficult situation but the conditions were so unusual as to bring him headlines.

Let us take the case from the beginning, for it is seeded with drama and bears a sound message of caution. There are two parts to the story: what is positively known and what is conjectured. Start with the known.

On October 15, 1954, a retired Southern Pacific carwhacker named Charles Bird reported to Polk County Sheriff Tony Neufeldt that four days earlier, while hunting near Fanno Mountain, he had seen a Plymouth parked on a road two miles below the lookout station. A few hours later a man from Aurora came into the sheriff's office to say that he had been to Fanno Mountain three times and had each time seen the Plymouth, parked on the wrong side of a curve. The first time he had looked into the car he had observed a sack lunch on the front seat. The bag was still there when he looked the third time.

The sheriff's office phoned the State department of motor vehicles. A check disclosed the car was registered to the Zeiszlers of Newport. Tony Neufeldt called the Lincoln County sheriff and learned that the family had been missing since October 9. They were supposed to have returned that evening.

The lost family consisted of Norman Zeiszler, 23; his wife, Esther, 33; and Esther's son, Harvey Hoff, 13, all natives of North Dakota. Zeiszler worked in a mill at Newport, on the coast, 80 miles southwest of Dallas.

On Friday, October 8, the Zeiszlers visited Esther's sister, Mrs. Elvin Wolski, in Corvallis, 24 miles below Dallas. They awoke at three o'clock Saturday morning and started for Black Rock, 18 miles west of Dallas, to hunt deer. It was to be a short trip. Esther's hair was still in pin-curls. They had two rifles, a box of shells for one of the guns and half a box for the other. Zeiszler had a hunting knife, cigarette lighter and some books of matches. For food they had only the sack lunch. Their clothes were the kind to be worn in the street, not in the woods.

There were several more things, that did not come out until later. Zeiszler had hunted only once before, and on that trip was lost. Esther and Harvey had never been in the woods. And Esther was between three and four months pregnant.

This is all that is known. Esther's brother thought the Zeiszlers had gone to hunt in eastern Oregon. Mrs. Wolski took it for granted that the family had returned to New-

port in time for Zeiszler to be at work Monday. No one
at the mill seemed to miss him.

In reconstructing the events that took place after the
Zeiszlers left Corvallis, there is much to be desired in the
way of evidence. But here is what may have happened.

In the rugged country west of Dallas the forestry department blocked off the mountain trail with gates, so that
gatemen would check every person going in. When the
Zeiszlers reached the gate leading to Black Rock, the gate-
man hadn't arisen yet, and the gate was down. Impatient
to get started, the Zeiszlers drove up an old Boy Scout
road into the Fanno Mountain area, perhaps trying to' find
Black Rock from the rear.

They parked their car, went down an abandoned railroad spur, and entered young timber. Fog followed them
into the thicket. In a few moments they were lost.

The terrain here is rugged and bushy, sliced with canyons
and dark in the thickets. There are places where you cannot
see five feet ahead of you. Night is cold. The temperature
had dropped below freezing on the first night, October 9,
and the next night was below 28 degrees.

Still, the country is laced with streams and logging roads.
Follow streams and you come to houses and farmers; the
roads lead to logging trucks and loggers.

No one will ever know what occurred. The Zeiszlers
probably zigzagged back and forth along the ridge. Before
reaching the river, they gave way to panic. Staring death
in the face, they couldn't give up. They lay down a few
hours, arose again to stumble on blindly.

Sheriff Tony Neufeldt, who died some years later, told
me what action his office had taken upon receiving a report from the Lincoln County sheriff, on October 15, the
day railroader Charles Bird sauntered into the basement
of the courthouse to ask if anybody knew anything about a
Plymouth parked near Fanno Mountain.

"That evening," recalled Sheriff Neufeldt, "we called in
the State forestry. The State police organized a search party.
We got about 150 men and started out the next morning
and made a drive. We didn't find a thing.

"Next day there's another group, about 250 men, plus

the local National Guard company. Men strung out 40 feet apart and we combed to the north and south of Fanno Mountain road. We lost a man that day. But he had the good sense to sit and wait until somebody came after him.

"Monday morning it was storming, but in the afternoon I called Dean Johnston of McMinnville, who has a heli-copter, and we flew in. But we saw nothing."

There was pressure to call off the hunt. Expenditures were mounting swiftly. "You'll never find them," some people insisted. Neufeldt replied: "We can't stop now." In Dallas there was talk of foul play. The town did not sleep. It was full of reporters, photographers and volunteers. Every-one looked to the dark hills and offered a theory.

In the maze of confusion there was agreement upon only one point: the Zeiszlers are on this side of the Luckiamute. They have not crossed the river.

Norman was in Yosemite, looking for a University of Cali-fornia student, when the first news of the Zeiszlers reached Los Gatos, where the Wilsons were living. He told it to me this way:

"When I got home my wife told me about the Zeiszlers and asked what I thought. At first, I figured it was none of my business. I had been fired from my job, couldn't get another, and in general felt like telling the world to go to hell.

"Friend wife, seeing what mood I was in, very carefully made sure that I would hear radio newscaster Sam Hayes at 12:30 p.m. the next day. Again he reported that an en-tire family was missing in western Oregon and there was little hope for their safety. Then friend wife dropped the bombshell: 'I'll bet our dogs could find them in 24 hours if they were given a chance.'

"I said, 'Sure, but you don't know where they are miss-ing or how long they have been gone.' She then started in on the deal in earnest but I was a little leery, as I knew I had everything against me.

"The next day Sam Hayes mentioned they were missing out of Dallas, Oregon. Friend wife said, 'Well, now you know where and how long.' Sam Hayes said they had been missing 12 days. 'What are you going to do about it?' she asked.

"At first I wasn't going to do anything. I started to crawfish, then thought to myself: How would you feel if it was your kid? At one p.m. I phoned the sheriff's office in Dallas. They said he was out but would call me back."

"I called back," Sheriff Neufeldt went on, "and I told him the folks had been lost since the ninth. He told me he would fly up to Salem. I said I'd meet him there and pick him up."

At 5:30 p.m. the next day, after being forced back twice by weather and twice changing planes, Norman and his dogs landed in Salem.

"Tony Neufeldt was waiting, along with the woman's father and mother," Norman recounted. "They asked me what I thought. I told them that after seeing the weather I had one chance in a million but I was willing to take it. The weather was foggy and misty and absolutely lousy for trailing. There were several newspapermen standing around with their tongues in their cheeks and laughing up their sleeves. I thought, if they're looking for a fall guy, here comes the sucker."

Tony Neufeldt asked Norm what time he wanted to start. "I'd just as soon get going tonight," Norm replied. After men and dogs had eaten, the party wheeled to Fanno Mountain. The dogs were started on Mrs. Zeiszler's clothing, which her parents had given the sheriff. Their huge, sensitive nostrils siphoned the odors from the garments and deposited the precise smell impressions on their memory banks. When they were satisfied they had the information they wanted they turned away.

"We figured Mrs. Zeiszler would be the first we'd find," Tony Neufeldt explained. "But the wind started blowing and everything was icy and the fog was coming in, so at one a.m. I came back to town to get some food and the others went to the lookout station and built a fire. We slept a few hours and came back to the Zeiszler car."

At five a.m. Norman and two foresters prepare to start. The party will carry two portable radios. Norman tells Tony: "We'll stay with it until we find somebody."

Norman pets his dogs, gives them the scent again; in the cold night it may have slipped away from them. Off they go toward the ridge and down into the brush and through thickets carpeted with ferns, around stumps and over fallen trees. The dogs grow alive, bound from one clue to the next. Something is up. Norman feels it in his bones.

But here is the Little Luckiamute, and everyone knows the family didn't get that far. Everyone but the hounds. They dart into the stream, come up the other bank, sniff and tug, sniff and tug . . .

At 11:47 a.m. Tony Neufeldt hears these words come over the radio: "We've found the boy." The lad had fallen for the last time 300 yards beyond the farthest line of the previous search parties.

The hounds fight to go on. It isn't Harvey Hoff they are seeking; it is Mrs. Zeiszler they are after. But Norman calls a halt. "We're beat," he tells Tony, talking about himself and the foresters. "I'd like us to rest up. I'm positive that if you get a search party in here you'll find the bodies of the others close by. If they aren't found I'll take the dogs in again tomorrow afternoon."

The next morning the search begins where 13-year-old Harvey's body has been found. An hour later Esther Zeiszler is discovered dead in a crude fir bed her husband had made for her beside a log. She is wearing his jacket and is covered with fir boughs to protect her. Her rifle is leaning against the log. She is found 500 yards northwest of the spot where her son had perished. Her husband's body, sighted 55 minutes later, is sprawled on its back 300 yards northwest of her, and only half a mile from the main truck road leading to Black Rock.

What happened to the family? There is only circumstantial evidence to weave into a pattern of speculation.

Lost, they became panicky. When the foggy chill struck them Esther Zeiszler grew bluish cold. She had come into the woods clad only in a pair of jeans, striped blouse, light sweater and light shoes. Zeiszler had tried to start a fire, but the branches were too large and too wet. With his hunting knife he could have peeled dry wood from a log. But he knew nothing of woodcraft.

Soon after they were lost Mrs. Zeiszler suffered two injuries to her right leg, spraining her ankle and incurring a bad bruise four inches higher. She probably went into labor pains the first or second day. Within 48 hours after she entered the woods she was dead. Her husband and son survived her by a day or two.

Those 48 hours must have been hellish ones. A storm hit the area the first evening and on the second and third days heavy rain fell.

Zeiszler may have told the boy to stay by his mother while he went for aid. Or he may have urged the lad to start off in another direction. Only this seems plausible: Zeiszler started toward the logging road after he heard some log trucks in the distance. Feebly he cried to them, lunging on until he collapsed, his rifle sliding to the ground. Frantic, he desperately crawled 60 feet. One shell was still in the chamber of his gun.

The boy started the other way but was soon swallowed up in fern six feet tall. He began walking in a circle, now completely disoriented, until he was too exhausted to stand. With life draining out of him he crawled, pulling himself a few inches at a time. One of his loafer-type oxfords and a sock were snagged off by ferns. He was found with his clawing hands full of twigs and ferns and his mouth full of soggy earth.

For Norman Wilson the Zeiszler search was a grueling experience but for the first time in his life he knew the plaudits of a community and the glory that comes to a hero. His dogs, it was said, had broken the previous record for bloodhounds following a cold trail. The old mark was 105 hours behind the hunted; Norm's dogs took a scent 315 hours cold and in eight hours solved a case that had frustrated hundreds of searchers for more than a week.

Wearily, Norman and his hounds returned to Los Gatos. But three days later they were back in western Oregon, this time to look for a 61-year-old Hillsboro banker, whose body was found at the foot of a bridge one mile south of Hillsboro. An hour after the hounds took to the fog-bound trail they located the spot where the banker had entered the Tualatin River, stones jammed in his pocket, to commit suicide. Search parties had been dragging the wrong portion of the stream.

As Norman was starting for home, the State forester offered him a job in the Polk-Benton division of the department. He talked it over with Phyllis. "Sure, why not?" she said. "We've got to eat."

In his first six weeks with the department, Norman and his dogs were dispatched on eight searches and each time were successful. But by then the glamour had worn off and people were looking elsewhere for momentary heroes.

For some reason, which was never made clear to me, Norm left the forestry department to take a job as a deputy sheriff. Soon he acquired a sleek, beautiful, vicious police dog. Only Norman, Phyllis and their son, Peter, born in 1954, were liked by the dog. Everyone else was an enemy.

Norman was now through with searches. "Too expensive," he muttered, "and nobody appreciates you." So he sold his bloodhounds, which he said he couldn't afford to feed any more.

There came a disagreement with Sheriff Neufeldt and Norm was an ex-deputy. He took another job, then found work as a welder in a Dallas factory.

For a while I lost track of him. We found each other again in the state capitol building. I was trying to elicit some information from an apparently irked secretary when I felt a heavy hand on my elbow and heard the growling words: "That'll be enough now." I started to protest: "Take your damn hands off me!" when I turned to see Norman. He was a sergeant-at-arms.

The family was still living in the farmhouse on a hill out of Dallas but they had given away the German Shepherd. "Too mean and expensive," said Norman. He looked very much overweight; not at all the man of muscle I had known in his bloodhound days.

Still, he retained the same sense of bitterness and helpfulness. He was contemptuous of legislators who were hypocrites and phonies and he swiftly opened doors that I might have battered against for weeks.

A few months later I learned that he had had a heart attack and was a patient at the Veterans Administration hospital in Portland. I found him pale, tired and grim, but as fatalistic as ever. Now he had two children and was worried about them but his wife remained his one abiding consolation: she had gone through a hundred hells with him and could manage by herself.

He survived that attack, and then another, and gave up his job as a sergeant-at-arms.

The last time I saw Norman he was a field representative for the Polk County Assessor. He was 43 now, wondering where all the years had gone, and resigned to a mundane life.

Every once in a while, in conversation, generally with a reporter, the search for the Zeiszlers is recalled. "Oh, yes," says the other person, a little unsure. "I think I remember it. Bloodhounds, wasn't that it? Broke some kind of record. Whatever happened to the fellow who had those dogs? Let's see now, what was his name?"

Norman couldn't care less. He never relished the moment of glory that was thrust upon him and perhaps he recalls the troubles that followed in the wake of fame. If he thinks about those exhausting searches—one in the Sierra was 56 hours long—or about the great bloodhounds who broke through the brush hot-nostriled for someone they had never seen, he does not talk about it. He has settled down to a sedentary life. The only call of the wild he hears comes from his television set.

Ernest Bloch

The Vacant Rendezvous

Only a matter of two dollars—or perhaps even a dollar —prevented me from meeting Ernest Bloch, one of the world's great composers. At least I thought so at the time. And now the opportunity has long past.

Only some months before, in the early spring of 1956, while residing in Eugene, I had written to Bloch, living at Agate Beach, asking to interview him.

He replied, in a hand-written note, that he was quite busy and preferred that I wait, but that if I could not wait he would see me. A magazine had requested the story on him, I answered, but I could understand the crowded schedule of a creative person and would explain the siutation to the editors.

Instantly he wrote back: "I appreciated deeply your very considerate letter—(It is so rare!) and I certainly will be glad to see you in Agate Beach.

"Only," he explained, "I am now slowly recuperating from delicate surgery, six months ago—my life was completely disorganized, my work interrupted. I have to come again to Portland for more medical treatment and, if all goes well, I plan to fly to Europe in three or four weeks. So I am not sure that there would be a decent time and no hurry when we could meet.

"I will be back sometime in late September—if this were possible to you, I think that in the fall we could talk more leisurely and . . . at peace—

"If not, I will try to arrange a meeting before I leave. Please, let me know—"

It would be all right to wait until the fall, I assured him, and added casually: "We will both be around."

Some time in the late spring or early summer—I cannot even remember the month—I had to come to Portland to cover an assignment and perhaps pick up a few trade stories. There I read that Bloch had again been taken ill. Promptly I dashed off a few lines, wishing him a speedy recovery.

I had come to Portland with only enough money to carry me over modestly for three days. (This was in the time of our hungry free-lancing and every penny was stretched to the utmost.) On the late afternoon of the fourth day, by an extra effort at skimping, I had sufficient funds left to fill the gas tank of our old Plymouth and buy a two pound rye bread, half of which provided the sum of my supper.

That evening the clerk of the Danmoore Hotel, where I generally stayed when I came to Portland, handed me a letter. It was from Ernest Bloch, saying he was feeling better and would be in Portland the next day, someone having volunteered to drive him up. He was coming to see his doctor, and would I meet him at noon in the Imperial Hotel for lunch.

All night long I struggled with the agony of the decision I had to make. Now I can see other alternatives: I could have, for instance, told him that I had had a very late breakfast and was not hungry; or that I had a prior luncheon engagement but would like to talk with him later that day. None of these simple maneuvers occurred to me. The problem was that I was broke, completely broke, with only half a bread until I returned home, and how embarrassing it would be if I ate with him and had to pay for my own lunch. Also, I reasoned, I could not permit him to pay for my food; it was I who had approached him.

Up until ten minutes of noon I was still gripped by indecision. How strongly I wanted to see this creative giant, regarded by many music critics as the greatest composer since Beethoven. Here was a story whose sale was assured. But pride, if that is what you want to call it, would not permit me to come as a beggar. So dolefully I crawled into my car and drove home, munching the dry bread to the last crumb.

Some years later I described this incident to Bloch's son, Ivan, the cosmopolitan consulting engineer. Somehow I expected Ivan to see the pathos or the humor of the situation. But Ivan, who has heard everything, just shrugged his shoulders and smiled wanly.

In the autumn of 1956 I wrote to Ernest Bloch again but the reply this time came from his secretary: "He is in Portland convalescing from an illness of a very serious nature." In the summer of 1958, while passing through Portland, I phoned Ivan and spoke to his mother, Margaret Bloch. She said her husband was in a hospital and that it would be best for me not to try to see him. "That man

is so restless, so worried about the work he has to do,"
she said. "Listen to what he said to me: 'I must get up
and create music.' But he is very sick." Three years after
I could have met him at the Imperial, Ernest Bloch died.

A year or two after his passing, we were driving up the
coast, looking for a motel. At Agate Beach we saw a sign
which indicated a place off the highway. We followed a
side road that slipped up a small knoll and just as we
rounded a bend we passed a mail box that bore the letters: BLOCH.

"Didn't Ernest Bloch live at Agate Beach?" my wife
asked. "Maybe this was his home." Until then I had not
thought of him for many months.

After we had settled at the motel I strolled back to the
mail box and turned into a lane leading to a large house
that looked somewhat like a hunting lodge and knocked at
the door. It opened and I was greeted by an ample, ma-
tronly figure of a woman, with a round but firm face and
strong but gentle eyes.

"Is this where Ernest Bloch lived?" I asked.

"Yes," she replied.

"I had some correspondence with him," I explained. "I
was supposed to come here to interview him at one time,
but it never materialized."

"What is your name?" the woman asked.

I told her.

"Ah, yes," she said. "I remember. I am Mrs. Bloch."

She gestured me into the house and we spoke for two
hours. I asked if I might bring my wife and child to meet
her that evening, and she agreed. Altogether I saw her
for about four hours.

This was the cherished home, on a bluff overlooking the
open sea, where Ernest Bloch had for almost two decades
lived with his wife and cats, ranging from seven to fourteen. ("I like cats," he once said, "because they relax so
beautifully, something I never learned to do.") Here, to the
muffled roar of the breakers and the sighing evergreens as
undertones, he composed, often in a lyrical and rhapsodical
style, themes expressive of deeply felt passions and ideals,
music filled with the tumult of a surging humanity and

coupled with a lifelong yearning for peace and the Brotherhood of Man.

Bloch was already universally renowned when he came to Agate Beach. His choice of this location was due to fortuitous circumstances, a lucky stroke for Oregon, for he gave to this state the most gigantic creative talent in all its history.

While driving from San Francisco to Portland, to visit Ivan, Bloch was halted at Agate Beach by a road block. "There's high water ahead," warned a policeman. "You'll have to go back down to Toledo, cross over to Corvallis, and then go up to Portland."

A bit weary, Bloch decided to call it quits for the day. He rented a modest tourist cabin, had an early dinner, and took a stroll on the beach.

His first impression fascinated him. The pounding surf, the rocky coastline, the rugged, wooded hills and the craggy peaks beyond sent joy surging through his heart as the vistas multiplied.

The discovery of agates bound him over another day, for Bloch had long been an ardent amateur lapidarian. On the second day he hiked into the woods and there, among the salmonberry bushes, he found an abundance of mushrooms.

A mushroom connoisseur since boyhood mountain days in his native Switzerland, Bloch's discovery of such variety and numbers of these fleshy fungi made Agate Beach even more interesting.

Only the question of a house remained and when he found it, a sprawling beach home, complete with great living room for a study, and large fireplace, he was sure where his future residence lay.

Into the living room came a huge desk, a grand piano and a table soon piled high with books and music. Paintings and sculptory filled the walls and shelves.

Only his bed was gone from the house when I visited Mrs. Bloch. "I could not bear it to be here after he passed away," she said. "It was the bed of death. I could not stand to be near it."

Mrs. Bloch talked often of the man whom she had known so intimately for so many years. But the words did not spill out; they came restrained, methodical, subdued, painful, casually informative and with vibrance, her mood shifting from answer to answer. She did not know how to begin to tell about her late husband, except in the generalities of flesh torn from flesh, for when there is so much to say there is often little said, and I might have learned scarcely anything about him had I not asked questions which indicated my own sincere respect for Ernest Bloch.

She described Bloch as a close student of history and politics, a man deeply aware of the world about him, a liberal thinker, vital and outgoing, kindly and approachable, zestful and zealous, a bundle of physical, intellectual, spiritual energy and passion that was overwhelmingly forceful.

Yet, curiously, I thought, although it was evident that she was enormously proud of him, there was not a single boastful word in all her speech. She had understood and cared for him, as a man and a child, as one who had serenely accepted his creative loneliness and whose entire married life was meshed to his will and ways.

"Where is Mr. Bloch buried?" I asked.

She lifted her arm toward the side of the room. My eyes followed a shelf until it came to an urn.

"His ashes?"

She nodded, and explained that some day, when the Bloch family could come together at Agate Beach, Mrs. Bloch, her daughter-musician, Suzanne, her daughter-artist, Lucienne, and Ivan, would carry the urn into the hills, or to the banks of a river, or perhaps to a point on the beach facing the sea, and there commit to Nature the last chemical remains of husband and father.

"Mr. Bloch hated funeral ceremonies," she said, as we sat in the shroud of a gloomy, chill October afternoon near the piano where Bloch had spent so much time. "He didn't want a public funeral, he didn't want to be buried, he didn't want a monument. He was insistent that his ashes be scattered to the winds or into the sea or among the tall trees he loved."

A year later Mrs. Bloch sold the house and on June 5,

1963, almost four years after the passing of her husband, the beat of her heart was also stilled.

"Whatever happened to the ashes?" I once asked Ivan Bloch. "Were they ever scattered to the sea?"

"Well," he replied, with an enigmatic smile, "it's against the law, you know."

Mathilde Grenier DeLore

"I Never Went No Place"

It was a teen-age girl, Mary Jo Pfeffer, who told me of 103-year-old Mathilde Grenier DeLore.

I met Mary Jo, a Portland high school student, at an annual banquet of the Sons and Daughters of Oregon Pioneers. She was there as the new Miss Oregon Pioneer and I was present to give what was euphemistically noted in the program as an address.

The program listed Mary Jo's genealogy of Oregon pioneers—all the way back to Etienne Lucier, the French-Canadian trapper who entered the Oregon Country in 1812. After service with Hudson's Bay Company, he became the first white settler on French Prairie and later participated in the historic "divide" meeting at Champoeg. According to legend, he and F. X. Matthieu, with whom he lived, placed themselves on the "American side," thus making the count 52 to 50 for Provisional Government.

Well, the great-granddaughter of Etienne Lucier was Mathilde Grenier DeLore, the great-grandmother of Mary Jo Pfeffer.

"You ought to talk to my great-grandmother," suggested Mary Jo when she learned I was interested in tape-recording old timers. "She lives in The Dalles"—and Mary Jo gave us the address.

About two weeks later we drove to The Dalles, to a modest frame house on West 9th St., to put on tape the words of a woman who was born while Lincoln was still president. It didn't turn out that way, but it was a pleasant day to be on the road, I've always liked The Dalles, and I did get to see a centenarian.

Imagine a person whose life has truly spanned the eras of stagecoach to jet flights or, more realistically, as in her case, from saddle horse and buckwagon to space ships. She was five years old when the first transcontinental railroad was completed, and married and a mother when the first train from the east reached Portland. She had been an adult years before electric lights flickered in Oregon; she was a grandmother when she first saw an automobile.

Mrs. DeLore was asleep on a hospital bed in the living room when we called. The house belonged to her daughter, Ethyl DeLore Bell, who declared she was 74, which I would never have guessed. A fine figure of a woman, with a handsome face, and tilting a cigarette at a jaunty angle, she appeared about 20 years younger. Except for the cane she carried, I would have thought her capable of waltzing around the room.

"Mama can't hear well," Mrs. Bell told us matter-of-factly. "I have to shout at her sometimes. Her eyesight is bad, too. Sometimes she doesn't talk but sometimes she'll talk on and on. Depends on how she feels. I don't think she's up to talking today."

I looked at the figure on the bed, curled up like a small child. A frail husk of a person, whom age had nibbled the stuff of life away on the inside and blotched on the outside, leaving a wrinkled, bony, scaly surface below a patch of white hair. This was the woman whose parents were adults when Oregon was not yet a state.

"Mama was never sick a day in her life until she was ninety-five," Mrs. Bell informed us casually and with an undertone of pride. "She was living at the ranch of my brother, her son, Mose DeLore, around Maupin. Then she broke her hip. I brought her down here and she's been here ever since."

When Mathilde Grenier was ten, her family moved to Juniper Flat, near present Wapinitia. She grew up there, on the high and naked plain, and when she was of marrying age she got hitched to a homesteader.

"There was no Wapinitia then," said Mrs. Bell. "No Maupin, nothing, not even fences, between my folks and Tygh Valley."

By the time Mrs. Bell was ready for school, Wapinitia had a one-room schoolhouse and a general store. It had become a hamlet.

"Mama was quite rugged when she was young," Mrs. Bell stated staunchly. "She and my father rode horseback across the Cascade Mountains to St. Paul and St. Louis, in the French Prairie country. They did that several times.

"Mama drove two wagons—a trailer-wagon, one wagon fastened to the other—and four horses over Tygh Ridge, when it wasn't any better than a cow trail," Mrs. Bell continued. "My dad broke his leg and Mama had to take his place.

"They were wheat farmers and they took the wheat down to The Dalles. It took two days to get from Wapinitia to The Dalles. The first night they made it just to Dufur. When the wagon was emptied of wheat, supplies were set in, and then the trip started back."

Mrs. Bell tried to remember other things about her mother. Finally she said: "We don't have any records or diaries or things like that of the past. We never thought of keeping any. My grandfolks sure had stories to tell."

Suddenly Mrs. Bell's eyes brightened. "My granddad's brother, Pete DeLore, he was sure a man! He blazed a trail with his hatchet from Wapinitia to the Willamette Valley. When the road was built, it followed his trail. My granddad and his brother Pete could tell stories all night. I've tried remembering them, but I can't seem to."

Well, I said, you were born before the turn of the century. Did anything interesting happen to you up around Wapinitia or Maupin?

"No," replied Mrs. Bell, shaking her head vacantly. "It was just livin', just work. Just one day after the other. I never saw anything exciting. But maybe Mama did. She was an early settler up there."

A moment later she added: "Mama has 14 grandchildren

and 34 great-grandchildren. I've got 29 grandchildren." And a smile touched her serious but pleasant features.

Just then Mrs. DeLore shuffled and blinked awake. I asked if we could take her photo and Mrs. Bell replied that she would first have to fix her mother's hair. She rolled up the upper half of the bed, so that the elderly lady was in a reclining position, notified her mother in a loud voice that someone wanted to take her picture, and began to comb her hair, which was long and smooth and lovely when combed out. She looked then, the mother did, like the matriarch of a tribe.

The centenarian stared at us, trying to fix us in her mind. When she saw the camera she blurted thickly, through toothless gums, "I'm gonna make a face." Everybody laughed and I thought I saw a corner of her eye twinkle.

Mrs. Bell called in a strong voice, "Mama, this man wants to talk to you about the pioneer days."

The old lady slowly, very slowly, with lips pressed together and nostrils flared, like a prophet who has been challenged, shifted her gaze to me, then returned her eyes to a neutral position, so that she was staring straight ahead, to the heart of judgment.

"I never went no place," she clacked, with a show of irritation. "Just stayed home. I don't know nothin' about the pioneer days."

There was still great strength in the long cheekbones of her leathery face. Her eyes seemed a bit bewildered but they were still soft, the blurred eyes of a child aroused out of a deep sleep. She must have been a beautiful woman in her prime.

There should be much about the old days she could tell us, I commented to Mrs. Bell.

Putting her mouth close to her mother's ear, Mrs. Bell repeated the message.

The old lady blinked her eyes and snorted: "I get tired of all the stuff I don't know nothin' about!"

And after that there wasn't anything else we could do but say goodbye and leave.

Joe Zatica

No Sheepdip for Him

There are a lot of myths in Oregon. Not as many as in California, and not as wild, but enough to keep life interesting.

One of the myths concerns sheepherders and sheep around Jordan Valley.

There are still articles written, some of them by state residents, about the great flocks of sheep which make the hills of southeast Oregon look like rough, grey woolen blankets and about the "quaint" and "picturesque" Basque sheepherders, each so happy to be alone.

And then there is the myth that Jordan Valley is so completely Basque that English is scarcely spoken there.

In 1964, when we called upon Joe Zatica, an early Basque sheepherder, in his modest frame house in Jordan Valley, there were only 1,500 sheep on the hills and only one Basque was still in the sheep business. (I understand that man sold out and that there aren't enough sheep around the area now to make any flock look larger than a doormat on a slope.) As for the tale of Jordan Valley being so all-Basque, the language is scarcely heard on the street and other aspects of the culture are looked upon as relics of a lustier day.

The first Basques came to Jordan Valley about 1885, give or take a year or three. They "got into sheep," as the saying goes, and when they had built their flocks so that they needed herders they wrote to their kinfolks and countrymen in the shadows of the Pyrenees, in northeastern Spain.

Joe Zatica received a letter which read, as he remembered it, "If you want to work sheep, herd sheep, come over here."

A lot of other men, all bachelors, also received letters; Joe was one of about 300 Basques who "jumped the ocean" late in 1910.

In New York, he recalled, "They keep us in one big house, because if you go out, go like sheep, stroll all over, but they keep us in one place. See? An' after that, come in Chicago, they gotta big depot, an' y'gotta eat, everything like that, but no sleep, we sleep on the bench, or on floor, 'til next mornin', next mornin' they load it, an' we come, to Nampa. Nampa, yeah."

He sat in his overstuffed chair, a bit bewildered by the attention paid to him by a visiting reporter, but pleased to have company on a hot day in August. The sun was too bright to wander outside and the house, while cool, was quiet, and Joe Zatica was a man who liked to chat with people. He would have talked more to his wife if she were not so busy around the house, which was spotless.

At Nampa the Basques separated, going to different parts of Idaho and Oregon. Joe took the electric train to Caldwell and then boarded a four-horse stage, which took two days to reach Jordan Valley, a distance I easily drove in an hour and a half.

"Stage driver, he say," chuckled Joe Zatica, "go walk, because horses, too much mud, can't pull it, he go like that, he mean, go walk. Understand what I mean?"

He made sure we comprehended before he continued, with a smile of satisfaction.

" 'N' we come in here, and got two hotels, Monaco Hotel I think one was, an' we come over here an' we see all stage drivers show the cook in hotel, an' we can't talk, and we put fingers that we wanna eat, to show, you know? Wanta this one, wanta that one, and we got the money, before come from Spain, we got to make American money, an' I ask him, how much he wants it, we can't understand, and each bill, we got in pocket five or ten, he picks that, an' we don' know how much he charge, but anyway, give it so much back, and glad. Jordan Valley. And all roads same way."

There is still another myth, that all the Basques in Spain were sheepherders and tended flocks as large as they were hired to guard in the Jordan Valley country.

Joe Zatica shakes his head vigorously. "Some Basques, before they come here, they never touch sheep. See but not touch. Don' own." As for his family: "We got a twenty-five heads in Spain, but gotta keep it inside the barn. See. In Spain, no room, so all farms, our country, maybe twelve, fifteen acres. Lotta places here, lotta big ranches. But our country small, lotta people, small."

He didn't stay in Jordan Valley long enough that bewildering day early in 1911 to know what it was like. Actually, he was passing through, on his way to Salt Creek, 22 miles from town. There he was given a band of 2,200 sheep to tend. It was four years before he saw Jordan Valley again, before he really saw it for the first time.

Then, half a century removed from where we stood, there were about 150,000 sheep in the hills stretching back from the Jordan and Owyhee Rivers. So there were quite a few sheepherders. But they rarely came in contact with each other.

"I was six years in one place," Mr. Zatica said, without humor. "Sometimes another sheepherder gathered, see. Maybe I got a band sheep there, and another sheepherder, maybe two miles, three miles, side, a sheepherder. Sheepherders see each other. But often alone. Months alone, maybe many months."

Did he like the lonely life?

He shook his head to his right shoulder and then to his left shoulder and made another round trip before he stopped at center position.

"Life herding sheep no good," he said with dour emphasis. "No-o-o, no good. Not good life, not like. No Basque like. That time, young people do everything, you know, no 'nough food, all the sheep mens not much money, and thirty dollars, wages. Thirty a month."

After six years of sheepherding he settled in Jordan Valley and bought some sheep of his own. But in 1922 he lost everything. "You don't know, you never remember that, but depression time. Can't find a twenty dollar bill Jordan Valley that time. Broke. And after that, started truckin' business, small truck of course, and after that, buy big one, hauling cattle and sheep in that. Do that until 1952."

Did you retire then, we asked.

He smiled wearily. "No, no retired. Tired. Heart trouble.

Kidney trouble. Broke veins. See that? Sharp veins comin' out both sides, foot. Can't do nothing."

In the old days, he said, which was about 50 or 40 years ago, the Basques had their own dances and clubs and socials. But there was never a Basque school nor a Basque newspaper and only seldom, when a visiting priest brought up in northeastern Spain came Jordan Valley way, were services in the lovely Catholic Church conducted in Basque.

Up in Homedale, Idaho there was a priest who still rendered sermons in Basque, said Mr. Zatica, but fewer and fewer of the old Basques from Jordan Valley were going up to hear him. Each year diminished the distance they wanted to travel, even with better roads and cars. They still lived by the mile, not time.

As for the young Basques, only a few of the children of Mr. Zatica's generation spoke Basque and hardly any of his generation's grandchildren did. A number of Basques were still around Jordan Valley, owning stores, running filling stations, working in the trades, holding state and county jobs. Quite a few had intermarried and Mr. Zatica was afraid there soon wouldn't be a sign of anything Basque around. "But, that life," he said quietly.

Will you tell in Basque how it was in the old days, we asked. He chuckled and shook his head. His wife, a sprightly woman with merry eyes, came dancing out of the kitchen to persuade him. She was remarkably light and graceful on her feet. "Well, come on," she prodded her husband.

Are you Basque, too, we asked. "Sure," she replied, with a proud swagger of her head.

The Zaticas conversed with each other in their rare and ancient tongue. Mrs. Zatica turned to us. "Well, what I goin' tell you?"

Just tell us how life was around here when you were young.

They again spoke to each other in Basque and Mrs. Zatica translated. "All the Bascos, maybe fifty, sixty or more, dancin' Basco dances, celebration."

Will you sing us a song in Basque, we requested.

"I don't know," Joe said. He and his wife once more chatted swiftly in Basque and ended in laughter.

"Yes, singin'," said Joe, "but you know what? Bascos, they singin' lot of dirty words too." There was more laughter.

Please, we insisted, let's hear you sing a little song in Basque. He started and was doing fine, singing deadpan, when his wife threw her hands above her head, screamed in laughter, and brought her head down into her apron, throbbing in a spasm of hilarity.

Joe stopped singing. "Eh, can't do it," he chuckled. "Lot of dirty words."

As we were leaving, we said: "Next time we come by we'd like to take you to a restaurant. How about lamb chops or mutton?"

"O.K. on plate," Joe said. "But you our guests, at home."

We take it, we said, tongue in cheek, that you didn't care very much for the romantic life of sheepherding.

Joe snorted, arising an inch from his chair, which held him prisoner. Then a grin extended his mouth deep into each cheek, bringing into warm relief the crinkles of age.

"You can betcha say again."

Nellie Miller

Catlow Was Too Quiet

You won't find Blitzen on the map. It hasn't been there for a long time. Like a lot of other sagebrush towns, it just faded away. Only a building or two remains.

For Nellie Miller, though, Blitzen would be a strong memory as long as she lived. That's what she told us as we chatted on a hot summer afternoon in the general store at Crane.

Blitzen, in the Catlow Valley, out by Frenchglen way, which is south of Burns, was settled in the last rush of homesteading. The town wasn't much, "just a little garage, and post office, and two little stores, and that was practically all," but it was a community.

"There was six hundred votes cast out there in the Catlow Valley when women's suffrage went in," Mrs. Miller said. "You'd have a hard time finding sixty people in the whole Catlow Valley now. The whole valley was settled up with homesteaders. Why, about four miles straight west of Blitzen there was a place they used to call Ragtown, because in the beginning it was all tents. That was a school district, they had a high school there. Nothing there now. You'd have a hard time knowing there was a place there."

Nellie Miller, who was born in 1898, moved out to Catlow Valley as a young bride. The big rush of homesteaders was on then, about 1915, but by 1920 most of the newcomers were pulling stakes.

"They just couldn't make it," Mrs. Miller explained. "You can't farm in this country and make a go of it. It was rough, with sagebrush and everything, and in those days you done everything with horses and teams, you didn't have no machinery."

The Millers were among the few who stayed on. After the homestead they bought a ranch in the valley and went into cattle raising. "I spent thirty-six years in Catlow Valley. That's why I know a lot about it," she said.

She had lived in Crane for 12 years when we saw her at the general store. Life was pleasant, even though she didn't have electricity in her home. "I've got propane, propane lights and everything, and refrigerators, and water heaters, and stoves, and I'm not trading it off for electric," she snorted between bursts of laughter. "They wanted thirty-five dollars a month to put the electricity in that old house of mine, and a I said no, I wouldn't use five dollars worth, and I work for my money and I'm not going to throw it away like that. And they haven't come down on their prices any, either, I don't think."

Mrs. Miller had lived in Harney County all her life. She had been brought up at Lawen, 11 miles west of Crane. "My grandmother," she recalled, "she run the store and post office there for about twenty years, and she also kept travel, and she had a double story, just a wooden frame house. And then grandfather, when he first settled in the valley, before that, he had a place three miles south, and he had a big log house, a double story log house, that he built himself."

Sometimes her grandfather would go into Burns, about 20 miles away, for supplies, and sometimes her grandfolks would drive a freight wagon clean to Huntington, way over near the Snake, and fill it up with goods for grandma's store. It was a mighty long trip, with the freight wagon team covering only about 30 miles a day, but folks weren't in such a consarned hurry to get places then, Mrs. Miller declared firmly.

Huntington was the big supply center because it was the terminus of a railroad that was creeping westward. "It would go a few years at a time," said Mrs. Miller, and each time it moved Harney County folks found the distance to supplies shorter.

"Well, the railroad came to Vale. And then later on it came to Juntura. And then on to Riverside, and then to Crane, and then to Burns."

Crane was just "mostly tents around here" when the railroad came—"I'm not sure whether it was 1914 or 1915. But I was here!" And she italicized that fact with a jut of her chin.

There was a big celebration when the engine puffed into the brand new terminal, establishing Crane as the big market town in the county. Mrs. Miller spoke of that day with pleasure.

"Several hundred people were here and we danced all night, on an outdoor pavilion, and everybody came with wagons and teams and buggies and horseback and we had big picnic lunches and it was a wonderful time for Harney County. Came from Burns and everywhere. We had a Ford at that time, we thought we was quite get up and go. It was the second set of Fords that came into the county, and my folks got one, so we came in a Ford, but most folks came in buggy and team."

A year or two later Nellie married and took off with her husband to homestead on the flats of Blitzen. Crane grew as a cattle shipping center. It had warehouses, stockyards, paved sidewalks, and a garage, hotel, bank, livery stable, several stores and some fine houses.

In 1920 the railroad moved again, with Burns the new terminus, and that took care of Crane. The general store, which was also the post office and the only place in town where you could buy gasoline, was the only private business in town we could see. If it hadn't been for the high school, the only boarding school in Oregon, with students coming from far off the ranges back of the rimrock hills, Crane might not even have been on the map.

Mrs. Miller and I walked outside and looked at the sidewalks all but covered by sagebrush. It was a quiet day, not a car on the gravel street or a car coming down the paved road that led to Burns or Princeton. The landscape beyond Crane was a sea of sagebrush and bunchgrass, where two trees comprised a forest and where the only sign of life was a jackrabbit flashing across the wasteland.

I turned in all directions, to see as much of Crane as possible. Apart from the students, I doubted if there were a hundred people in and near the town.

"Do you ever miss Catlow Valley?" I asked.

"Heck no!" Mrs. Miller exclaimed. "That place is too quiet. I like a place that's got some people and pep. That's why I come to Crane."

Joe Thoma

"They Was All Nice Fellas"

Louis La Bonte was supposedly the first retired Hudson's Bay Company trapper to settle around the present town of Dayton. The 19th century was but three decades old.

Half a mile down Neck Road from where La Bonte had built a dwelling on his Donation Land Claim I found Joe Thoma, who said he knew La Bonte.

La Bonte was getting on in age when he knew him, Joe Thoma said. "Pretty near hundred years old when he died."

So Joe Thoma, who was born in 1880, on the same farm

he was living on when he was 85, had been a boy when he knew La Bonte. He remembered the ancient trapper as "a half-breed—two-thirds Indian I guess he was," who spoke "mostly English and French both" and died in St. Paul, "on the other side of the river."

Joe Thoma, who called himself "the oldest old timer around in Dayton anymore," lived in a house that was built in 1905, he said. It looked to me at least 50 years older. A brief tour of the inside just about convinced me that the old man had saved every newspaper, magazine, garment, broken cup, tin can and potato peel he had laid fingers on since the house was built, and maybe before then. He had never married and early in manhood had acquired the backwoods bachelor's penchant for packratting.

His parents settled here in 1873, buying the land from Charlie Terry, first man here under the Homestead Act, Thoma said. He didn't say it all at once; it took about three questions to pry this information from him. He had lived so long alone that he either regarded words as something you could do without or as too precious to be passed out by the mouthful. Sometimes I had a feeling he meant it one way and other times I was sure he supposed it the other way.

Here was a man who was a living link to early Oregon history, but all he remembered of La Bonte and of General Joel Palmer, who was in charge of "Indian Affairs" before Oregon achieved statehood, who founded Dayton, and whose handsome two-story house, which he built in Dayton in 1852, still stands, though muchly modified—all Thoma could remember of La Bonte and Palmer was that "they was nice fellas."

He had to be quite young, of course, when he knew them. He did volunteer that he "knowed Palmer's son, Will, knowed him well."

And what kind of a man was Will?

"Nice fella."

Is that all you can remember of him, I asked.

The old man looked at me long and stroked his rough chin, probably wondering what kind of an educated fool I was that I couldn't understand the English language.

"Nice fella," he repeated, and laid the palm of his hand hard on the porch.

All around the house were trees, some of them standing when Joe Thoma's parents took over the homestead from Charlie Terry almost 100 years ago. Mostly they were maple and ash. The old man pointed to a cherry tree and said: "See that? The one over there? My father planted with a pit."

A tangle of trees screened the Willamette River, below a high bluff, from view. Joe Thoma knew the river well. As a boy he had fished in it for bass and catfish. For about 15 years, starting around the turn of the century, he had run a ferry boat across the river, until a bridge put him out of business.

As I said, Mr. Thoma was not exactly what you would call a talkative man, and you can judge the truth of my statement by part of the taped conversation, with Mr. Thoma answering the questions.

"You're not far from Champoeg, are you?"

"Down the road a piece."

"That's a pretty historic place in Oregon, isn't it?"

"Yeah."

"When you were young, was Dayton pretty much of a Saturday night town?"

"Oh."

"Was it full of horses and buggies?"

"Horses and buggies. Couple of livery stables. Two or three blacksmith shops."

"How long did it take you to get to Portland in those years?"

"Well, I didn't go to Portland only by train or steamboat."

"Were there steamboats here?"

"Oh yeah, every day four or five of them."

"How long did it take to get up by steamboat?"

"Portland?"

"Yes. How long did it take to get to Portland?"

"Oh, it'd take about three hours."

"You took the train sometimes?"

"Oh, yes."

"You caught the train at Dayton?"

"Yes. The tracks are still there."

"How long did it take from Dayton to Portland?"

"About an hour. Little over an hour."

"Did Dayton have more people than it has now?"

"Oh no. Got a little over seven hundred now. I don't think it was over a hundred then."

"Is that right?"

"Dayton right now is dyin' out fast. Hardware store went out. Drug store went out. Variety store went out. Lunch counter went out. Just lately. Everything's goin' out."

"Where do you do your shopping now?"

"McMinnville."

"How do you get there?"

"Oh, just hop into the car and go."

I asked the old man if he had any diaries or records his parents might have left him or if he had any documents or magazines or newspapers going back to his boyhood.

"Could be, I dunno," he said, but he wasn't about to start looking, and I couldn't blame him. I thought that if he found anything he was searching for in his heaped, cob-webbed house it would be by accident.

Before we left I tried once more to prime the pump of history. "A lot of the Hudson's Bay Company trappers and traders settled around here, didn't they?"

The old man nodded.

"Some of them lived pretty long lives and I reckon you knew a few when you were a boy."

"Reckon," he agreed.

"Did they ever talk about their early days?"

Joe Thoma pondered. "Never asked 'em. Mostly talked about crops and weather. But they was all nice fellas."

Jonas Mosser

Hermit of Adventist Creek

One of the serenest men I ever met was Jonas "Grandpa" Mosser, the gentle hermit of Adventist Creek.

He was edging on 80 then, but his mind was sharp as a blade, there was laughter in his eyes and a hymn for life in his heart. His clothing looked like they had come out of a town dump where only poor people discarded what absolutely could not be salvaged and his living quarters probably would have shocked the week-end nature lovers who relish in "roughing it," but Grandpa behaved as though he hadn't a personal care in the whole wide world.

When I saw him last, some years ago, he hadn't paid land taxes for about 35 years and he was living on less than $100 a year, which he earned by selling wool blankets he made with the most rudimentary tools.

All this time, three-and-a-half decades, the white-bearded, blue-eyed Jonas Mosser had been squatting unmolested on federal soil. A man from the government offered this logical explanation: "Grandpa just being there is worth all the taxes we could get out of him. He keeps down fire hazards. Anyway, we like him."

The Mosser "homestead" occupied an idyllic setting on the crest of a rolling hill looping into the Coast Range. It was more than 15 miles from a paved road and four miles from a dirt road, which ran out at the farm of Grandpa's son, Noah. When Grandpa wanted to go to Willamina, the nearest town, he'd hike down to Noah's place and wait until Noah finished his chores.

Only a trill from Grandpa's cabin were virgin woods, aswarm in summer with songbirds, and the habitat of deer, bear, coyotes and other wildlife. From these woods he gathered huckleberries and rhubarb for eating and cascara "for medicine."

The cabin lacked all modern conveniences. There was no electricity, but Grandpa found nothing wrong with kerosene lamps. There was no indoor plumbing or pump; Grandpa used a creaky Chic Sale whose tired boards were beginning to come apart, and hauled water from the brook at the edge of the forest. An ancient iron wood stove supplied his cooking needs.

Jonas Mosser had no radio and subscribed to no publication. (He didn't have a mailbox.) But he was an avid reader. He studied the Bible daily, closely scanned newspapers friends brought him, and read books "worth reading." One of these was Thoreau's *Walden*. Grandpa thought Thoreau had the right idea.

A small flock of sheep provided the gentle hermit with wool for the four-foot by six-and-a-half-foot blankets he knitted, averaging one a month. He also derived some revenue from the sale of surplus sheep.

Grandpa did all the blanket making by hand, from shearing to knitting. In place of a spinning wheel he used a hand-made "Peruvian Indian spinner."

Not all of his blankets were sold. He had knit blankets for every one of his 20 grandchildren and six great-grandchildren. The blankets he toted to Willamina were eagerly purchased by the townspeople.

With the purchase money, Grandpa bought rye, barley and corn, from which he made bread, using a hand grinder. But his favorite staple was soybean meal, "wonderful" for flour and milk. "It just fits in with everything," Grandpa offered enthusiastically. "It goes in good with fruit, you can put it in gravy, it's just fine for seasoning. You see, the Chinese and Japanese have lived over there during famines on just soy beans."

Field peas he obtained from the canneries, which were glad to get rid of discards. Grandpa cracked the peas, seasoned them with onions, and cooked them whole. They tasted like lentils.

Some vegetables Grandpa raised in his own garden. Carrots and potatoes were given him by Noah, whom Grandpa helped work a plot. Apples, grapes, prunes and other fruit were brought by people who were fond of him. Some came from 50 miles away. These were mostly men and women who were knocking themselves out to pile up more money to pay more taxes and were so busy keeping their noses to the grindstone they weren't seeing much beauty in life. They envied Grandpa, him doing some of the things they wished they had the courage to do, so by helping Grandpa they were pointing to their own frustrations and showing appreciation for a man who didn't have any.

"I dry about three times as much fruit as I can use and give the rest to poor folks," Grandpa said. "I'm active all the time. When the weather is bad I knit and spin, knit and spin. And ponder."

It seemed to me Grandpa did a lot of pondering. He sounded like Henry Thoreau might have a hundred years after Thoreau died. But Grandpa was so sweet and mild that if he had stood on a street corner and delivered a modern day version of the Sermon on the Mount, few would have been offended. There would have been, I suppose, some who would have grumbled about his lack of "patriotism" and maybe one or two would have called him a senile beatnik. But most of his listeners would have just thought the old man odd and quaint.

Born in a sod house on the banks of the Platte River in Nebraska, Jonas Mosser started doing man's work while yet a boy. At 18 he left home to herd sheep in Wyoming. In 1904 he became manager of a grain elevator in new-found Ashton, Idaho, and there married his childhood sweetheart, Cora Davidson.

"The snow in Idaho was too big for my family," Grandpa recalled, "so we moved to Oregon." That was in 1912. After going broke in a chicken farm near McMinnville the Mossers began a slow drift westward, farming as they went. In 1924 they settled near Grandpa's "hermit homestead," but two years later they were told they were on private property. The family trekked a quarter of a mile south and built again.

"The government canceled the Homesteading Act, so I was left twiddling my thumbs," explained Grandpa. "When

I came into town to prove up on my land, I found there wasn't any more Homesteading Act. So I put it out of my mind."

Jonas and Cora had seven boys and three daughters. Eight were living, seven in Oregon, when last I saw Grandpa. Cora had left him many years ago, to take the six youngest children to Medford, for schooling, which Jonas insisted he could himself provide.

"Once in a while," said Grandpa matter-of-factly, "my wife came up to see me and tried to talk me into leaving and living in a town. She said it was no place for a man my age. I reckon," he chuckled softly, "she thinks I'm teched in the head." I gathered she hadn't been around for several years but had managed, perhaps through Noah, to keep track of Jonas.

Grandpa received no old age pension, social security or any form of public aid. Since he did not regard himself as destitute he had never sought assistance. "I have a peace of soul," he declared with saintly calm. "If you manage poverty right you won't be bad off."

This philosophy, Grandpa agreed, could be applied to only a few people. After all, how many Mossers would society tolerate? But at least he had been successful at it, which is saying something.

Only one thing bothered the hermit of Adventist Creek. For two years he had been hearing rumors that the state intended to build a road past his cabin. "If they do," he vowed, "I'll have to move back. Civilization would kill me."

Later I was told, by what I hope is an inaccurate source, that the road was built. I never tried to find out, because I was afraid the report might be true. Perhaps, then, there wasn't any new ground Grandpa could build on again. Maybe I'm wrong not to have inquired but I prefer to remember Jonas Mosser in his tranquil setting. In my mind he remains there: an arm's length from woods flashed and filled by the color of friendly birds, bushes coated by berries, wildflowers dancing on the banks of the creek to the applause of the stream tumbling over polished rocks, and sheep that came to him as pets.

"I'm a lucky man," said Grandpa. And one of the happiest, I thought.

Stephen W. Matthieu

A Memory of Champoeg

On the wall of attorney Stephen Matthieu's law office in downtown Portland there is a framed clipping of Ripley's "Believe It Or Not," dated October 26, 1956. Accompanying a head sketch are the words: "One vote cast by Francis X. Matthieu, a Canadian, gave to the United States Oregon-Washington-Idaho and parts of Montana and Wyoming."

Stephen Matthieu, who was born in 1899, is a grandson of Francis Xavier Matthieu. According to history or legend, depending upon your inclinations, Francis X. Matthieu, together with Etienne Lucier, cast the deciding votes at the famous "divide" meeting at Champoeg on May 2, 1843. Thus, in effect, their ballots—they voted with their feet—determined that the vast Oregon Country would have a provisional government under American rule.

One could ask some pointed questions. For instance, if the vote had gone 52 to 50 against, rather than for, provisional government, would the American settlers have considered the matter closed? Would the United States have surrendered its claim to the Oregon Country on the basis of that rather confused meeting? Would Great Britain have marched in troops, claiming that rejection of provisional government meant popular support for the King?

But all that is something else again. Francis Xavier Matthieu needs no irritable questions of historical analysis to make his appearance here. His own life, as told by his grandson, Stephen, who was a teen-ager when the old man died, is colorful enough.

Matthieu the pioneer was born on the second day of April, 1818, the son of French parents (his mother from

Brittany, his father from Normandy) in Terrebonne, a village near Montreal, in the Province of Quebec.

In 1838, when he was 20, he "skipped from Canada into the United States" after a rebellion, in which "he'd been running arms," collapsed. He was a grocery clerk at the time.

So he came to Albany, New York and worked as a candlemaker for six months before drifting west, where he took employment with the American Fur Company. His territory was what is now South Dakota and he lived among the Sioux—the Hunkpapa, the Miniconjou, the Sans Arc and the Oglalla—as a trader.

He sold whiskey, "among other things," and collected furs. He liked his life among the Indians and was fond of reminiscing about them to his grandson, but Stephen Matthieu remembers little of what the old man told him about the Sioux. One can forget a great deal in 55 years.

In 1842, with two Mountain Men he had met, Francis Matthieu hitched up with a wagon train bound for Oregon. "He terminated his employment, and turned in his equipment, and he simply had a horse, a blanket, gun and cup, and that's—well, and these he had on his back," said Stephen Matthieu.

Francis X. Matthieu, now 24, strolled into Fort Vancouver and presented himself to Dr. John McLoughlin, the fabled "Whiteheaded Eagle" who was Chief Factor of Hudson's Bay Co. for the company's far-flung Northwest operations.

In his anecdotage, the old man sometimes talked to his young grandson, Stephen, about the "highly competitive" situation which existed between the American Fur Co. and Hudson's Bay Co.

"He said that he thought it was very nice of McLoughlin to receive him so well, in view of the fact that he'd been with the American Fur Company, and he said that McLoughlin drew no distinction," Stephen Matthieu told us, bent over his desk as he slowly sought to trace the years down to boyhood.

"And he said, I remember he said: 'You know, that's the first potato I had seen for a long time.' He had a big dinner at McLoughlin's house, and the principal item was potatoes."

The old man remembered McLoughlin very well. "Grandfather said," Stephen Matthieu recalled, "that he was seemingly a very stern and precise man, but that he was actually a very understanding and considerate man, that he was personally very fond of him and they had a friendship that lasted for a long time."

Leaving Fort Vancouver, F. X. Matthieu journeyed down to Oregon City. "He did nothing at first," declared his grandson, with a slight laugh. "He was supplied by Dr. McLoughlin, who extended him some credit and let him have some equipment."

Then Francis Xavier Matthieu moved a bit southwest, to French Prairie, between Butteville and Aurora.

It was called French Prairie, the grandfather related when he was 90 or so, Stephen Matthieu said, "because the Indians had kept the shrubs and brush and everything burned down, and therefore it didn't pose a problem, for it was really open country, prairie land."

The "French" part is there, I would assume, because of the French-Canadians who had retired from Hudson's Bay Co. and taken to farming on this open land. One of the first *voyageurs* on the prairie was Etienne Lucier, who was "considerably older" than the young Matthieu, whom Lucier "took in his cabin, and they lived together.

"Lucier was very kind to my grandfather, and that was about the only trait of Lucier my grandfather mentioned," stated Stephen Matthieu.

We come now to the famous meeting at Champoeg. The division, according to Francis Xavier Matthieu, as told by his grandson, was between the Americans on one side and the Canadians on the other. "And he and Lucier, he said," narrated Stephen Matthieu, "had been talking about the question of provisional government, which had come up previous to the meeting on May second, 1843. My grandfather had more education than Lucier. He'd had some very substantial schooling in a parochial school. And he was very partial to the United States. He claimed it was for two reasons; number one, his training; number two, he had of course skipped from Canada because of his revolutionary activities in the rebellion."

The cabin Lucier and Matthieu occupied was not at Champoeg; Stephen Matthieu does not know where the cabin stood, except that it was somewhere between Butteville and Aurora.

Joe Meek, the tale-telling Mountain Man, who was always first in the chow line and always quick to flatter ladies stirring a pot of food, was at Champoeg and must have done some bull-nostril exhorting. Big, burly Joe shouted, in a roaring voice that would have set buffalo stampeding, "Who's for a divide? All in favor of the report and an organization follow me!"

"Grandfather described Meek as a very fiery character," Stephen Matthieu commented with a judicial smile, as though saying in his lawyer-trained way: It's a judgment, not a fact.

Joe Meek did draw a line, as Francis Xavier Matthieu recalled the day to his grandson about 70 years later.

According to history, or legend, after Meek scrawled a line with his boot, the men divided and the count came to 50 on one side and 50 on the other. Then, supposedly, Matthieu and Lucier stepped from their neutral ground to the "American side," and the day was won for provisional government.

But Francis Xavier Matthieu remembered that event otherwise. "He did not actually say that there had been a nose count, so that they knew that he and Lucier were the deciding factors," Stephen Matthieu told us, "but he said they decided—Lucier hesitated a moment, and he said, 'Come on, Etienne, let's get over here,' because he certainly didn't want a government organized under the British, since he was a fugitive.

"My grandfather didn't say that there were fifty people and fifty people standing and looking at each other, with a line drawn between them, and him and Lucier standing at the side," Stephen added. "I never heard him say that. He said they simply moved over to the American side. The count was 52 to 50. He repeated that many times."

And this is all that Francis Xavier Matthieu ever told his grandson about that day at Champoeg, or else this is all his grandson recalls the old man saying of that historic event.

Almost a year after the "divide" meeting, Matthieus left the cabin of Etienne Lucier to marry Rose Osant, daughter of a trapper. Both her parents were French-Canadians.

Francis and Rose took up a donation land claim a mile and a half from Butteville on the road to Woodburn. The east half of the 640 acres went to Francis, the west half to Rose. The cabin he built was a rude thing, without windows, with a dirt floor, and lit by candles.

"Practically all transportation was by water," the old man had told his grandson. "He said there were no roads," Stephen Matthieu recalled, staring intensely through a cloud of cigarette smoke. "For instance, they'd go from the French Prairie district to Oregon City, where there was a Hudson's Bay post, and then over to Vancouver, and it was all done by canoe."

Francis X. Matthieu lived most of his life on his farm. He did not leave it until 1905 or 1906 when, cataracts having built a wall across his vision, he moved to Portland to stay with the family of Stephen W. Matthieu.

Some years after settling the donation land claim, he opened a general merchandise store at Butteville. The farming was done mostly by his kids," Stephen Matthieu told us in a hoarse, labored voice that even when faltering into raspness was always courtly, "And he sat on the front porch of the store as far as I can make out. It's the kind of work I'm looking for." And he editorially smiled. This was judgment and fact, the best of combinations.

In 1900 Oregon became acutely conscious of its Champoeg roots and sought to locate the site. Only one of the survivors was still alive: Francis Xavier Matthieu. He led the Governor of the state and the secretary of the Oregon Historical Society to the "precise point," and there a monument was later erected.

How, after more than half a century, did your grandfather know exactly where the meeting was held, we asked Stephen Matthieu.

"The only thing that he could say as to the exact point," he replied, "was that it was necessary that the meeting be held on high ground. This was up above the river level."

And so are "precise points" determined. But does it really matter?

After Rose Osant Matthieu died, her husband relinquished his claim to her half of the farm—320 acres—and it was divided among their 13 children.

When Francis X. Matthieu came to live with one of his sons—Stephen's father—he was already 88 but his grandson remembers him then as an alert man: "He was never senile, his memory was excellent."

And the grandfather is also recalled as a short, sturdy man, with white hair and blue eyes. "He was an extremely polite, well-mannered man, soft-spoken, and given to—he liked to talk about the past."

Stephen Matthieu paused a moment in reflection, squinting through a haze of smoke. "The conversations, some of them, were with me," he continued, "and I made some notes at the time, but like all things, these were the notes that I took when I was probably eleven years of age and . . .", his voice trailed off, "and they disappeared.

"When my mother's house was sold some years ago I looked high and low for those notes and I never could find them, they were on little cards."

In 1913, Stephen's mother was unable to continue to care for her father-in-law, and Francis Xavier Matthieu moved back to the donation land claim, to the house of a daughter, and there a year later he passed away. His funeral was held on the prairie, where he had settled seven decades before, and he was buried in the little cemetery at Butteville.

Today, in all the divided and subdivided plots of the original square mile holding, not a single descendant of Francis Xavier Matthieu resides.

Stephen Matthieu would like to purchase some of that land: "Oh, just a couple of acres, for sentimental purposes." But he hasn't gotten around to it.

Francis Xavier Matthieu left three material things with Stephen's family: a gold-headed cane, that he always carried; a watch; and a davenport. Stephen Matthieu does not know where the cane and watch came from, but he is certain about the davenport. "It was one of the four that grandfather and John McLoughlin and others bought and that were carried around the Horn by trading ship."

The davenport was given to the Oregon Historical Society.
The watch was presented by Stephen Matthieu to his cousin, Willis Matthieu, of Aurora.

And the gold-headed cane disappeared.

Mary Gerber and Pauline Corriery

The Sisters of Bethany

Mrs. Mary Wyman Gerber was born in Bethany in 1879 and her sister, Mrs. Pauline Wyman Corriery, was born in the same house two years later. We found them in an old stagecoach house which Mrs. Gerber had occupied since 1914. The house, on the site of Old Bethany, was two miles from where the sisters were born. So in more than 85 years, Mrs. Gerber had moved two miles from her birthplace, and she thought that was far enough. Mrs. Corriery, who believed in seeing the world, lived in Portland.

It's a short and easy drive now from Portland to Old Bethany, but when the sisters were the young Wyman girls it was a four hour drive by horse and wagon, over a choppy dirt road, to the big city.

We sat in the simple, old-fashioned kitchen of the sleepy stagecoach house, looking out at fields still not surveyed for shopping centers and housing projects. Mrs. Gerber, resting near a big iron wood-burning stove, which she still used, listened and nodded as her sister, a peppery, plain-spoken woman, talked about how the country had changed since they were kids.

"It was all woods, nothing but woods," she said, "and people that come from the old country, they went in with a big hoe or whatever they could get, no dynamite. Cleared all that land around by hand, man and wife; they had one kid after the other; and then, the woman, as soon as the kid was a little bigger, she'd go and scrub again. And that's the way it built up.

"Then they farmed, for a little potatoes and they'd get maybe a pig, and then they'd butcher the pig and we'd eat, sauerkraut and potatoes and bread. Never seen no candy, only at Christmas time we seen a few pieces of candy."

The sisters remembered having mush and milk for breakfast when they were small, but no eggs. "We had to sell the eggs, to get something else. You know," said Mrs. Corriery.

The eggs were sold for 15 cents a dozen. Potatoes they grew were sold for 35 cents a 100-pound sack. Sometimes the eggs and potatoes were bartered for groceries. Not canned goods—they were too expensive—but sugar, coffee and flour mainly.

"We took our stuff to Portland," said Mrs. Corriery. "Some eggs, some potatoes. My brother and I, we were about ten, fourteen years old, we took them into town. Then the people from the store, they'd have to come and help us take the potatoes out of the wagon. We couldn't manage 'em. It was an all day trip. The road was crooked, and when it was muddy—well, we had to go along the best we could."

For lunch there was bread and vegetables, home-baked and home-grown. We think of supper as the big meal on the farm, but it wasn't so at the Wyman place. "There wasn't much," said Mrs. Corriery, her eyes glistening in emphasis. "We didn't get too much meat, y'know. Just pork sometimes."

Once in a while there was butter, hand-churned, and on rare occasions jellies and jams. "It took the sugar and we didn't have it," Mrs. Corriery explained.

At this point Mrs. Gerber asked her sister how much their parents had given for their 40 acres in 1876, when their parents had settled here. Before a reply came she had the answer. "Five thousand dollars. Very little we paid for the land."

Was the land sold? Mrs. Corriery chuckled. "Not all is sold, part is still there. My brother had it, and then my mother and grandma give it all to my brother, see? We didn't get nothing. We got a kick in the——well, you know where."

When she was seven, Mrs. Corriery said, she worked for a neighbor, pulling weeds and picking potatoes. She put in about eight to ten hours a day and at the end of the six-day week her neighbor put a dollar and twenty cents in her hand and admonished, "Now don't open it until you get home."

Her mother took the money and used it to purchase food and cloth. "We never bought clothing," declared Mrs. Corriery with a pinched smile. "Clothing we made. Y'know. Buy a little piece of cloth and make it."

Where did the boys and girls go courting when the sisters were teenagers?

"Oh, I don't know," replied Mrs. Corriery indifferently. "At home. The neighbors come. We didn't go no place."

The sisters didn't remember sewing bees but they vividly recalled church picnics.

"Fun, good fun," Mrs. Gerber hoarsely whispered.

"We had an awful good time!" exclaimed her sister, almost shouting the word "awful," to show how much she really liked the old church picnics.

"Old and young together," continued Pauline Corriery. "We were young and some of them were fifty, sixty years old. We thought they were so old they oughta die!" And she pointed to herself, almost touching eighty, and laughed and laughed.

William L. Preston

Saga of a Simple American

William L. Preston, whom we found in a worn shack in tiny Barlow, was just about one of the most interesting and loquacious old timers we ever sniffed out. In his wanderings and rootings and displacements and ups and downs across the face of this midwestern and Oregon land he had led such a rich but unpretentious life that I thought of his story as being the saga of a simple American.

By simple I mean one of the unsung close-to-earth people who built this country, a man who was never a celebrity and never had desire to be one. By his own reckoning, he had done well: he had led a productive life, had faced up to adversity and backed it off, had stayed married to the same woman until she passed away, had reared a good set of children, and owed no man a dime or apology.

I am going to let Mr. Preston tell his own story. Sections of the taped interview were transposed to provide a continuity but the words remain those of Mr. Preston. From here on, it is he who speaks:

Well, I was born in the state of Kansas, September 30, 1879. The last herd of buffalo went through three years before I was born. The plain was littered with bones. Big old white skulls, and black horns about that long, and that big around at the skull, and you could polish them and oh, they was beautiful. But the prairie was just, oh, just all kinds a-layin' there, carcasses, the buffalo carcasses layin' all over the prairie.

And there was sod houses. I've got a picture here of a sod house in Kansas. I've helped build a-many of them. You lay 'em just like you do brick. Yeah, you could cut a house right out of a bank of a hill. I've seen lots of 'em. At Colby, Kansas there's a sod house there. And they wrote me a letter here, a year or two ago, and wanted some of the history of that part of the country.

And I herded cattle there, barefooted, in the cactus, and prickly pears, and sandburrs and cocoburrs, when I was a little boy. The herders, the cowboys, they were called brush busters in the early days on the plains.

The cowboy then, he wore leather pants and high top boots and a wide-rimmed white hat, a felt hat, same as to-day, and jeans, only they were kind of a gray color, and shirts of different colors, different kinds, about like what we do now. They had chaps and spurs and a few of 'em carried guns and what I remember most is, most of the cowboys them days wore a mustache.

Yes, I remember a stampede, too. Went through a corn field and just blown through the field, and tore down fences and they was four hundred head, I think, and it was about two weeks before they found five or six, and they was fifteen miles from there, and they was a long horns outfit.

Well, the missus and me, we tied up when she was a few days past eighteen and I was twenty, but I was on my own from a little boy. And we went to ourselves, and then it looked like boys took better care of themselves than boys do today, and I was pretty well fixed. When I was married I had two of the best teams in the country and a hundred-and-ten dollar top buggy, that was a Cadillac car today, pretty near brand new Moline wagon, two sets o' harness, some farm tools, a hundred and ten acres o' corn in, and some household stuff, and I made it all. I practically lost that crop and the next crop. And I sold out and went back to Hoosier State, Indiana, the worst state in the Union. Maybe you're a Hoosier, I don't know, but—on the banks of the Wabash, far away. And the next oldest daughter was born there, and the water run me out of the house on the 27th of January, when she was five days old. Stayed there a year and I came back to northwestern Missouri. I was there a year and I came back to Logan, Kansas, where I was born, my credit was good, I was practically broke. I went into the bank and old Jake Wilcox staked me; I could borrow money on my note, and my stock.

In three years I had one hundred sixty-five acres of land paid for on the Smokey Hill River in Kansas and I traded the farm for mules, cattle and money and that year I rented a farm and I had forty-five hundred bushels of corn. I run twenty-eight head of baby beef, Herefords, and Black Poll Angus, and to fatten 'em up I fed 'em shell corn and alfalfa from October to February and I expected thirty-five cents for corn and it went up to fifty-six. And they had a boycott of meat in Kansas City in February, weren't going to eat any more meat till meat come down, and I lost seventeen hundred dollars. Them days seventeen hundred dollars was like ten thousand today. I shipped one hundred-forty head of poor old steer into Kansas City for John A. Ardman, and I forgot how many carloads of hogs he had, he lost fifteen thousand dollars.

I had a big crop that year. In the middle of July come a hailstorm and pretty near died. And my wife was sick. About the second of October it come up a terrible storm one night, and I had some very valuable horses and mares and cattle and I was setting in the kitchen, and my wife was laying on the bed, feeling bad, and it lightened and thundered and I heered a cow bawl. So I just figgered the next morning I'd go down and no telling how many I'd find dead. So I got up and went into the bedroom and set down at the side of the bed, and it come another one, o-o-o-oh it just rattled everything, and the light burning, and the flash of lightning would blind you, and I said to my wife, I said, I'm going to leave here. She said, Where are you goin'? I said I'm goin' to the Willamette Valley in Oregon. She said, When are you goin'? I said just as soon as I can get ready to go. In February I had my sale, and a big crowd, the auctioneer for twenty-three years said it was the biggest crowd that he'd ever had and sold it for the most money he'd ever sold. And we landed here.

Come by train. Took three days and three nights. We had six children. The baby was five weeks old.

Nineteen-eleven I came out here, and didn't do much the first year, and I went into the hop business. And I made a pocket of money. And 1914, war broke out. Nineteen-fourteen, 1915, the two crops of hops broke me. So I went into the loggin' business. And I logged for twenty-nine years. And I had quite a bag of experience. I had sickness, and doctor bills, and five operations in the family, three cases of typhoid fever, and two deaths one right after the other. But I got nothing to complain about. There ain't anybody healthier in the United States than I am, I'm eighty-five. I think I can outjump any man or boy standin' flat footed today. And I've been through a lot of hard work and worry, but I've got nothing to complain about whatever, I'm in the clear and guess I've got enough to take care of me until the Judgement Day, and a clear conscience and a good night's sleep is worth more to me than all the money in the United States. And I've been in lots of court rooms, and been on the jury lots, and had quite a bit of experience, quite a bit of experience, but I've got nothing to complain about a-tall. I believe I've got the best son-in-laws and daughter-in-laws that any man could have. I never whipped my children and we never got in one another's hair, and we never used the breakfast table to fight over all them sixty-four years.

You might want to know how Barlow was when I come in 1911. They was some wonderful people here. The town was flourishin'. There was a big business here. Yes sir, big. They was two stores, two saloons, a blacksmith shop, a livery barn, and a hotel, and the old timers is all passed, there's only one left, he was born here, he's just past eighty-four. But he's probably, maybe had a little trouble, but he mighta had a little too much to drink, so bein's that—well, that's that. Anyway, look around. Hardly nothin' now.

I've got no property now whatever. I couldn't handle it if I did. But I had to up and sell everything on account of the woman, she couldn't take care of the house, fell three or four times, and it hurt her, and I got her out of it. So I went down to my daughter's, she has a big apartment house this side of the Ross Island bridge, and we was there a couple of years, and we got lonesome to come back out here, and we rented this little shack because the floors were level, and we just picked up a lot of second-hand stuff, and moved in. And that's how I come to be here, and now I don't want to leave it till Gabriel blows his horn.

Lookin' back, I think that in ways the old days was better than now. I'll tell you, a man's word, it seemed to me like, was better than they are today. If I come to you and you got ten or fifteen dollars you'd let me have, say, for four weeks or something like that, why yes! Well, a man's word pretty near had to be good or he wasn't going to make it. And if you run out of flour and I had a sack of flour, why sure, you could have part of it. I can't get to town for a week or two. All right. They lived for one another, and they had a helping hand to help each other. Everywhere. In case of sickness or accident or anything, the neighbors was right there to look after yuh. And if you had crop in hand and you got hurt or somethin', they come right in and tended yuh, and took care of it for yuh. Well, they don't do it today. And it's greedy, greedy, the people is more greedy today than they were them days. Selfish.

Well, today, you know, it's the dollar, the dollar. They have no care for one another. But I was raised different from that, and the helping hand was out there, and if you have a misfortune or anything, I feel it's my duty to go and do all I can for yuh. And not asking for your purse. Help one another. Just help one another.

And that missus of mine would go and nurse the sick when she was sick herself. And she nursed all over the country here, clear to Salem, she was a practical nurse, and they turned nurses off that was really nurses to get her, and she never refused, never. And I never heerd her say a harmful word about anybody, she wouldn't talk about anybody, and gossip, she didn't care for that a-tall, and she always wanted to help somebody, and if somebody come, during the depression or such as that, for something, she seen they got something to eat. Never turn 'em down.

Well, I think I've got enough to run me the rest of my days. And if I ain't, I've got son-in-laws, daughter-in-laws, grandchildren that I can depend on, I know. So I've got nothing to worry about, you reap what you sow, the Good Book tells you that.

Well, I was over to the coast last Saturday night, and I got two sons that lives over there, and they just pretty near kidnapped me, they wouldn't let me come back. And my granddaughter, she's married, she's about twenty years old, she said, you're gonna stay with me. No, I says, I ain't. I can't. I've just got to come back here. Well, I have a daughter got a trailer court down at Oregon Springs, know where that is, I reckon, on the Deschutes, up the river there, and she went to Idyho, her granddaughter was a-gettin' married last Sunday. And my daughter decided, well, I have the apartment house at this end of the Ross Island bridge, and they went up to take care of things while she was up there. I was up to Warm Springs, but I wouldn't go on to Idyho, I didn't feel like I should go. Well, it's quite nice when you know that you're insured, that your family will help you out. Mom's last request was, one of her last requests, she said, I want you to be a good boy and go to church. She told the children, Now I want you children to look after your father, he took good care of you and I want you to take good care of him. And they—peace of mind, is worth a lot to you, peace of mind.

John Conroy

The Harsh Land

From a distance, the Conroy house looked like a gaunt scarecrow. Close up it wasn't any prettier. An unpainted, awkward frame house whose sides seemed blackened by soot or bleached by the sun. It stood, taciturn and esoteric, on the bleak, windswept plain of central Oregon, two-and-a-half miles from the nearest home, which, 60 years before, had been erected as a schoolhouse.

The old schoolhouse, now a shanty on the harsh plateau, was a mile west of Sherar's Bridge, where Indians still netted salmon from platforms perched over the frothy Deschutes River, and about five miles east of Tygh Valley, the closest store. The trace up to the Conroy house was rocky, twisty, bumpy and full of chuckholes. Along the way there were a few empty corrals, shacks and barns, all relics of the big land rush.

In the first part of the twentieth century, tens of thousands of people, hooked by vivid advertising and tall tale promises, massed upon central and eastern Oregon to take up homestead rights. Most of the land was useless, little better than desert. Only a few of the comers hung on. John Conroy was one of them, and he was joined later by his brother.

Conroy was a young man in his native Ireland when he was attracted by stories of "free and wonderful land." "We were bombarded with literature about Oregon by the railroad and some companies," he remembered. "Oh yes! They flooded us with literature about Oregon, in fact about the entire West."

He came steerage across the Atlantic and for $60 purchased railroad passage to The Dalles. "It was what was known as the emigrant rate," he remarked.

When John Conroy first homesteaded in these parts, in 1904, his nearest neighbor was four miles off. That wasn't too bad. But when another homesteader settled three miles from him, John Conroy up and left, moving farther away. "I was crowded out," he explained simply.

Now, when we saw him, he was glad to meet people and to talk with them, though it was quite evident he could survive spiritually without the social bread of company. He had for comradeship his brother, also about 80, who was blind. They had been together a long time—neither had ever married—and had grown accustomed to few comforts and little conversation. The harsh land had purged them of pity and turned them taciturn. But when they did speak to each other it was with courtesy and respect, and with a formality that somehow seemed out of place in this rude dwelling and wasteland atmosphere. Most of the time they lay on their bunks, one on each side of the front door, and passed the time listening to battery powered radios, although John sometimes read magazines and newspapers.

Life had never been easy on the curt and naked plateau. For years there was no sense growing wheat, because there was no transportation to market. So John and his brother ran some stock, worked out some, and somehow made ends meet. They had never been, as John said with a twinkle, "more than a step ahead of the sheriff," but they had grown a love for the land that was fierce as the land was.

"Sometimes I hate it," John Conroy said, "but it's all the beauty I know. I guess they'll bury our bones here, right next to some other coyotes that belonged."

All around them was historic ground. Sherar's Bridge had once been a great crossing point in Central Oregon. John Conroy knew Shaniko, which in his still rich Irish brogue he pronounced Shyniko, when it was the wool-shipping center of the world. He still drove there, when he felt in the mood. Half a mile from his house was the scrawl of the Tilkenny

Toll Road, in its time the main pike between The Dalles and Canyon City. And between his house and the ghostly old toll road were a pair of graves rooted deep in Oregon lore.

In his early days here, when he had to go into The Dalles, John Conroy legged it to the toll road, waved down a stage-coach, and hopped in. Four hours later he was in The Dalles. Or he rode horseback—and that took four hours, too.

Toll on the Tilkenny Road was 50 cents for a saddle horse, a dollar and a quarter for a two-horse team, a cent a head for sheep, "and so much for cattle." He didn't re-member the cattle fare; most of the stock he took down the road was sheep.

The graves were on a hillock which couldn't be seen from the house. They were marked by two small rock piles and a blanched pole. The graves had been dug by a part of the Lost Emigrant Wagon Train, connected in legend with the Blue Bucket Mine. The pole had been put up the year before we came by some descendants of some members of that part of the wagon train which had dug the graves here.

The Conroy house had electric lights, powered by a gaso-line generator. There wasn't any telephone but John could communicate with other ranchers by way of a battery-powered two-way short wave radio. And every few days somebody came by, just to see how the feebling brothers were getting along.

"We never had it so good," John said, with a short laugh that could have been funny or bitter or sad. "A little more and we'd be spoiled."

Our People of Hells Canyon

No Bats in Civilization

The mountains to the north of Homestead looked as though a jagged can opener had ripped apart the basaltic mass. Actually, the gap was caused by the mighty Snake

River, which for eons had twisted and slithered through the volcanic fortress, gouging earth and stone that barred its path. For 100 miles, below Homestead, the lonely stream roared between barren mountains rising thousands of feet on each side and, for 40 miles, Hells Canyon averaged 5,500 feet in depth.

This was in 1955. The Idaho Power Company dams that have tamed so much of the Snake had not yet been built. The area, stamped with the rough mark of the frontier, was braved by only a scant handful of settlers. Homestead, which consisted of a few rude shacks and a little store-post office, that received mail and groceries three times a week, was the end of the line.

We had come to Homestead from Cornucopia to do a story on Hells Canyon. But just outside Halfway—12 miles south of Cornucopia—where we had lunch in a boarding house, before chancing the drive in the July 100-plus temperature, we weren't sure we had chosen the correct road to the Snake. The trace led to the river, all right, but after checking the sign, which I recall reading something like: County Road, Proceed At Your Own Risk, we felt maybe we ought to backtrack to Richland, which we had passed on the way up from Baker. Then we could follow the wavy road that dipped down to the Snake, and go up to Homestead on a dust-choking spread of washboard gravel that covered what had been built as a spur line of the Union Pacific.

For some reason, it may have been the heat getting to our heads, we took the Pine Creek Road. It was 20 miles of jolting, fearful, stop-and-crawl agony. The folks in Halfway, who had breezily assured us that that narrow scrawl of dirt, riding above the mocking waters of Pine Creek, would prove no trouble to us, either underestimated their own sense of humor or overestimated ours. Later we learned that not one of the half-dozen counselors, each so free with recommendation, had traveled the road in at least two years. And time can soften terror.

The road was so narrow we kept to the middle, which didn't leave much space between the precipitous slopes plunging down to the creek and the high banks full of large outcropping rocks. Most of the bigger rocks looked like they were just about ready to extricate themselves from the grasp of earth, and if they had fallen on the car or directly into our path, before we had opportunity to halt, we would have had to hike back to Halfway for a tow truck.

Rocks on the road there were plenty of, some of them pretty hefty boulders. Since I considered myself the better driver in this difficult situation, my wife was the one who nudged the rocks off the road. She must have pushed a couple of hundred before we came to the gravel road at the site of Oxbow, where Copperfield had stood four decades before, as the roaringest town in Oregon.

Where there weren't rocks protruding out of the banks there were waterfalls, that spouted thick streams at us. So one window, on this blast furnace afternoon, had to be closed. Apart from the rocks in our path, the spouting water, the thousand chuckholes and the roughness of the surface, that shook the car into spasms when the speed was increased to 15 miles an hour, it was a lousy road.

Luckily, we passed no car. We did drive by a few dwellings, maybe three or four, nearer Oxbow than Halfway, and at every place there were folks outside, just sort of standing around. When they saw us, they stopped talking to each other and stared, probably wondering how stupid some people can be.

At Oxbow, where the Snake doubled back upon itself, and where Copperfield had sprawled—there wasn't a trace of it left—we turned north on the gravel road that came up from the Richland junction and sighed our way the four miles into Homestead.

That early evening, at the store, which was run by Mrs. Dan Cole, who said she was out in the wilderness because she hated civilization, we learned that the natives called the Pine Creek Road "Oil Pan Alley." We hadn't lost ours, knock on wood, but we could readily understand how it got that name.

Late in the afternoon we laid down our sleeping bags, near an old-fashioned hand-propelled water pump, and made ourselves to home. I wandered up the gravel road and found something I hadn't expected to see, a small apricot orchard.

I tried several cabins close by to ask if I could pick some of the fruit but the shacks were all bare. It seemed obvious to me, as an old fruit tramp, that the trees, which were pretty spindly, hadn't been pruned for a long time and maybe the apricots hadn't been harvested for a couple of years, either. So I picked about a dozen and they went well with our supper of bread and tinned beans.

It was so warm there down by the Snake, and no breeze to speak of, that we didn't crawl into our sleeping bags at all. We spread ourselves on top of them and sleep came easily, to the husky chant of the river.

The next morning Steve Stegall, who was nicknamed Curly, because there wasn't a self-respecting hair on his head, came down from his home at Cuprum, Idaho in his four-wheel-drive jeep, and we spent the day with him, exploring Hells Canyon from its overlooks.

In those days Kleinschmidt Grade, the only "direct" road from Homestead to Cuprum, was an even worse road, far worse, than the "Oil Pan Alley" of Pine Creek Road. Within seven miles it lurched maniacally almost 4,000 feet uphill. Some of the hairpin turns seemed to dive down the mountain; several of them were so shallow they bore such expressive names as "Doorhandle Curve."

I had been on the Kleinschmidt once before and I could believe the stories Steve Stegall told us about all the people, first time on the road, who had literally become terror-stricken. They halted their cars and sat frozen at the wheel, unable to budge. When they reached Homestead, if they were going downhill, the women were half-hysterical and the men convulsively shaking and ashen.

For the natives, Kleinschmidt was part of their lives. That night out in the open, alongside the Snake, we had seen lights on the mountain grade, stabbing the darkness with rapier thrusts before being scabbarded by the maws of the curves. Some of the natives thought nothing of driving up to Cuprum for a beer or two or visiting a friend and then, about midnight, driving back. The thought of it was enough to chill me.

Steve had been up and down the Kleinschmidt hundreds of times. He knew every curve and nuance of the road. He could drive with one hand—which sent my wife's heart racing in fear—and with the other point to a ravine shape, a couple of thousand feet down a slope, and comment, as though he were talking about the weather: "A car rolled all the way down there last summer. Three people in the car but they jumped out before it slid down. And do you know what that crazy dog of theirs did? It chased that blamed car all the way down to the bottom. And then the dog couldn't get back, I had to go down and fetch it."

We had made arrangements in Baker for Steve to show us Hells Canyon from above, and he sure did. Most of what we saw I have described in *Oregon For The Curious*. But I did not tell how we got to Sheep Rock, which I considered afforded the finest view of the overpowering chasm.

Steve sent his jeep clawing up a 45 degree hill and then we bounced along a ridge until we had run out of width space. "We'll have to shank's mare it the rest of the way," Steve announced blithely. My wife took one look at the mountainside we had to ascend and said she'd stay put, right by the jeep. So I took the camera and followed Steve.

"I'll take it easy," he called, as we started up a wildflower-studded path that couldn't have been a foot wide at its most bountiful latitude. "Watch out for loose earth. This is slippery. You fall and it would take a week to bring your body back up."

What Steve didn't know was that I had good balance and stamina. Soon I had stepped around him, was pushing uphill, and gesturing for him to hurry on. When we reached the top he was puffing hard and eying me with a bit of wonder. Upon our return to the jeep he said to my wife, "Say, did you know that that husband of yours is a mountain goat?"

Of course, I couldn't do anything like that again, but it's nice to remember.

Coming back through Cuprum we paused at Steve's house, part of which was a small cafe. The manager, cook and bottle washer was Steve's wife, a lovely, soft-voiced, long-legged Australian girl, whom Steve had met and married during the war.

Cuprum, with its few sleepy houses and a store or two, perched on the edge of one of the largest primitive areas in the country, was such a far cry from the big city down under where she had been raised and was working when Steve came along.

Do you like it here, we asked. "Well," she replied pensively, "I think I'd be happier where there are more people and things to do, but Steve likes to be independent and we can make a sort of living here."

About 4 p.m. Steve returned us to our car, at Homestead, we shook hands, and he cheerfully set out for home, his fourth run on the Kleinschmidt that day.

We were getting ready to unpack our victuals for supper when a fellow in a pickup stopped and asked our names. "Oh," he said, with a broad grin, when we told him, "we've been expecting you. You're going down the river with Blaine Stubblefield tomorrow. My name's Ray Holt. No point staying here. Might as well come to our place. The missus has a good meal ready and we've got a spare room."

No, we said, we don't mind it here. It's nice.

He wouldn't accept that. First thing we knew he was reaching into our Plymouth for our suitcases and piling them into the pickup. "Put your gear in your car, lock it up, and leave it here," he directed. "Nobody'll touch it."

So we went with Ray Holt to his home, and darned if he didn't live up the Pine Creek Road.

Ray told us he was a retired Air Force sergeant and worked with Blaine Stubblefield, the chamber of commerce manager at Weiser, Idaho, who ran a boat and float guide service on the Snake. Came the end of the tourist season, Ray and his wife would work on their house. In winter they took it easy, just doing enough to keep them comfortable.

The first thing that struck me about the Holt house was that it was lighted and powered by propane. Propane lights, propane refrigerator, propane range. How come, I asked Ray. Why don't you have electricity?

"Too expensive," he replied. "Idaho Power wants a lot of money to hitch us up to their lines and their rates are too high for us. It's not too bad. We get along fine."

They didn't have a radio but they got a newspaper from Baker and that kept them as up to date on what was happening as they cared to be informed.

Mrs. Holt served up a sumptuous meal and after we gabbed a bit it was time to hit the sack, since we had an early morning appointment with Blaine Stubblefield.

After my wife and I had undressed and gone to bed we commented on the brightness of the moon, which slipped down a draw and through the curtains to fill the room with a lemon hue.

Suddenly my wife asked: "What's that shadow on the wall?"

"Maybe a spot of paint," I replied.

"Unlikely," she said. "Doesn't look like a spot of paint."

I picked up a flashlight which I had taken with me and directed a beam at the wall.

"A bat!" my wife exclaimed. "What do we do now?"

So I put on my pants, opened the door, and hollered, "Ray, I think there's a bat in this room."

"Oh—gee whiz—my gosh!" I heard him gasp. There was a rustle, which told me he was getting his pants on, and he hurried into the room holding a big cloth. Standing on a chair, he pulled the bat off the wall and threw it out of the house, all the time muttering, "Golly, gee whiz, that's awful."

The next morning he and his wife continued the apologies but we shrugged it off. "We're old hands with bats," my wife explained gaily, which was a bit of an exaggeration, because only once before had we shared a room with a bat, in Cedar Rapids, Iowa. We didn't discover the bat until next morning and it was still snoozing on the wall when we casually announced the fact to the hotel manager as we were checking out.

Blaine Stubblefield, a crisp man who drove himself like blazes, took us down to Kinney Creek Rapids in a twin-engine power boat. It was quite a mad ride, something like a roller coaster gone out of control. Still, my wife and I were willing to go on, but when we reached the bolting current Blaine said it was as far as he could go without jeopardizing all our lives.

So we beached the boat and stomped through thickets of underbrush and wizened trees, plucking wild berries and looking straight up at the zooming walls of the canyons. "Keep an eye out for rattlesnakes," Blaine warned, picking up a bough for defense. That must have been the signal for action, for the last word had hardly left his mouth when we heard a crackling in the bush. Out wound a rattler, long and thick, and with a mean tread. He was all business, the way he traveled, but fortunately he was bound in another direction.

"Let's get him!" Blaine shouted, raising his club and pushing toward the spot we had seen the rattler whiplash out of view.

"O.K.!" I replied, scrambling after him, but keeping about five feet back.

"Don't leave me!" my wife shrilled.

So we gave up the pursuit, returned to the boat, and hurdled back to Homestead. All of us drove to Ray's house for lunch and then the wife and I sagged into our baked Plymouth and bounced down the Snake River road to Huntington and U.S. 30.

We've been back to the Hells Canyon country since but never met the same people and, somehow, no trip was as interesting as that one, in 1955.

A lot of Snake River water has flowed through the gorge since that summer. Idaho Power has three dams on the stream. A fine paved road connects Brownlee, 16 miles below Homestead, to Cambridge, Idaho, on U.S. 395. It eliminates 50 miles and cuts out a lot of rough traveling. Pine Creek Road is paved, too, and shortened by three miles. Kleinschmidt Grade has been widened and smoothed and a lot more turnouts added. Anybody used to unsurfaced mountain driving should be able to handle it without too much trouble now.

Twelve years after that summer I checked on some of the people we met then. Mrs. Dan Cole, who wanted to get as far away from people as she could, has moved her post office to Oxbow. She had to, since Homestead now lies under the Snake, which is a reservoir there.

Blaine Stubblefield died a couple of years after we shot a piece of the river with him. Curly Stegall continued guiding, while his wife operated a cafe, tavern and some cabins, until October, 1964, when she became very ill. They sold out and moved down to Fruitland, Idaho, where she passed away 14 months later. In 1966 Curly remarried.

After Blaine Stubblefield's death, Ray Holt went into the float guide business, running rubber rafts from Homestead clear down to Lewiston, Idaho, on five day trips. His customers, who came from many parts of the country, got all the thrills they were looking for, especially in those trampoline rapids.

Ray retired in 1963, the dams having flooded him out. But he and his wife are doing all right. They have electricity and all the latest gadgets, including television.

Twelve years after we stayed at his home I phoned him. He didn't recognize our name but he remembered the bat.

"I'm sure sorry about that," he said. "Gosh, I hope it didn't disturb your sleep."

"Forget it," I said, "I was just kidding you."

"Well," he replied, "Y'oughta come down and stay a spell with us now. We get all the good programs you folks in Portland see. We got real suburban living here. And we ain't had a bat for years."

Erskine Wood

The Boy Who Knew Joseph

Few of us can really claim close association with one truly great person. But Erskine Wood, who has been a Portland attorney since 1912, lived with two supremely gifted men.

One was his father, Charles Erskine Scott Wood: soldier, poet, artist, lawyer, essayist, philosopher, libertarian—perhaps the most universal man to ever call Oregon home. ("I think of your father as the Leonardo of Oregon," I once remarked to Erskine Wood, and he replied with an appreciative chuckle, "That's a fair statement.")

The second great man was also an Oregonian, Chief Joseph, whose tepee Erskine Wood shared for a time when he was a boy.

Though Erskine Wood's association with the Nez Perce leader ended three-quarters of a century ago, it is doubtful if there is anyone else alive whose life was so meshed with the affairs of Joseph.

Erskine Wood's father, then a lieutenant in the Twenty-First Infantry, took down verbatim Joseph's famous surrender speech, ending with the classic line: "From where the sun now stands, I will fight no more forever." His grand-uncle, Gen. John Gibbon, had as a colonel led a column against the Nez Perce in the bitter war of 1877. And Erskine Wood's godfather, Gen. Oliver O. Howard, was the man who directed the pursuit of the Nez Perce. Later, Howard was commandant of Vancouver Barracks, where Erskine Wood was born on Sept. 1, 1879, in the Territory of Washington. (There is the flavor of pride in his voice when he says "Territory of Washington." The tang of the frontier is in those words.)

"About" 1884, C.E.S. Wood moved his family to Portland, where he "hung up his shingle" as a lawyer. "The Army was no place for him," says Erskine Wood of his father. "He was too much of an individualist."

CES Wood, as he came to be known, had developed a strong admiration for Chief Joseph, whom he had met as a defeated warrior in the Bear Paw Mountains of Montana, and had strongly protested the removal of the Nez Perce to the barren lands of the southern Great Plains. When Joseph was returned to the Northwest, eight years later, it was not to his green Wallowa Valley homeland but to the tawny Colville Reservation in north central Washington.

In 1891, Joseph "and some other chiefs" came down to Portland "on some business of the tribe" and were invited to the Wood home for a mid-day meal. CES Wood asked Joseph if Erskine could sometime come up and visit him. Joseph nodded and the discussion was closed. The following July, Erskine "found it a good time for me to accept Joseph's invitation."

By train, hack and dugout canoe he traveled to the Nespelem Valley of the Colville Reservation and on the banks of the Nespelem River pitched his little canvas A-frame tent alongside the tepee of Chief Joseph. With parental solicitude, Joseph and his two wives took Erskine into their family shelter, where the boy slept beside them.

The Indians did not use the word tepee; "they said *E-neet*," recalled Mr. Wood, a solid man with a craggy face and a shock of salt and pepper hair reaching over his forehead. With his bow tie and horn rim spectacles he resembled very much an old-fashioned lawyer of the Clarence Darrow type. It seemed to me he looked quite a bit like Darrow, whom I had seen as a boy.

A number of times I asked Mr. Wood how to spell the Nez Perce words he used, and invariably he replied: "Any way you wish; it would be as good as mine." But, after a while, on each occasion, he complied with my requests—somewhat wearily, I thought. Almost seven and a half decades had passed since his boyhood days on the Reservation and how could anyone expect him to keenly remember sounds and details?

The Indians with whom he lived were not the Nez Perce *tribe*, Mr. Wood made clear, speaking slowly, and pausing between sentences, but only Joseph's band of the Nez Perce —"the dwindling remnants of those whom Chief Joseph had led in the 1877 war." The band numbered about 150 persons—"no more than that," he declared firmly.

"Throughout the main part of the year," Mr. Wood narrated, "the Indians camped in individual tepees scattered through the Nespelem Valley, strung along it for two or three miles, mostly above the Sub-Agency at Nespelem. When they went on the fall hunt they split up into little groups of perhaps six or eight or possibly ten families and went into the mountains, up toward the Okanogan country. The fall hunt lasted perhaps two weeks. And on that fall hunt the individual tepees were combined into one long tepee, occupied by the whole group. Instead of one fire in the center of the round tepee, there were four fires, strung along the whole length of the inside of the tepee. The Indians moved their tepees around; they couldn't hunt in one spot all the time. When they came back from the fall hunt, that is, moved back to Nespelem, they continued the prac-

tice of living in the long tepees, because winter was setting
in and it was more suited for winter living. And those long
tepees were not scattered up and down the valley as much
as was the case of the individual tepees in the summertime.
In spring, the Indians moved up the valley and divided into
individual tepees."

We asked Mr. Wood to describe an individual tepee. He
took a deep breath and began:

"It was circular, of course, supported by lodge poles, with
a diameter of 25 or 30 feet. The floor around the center,
where the fire was, was dirt. The rest of the floor was usually
covered with dried rye grass as a base and then covered
with canvases or blankets. The outer circumference was
where they stored their bags and their belongings. Those
made it comfortable to lean up, recline against; also, they
kept out the draft. It was not comfortable to stand up in the
tepee for any length of time because the smoke would get
in your eyes. If you wanted to be comfortable you were
sitting down or lying down anyway. You don't stand up in
a little place like that."

During the fall hunt, he said, venison, which had been
cut into thin slices, was hung on racks standing about head
high, above the tepee fires, and slowly smoked. The meat
was then stored in bags which "had flaps folded over and
laced up."

In summer, Mr. Wood recalled, the Indians "cultivated a
little ground, raised little patches of grain, I think, because I
do remember we thrashed grain by trampling it out with
the horses. Some of the squaws went to the hop fields to
pick hops and earn a little money. Some went to the berry
patches to pick huckleberries. Every Sunday we celebrated,
in the summertime. Sometimes Joseph would invite a few
men into his tepee for a Sunday breakfast. And we had
many Sundays when we went horse racing in the afternoon
—four or five miles from camp. It was very exciting, very
dramatic, and picturesque. *Cool-cool-smool-mool* and I had
a special summer job, looking after the horse herd, riding
out into the surrounding low hills, through pine timber, and
finding the herd, driving them to water in the Nespelem
River, turning loose the horses we had ridden and catching

fresh horses. Joseph had about 60 or 70 horses, maybe more. He never sold any that I know of. They were for camp use and for riding and packing. He always had a pony herd so that he'd have fresh horses all the time. If you read any books on the Nez Perce War you would know that they had herds of horses, a thousand or more, and it was finally when their horse herd was driven away at Bear Paw Mountains that the Indians were afoot, couldn't move any further, resulted in their capture."

The horse-racing Indians used no saddles. "They usually had a hair rope under the horse's jaw and that was the bridle. Sometimes they had a hair rope around the horse's girth. The rider was on bareback. He'd slip his knees under that rope and he had a better grip of the horse."

Some functions of the Indians impressed young Erskine Wood more than others. He vividly recalled the "very cleansing method" of bathing.

"They took steam baths. They would erect what we whites call sweat houses, which would hold anywhere from four to eight Indians, depending on how large a house they built. The Indians would go in, close the little door, and then they would dribble water over heated stones and that would make clouds of steam—very hot—which would fill the house completely and envelop the bathers' bodies completely. You wouldn't be there more than a minute before you were in a sweat. If you were there five minutes the sweat would be rolling off you. After about ten minutes they'd come out and jump in the Nespelem River or a creek. They'd do that as their fancy dictated, about two or three times a week, during the summer. But on the fall hunt they did it religiously every morning before daylight, to remove all scent from their bodies. The streams then were cold; sometimes we had to crack a little skim of ice to get in there. And we didn't stay in long!"

Mr. Wood could not remember what the Indians called themselves "but they used the word *Tee-taw-kon*. I don't know whether that meant people or whether it meant the Nez Perce people."

Joseph's name was *Hin-mah-too-yah-lat-kekht*. "Its meaning has been variously disputed," Mr. Wood said. "My father called it Thunder-rolling-in-the-mountains and other people have called it Thunder-striking-from-the-water. It seems to be a rather mysterious meaning. No Indian I ever talked to has been able to tell me exactly what it has meant."

Joseph lived with his two wives, who "observed harmony and shared his bed." The elder was *Wawin-tip-yay-la-tal-e-cotsot;* the younger, a plumpish woman, was *Iyat-too-we-a-net-en-my.* In our conversations Mr. Wood referred to them as *Wawin* and *Iyat.* Both treated him "wonderfully" and *Iyat* made for the boy "some beautiful beaded moccasins and leggins." Later, Joseph helped Erskine make a muskrat hat. Only the leggins are still in Mr. Wood's possession.

The tepee was also occupied by an Indian boy first known to Erskine as *Nicky-Mowitz* and then as *Cool-cool-smool-mool.* Mr. Wood said he did not know what the names mean. Nor does he know what the lad was to Joseph. "Perhaps a distant relative, maybe a nephew, or maybe he was an adopted boy."

One thing seems for certain: Joseph had no children of his own on the Colville Reservation.

Wood called Joseph Joseph. Joseph called him Erskine "as well as he could pronounce it. Uskin, probably," and the venerable attorney chuckled. "I don't remember that too well. I was generally referred to throughout the camp as *Soo-ya-poo,* which means White Boy."

Sometimes, in jest, the Indians called him *E-shem-tipis-ilp-ilp* (Red Moon) or *Sut-sis-mox-mox* (Yellow Porcupine).

Joseph evidently could not speak English. "If he could he didn't." Erskine found communication presented few difficulties. "I picked up the language," Mr. Wood said matter-of-factly, "which you could very easily if you were young and you heard nothing but Indian around you, and a bit of Chinook jargon and some sign language."

In 1892 Erskine Wood stayed on the Reservation from July through November. The following year he returned in September and lived with Joseph until late December.

"I came up for the hunt," he said of his second visit, "but I didn't add much to it. There was always one or two men or boys with me. If I had gone alone I'd have been lost in the mountains."

He was 14 when he saw Joseph for the second time— "but I was just interested in fishing and hunting." He never tried to converse with Joseph about the Nez Perce War. "I wish we had," he said resignedly, "but I wasn't old enough to appreciate the opportunity. Besides, I don't think he'd want to talk about it. It was a very sad part of his life."

Chief Joseph was in his early 50s when Erskine Wood knew him. The elderly lawyer described the great Indian as "about six feet tall, a very fine figure of a man, straight, broad shoulders. Of course, he was getting a little heavy at that age. A fine head of black hair, with a forelock rising upward from his forehead and falling gracefully over to one side. It shows perfectly in the medallion on my wall." And he turned to a large medallion, which had belonged to his father, and which shows Joseph in noble profile.

"The main body of his hair," Mr. Wood continued, "was braided, one braid on each side, and falling down over the front of his shoulders and collarbone."

Mr. Wood mused at his desk for a moment. "A most intelligent and eloquent man," he went on. "A gentle man. A natural leader. The Nez Perce on the Reservation regarded Joseph as their leader. They had great respect for him and followed his decisions. He had a quiet authority in everything he did."

The love for Chief Joseph shone through every word the 88-year-old Erskine Wood uttered.

Wood compiled a diary during his second visit to the Colville Reservation. It is titled *Days With Chief Joseph* and was published as a book many, many years after the 1893 visit and many years after Joseph's death, on the first autumn day of 1904.

For weeks—one day after the other—he had sat stoically at his campfire, breaking his brooding silence only with the murmur of *"Halo manitah"*—he would not see another winter. On September 21st the deepening sadness devoured his last thought. The Agency physician reported: "Joseph died of a broken heart."

Wood's diary provides little insight into the culture of the

Indians, as Wood is the first to admit. What emerges of value is almost incidental to the main theme: the hunting and fishing and horse activities that seem to have consumed almost the entire attention of the energetic boy. But here and there one finds some precious passages, which reflect the lad's lively curiosity and sharp sense of observation.

Consider this gem, which Mr. Wood kindly gave us permission to reproduce here:

"After we had washed with snow and eaten what bread, kows and camas that was left we caught our horses which we had hobbled and put the saddles on then we dug some holes in the ground and proceeded to get some water. . . . The water was kind of dirty and tasted of the fir twigs but it was pretty good. The wolves were howling down the mountain and thinking of Itchala-haykt [who was lost] it was pretty dreary. It snowed all night and was snowing and blowing now. Well we got in the saddle and started off Joseph had discovered a trail while hunting the day before and we now followed it. It led in the direction of the teppe and was lots nicer than going through the brush, getting snow down your neck, having your hat swept off going through young fir thickets and tearing your clothing to pieces all of which I went through yesterday. We went up a mountain and it was so rocky that we had to come down aways and struck the trail and followed it across a canyon down which flowed a little stream partly frozen. Half way up the mountain that this canyon formed we stopped and got off our horses took off the saddles and hobbled our horses and turned them loose then we built a fire and warmed ourselves and then the men started to hunt for deer and Itchala-haykt. Cool-cool-smool-mool and I stayed behind with directions to keep up the fire to keep the horses in camp and after a while to holler at intervels. Then the men went off and we got some wood and put it on the fire. Then we sat down and took off our moccasins and warmed our feet and then we dried our rifles and wiped them off. After the men had been gone about half an hour we hollered and about 15 minutes later we hollered again and Joseph down the canyon hollored like a wolf. After a while Joseph came panting up the trail and told us not to holler any more and maybe a deer would come along. We got some more wood Joseph sat down on a saddle blanket and I drove the horses that had strayed back and then came back and sat down with my back against a big fir tree. In a little while Joseph motioned Cool cool smool mool to move his head and I looking around my tree saw a big buck about 20 yards off. I reached for my rifle and had a fine shot at his head but I expected Joseph to shoot every second and so I only held myself ready to shoot if Joseph should miss. But he was so slow that the buck with a snort wheeled around and dashed up the mountains the trees hid him from me but Joseph took a running shot at him without any effect. In about an hour the men came in. How wow a new had killed a buck and he caught his horse and went and got it and then we all cut some meat and fat off and each one cooked his own dinner. I was awful hungry and the fat just melted in my mouth. When we had all eaten enough we caught our horses put the saddles on them and then News new cohet divided the meat and we started off. It had stopped snowing now and we rode around the mountain but kept about half way up all the time. At about 7 o'clock in the evening we reached the teppe without anything happening worth telling."

One almost feels like adding an editorial note—nothing worth telling?!—to this notation of Friday, November 3, 1893. As for the spelling and the punctuation—or lack of it —only a sterile English teacher would be alarmed.

We asked Mr. Wood to read part of that passage so that we might tape record it. He read quietly, poetically, with freshness and depth.

After you left the Reservation in 1893, I asked, did you ever have contact with Chief Joseph again?

Mr. Wood arose and paced to the window, his back toward us. "I never saw Joseph again," he said tightly. "I never wrote to him. That's always been one of my regrets. Too many things happened. Too many things, and by the time I realized I had not seen or heard from Joseph in years, he was dead."

Do you ever think of those days with the Nez Perce, I

asked. Do they ever come back to you? What do you think about?

"Yes," replied Mr. Wood softly, dreamily. "I remember various episodes—deer hunting . . . horse-racing . . . herding the horses and taking care of them . . . hunting with my shot gun for pheasants and ducks and grouse . . . going on the deer hunt with the men . . ."

Joseph the meditative man is not one of his youthful recollections. The greatness of Joseph was perhaps sensed in the tepee but the historic figure of Joseph was realized only in retrospect. "If I had been a mature man," Mr. Wood sighed. "But at thirteen, fourteen? My mind was elsewhere."

Grover Jameson

A Trial to Remember

In 1898, when Grover Jameson was 12 years old, he attended the jam-packed trial of Ed Oliver, the homesteader who slew cattle king Pete French.

"I remember it quite well," said Mr. Jameson, an intense, cautious, courtly man with sharp eyes and an insistence upon having us understand exactly what he was saying. Sitting in the realty office at Burns, where he was employed, Mr. Jameson told us something of the trial, the most celebrated in all the history of the Oregon cattle country.

"It lasted two or three days, is all, but I was there every day it was on, every minute of every day. It was pretty emotional at certain times. The defense had a great attorney, from Portland, L. R. Webster, and he was not only an elocutionist, but he was a very dramatic sort of man, and during the final plea to the jury—I'll never forget that as long as I live—he had this fella's widow, the fella that shot French—she had three little children, I guess, ranging in age from oh, I'd say, from eight years down to six months— and he had them sitting right there every day. Well, during his argument to the jury he was the most dramatic, eloquent fella that you ever heard in your life, and he had all that jury in tears when he got through talking. And all they had to do was retire to the jury box, and on the first ballot it was Not Guilty.

"The jury was sympathetic to the man that shot French," Mr. Jameson continued, speaking about the trial as though it had been held yesterday instead of almost seven decades ago. "Of course, he was a homesteader, and in those days some of the big cattle men apparently made it hard for a homesteader to get along. In the early days here, why they would send their buckaroos and their ranch men out and scare 'em off."

What happened to Oliver, the homesteader who killed French, after the trial?

"The story is," replied Mr. Jameson, "and I think it's absolutely true, he ran off with another woman. Left his family and left the country, Oliver did. No one ever heard of him since. There was a fella by the name of P. C. Peterson married the Oliver widow and raised the children."

It was interesting the way Mr. Jameson referred to Mrs. Oliver as a widow. Actually, Oliver may have been very much alive for many years after he took off but the fact that he disappeared beyond the pale of life, as far as Burns was concerned, may have prompted the town to write him off as dead.

Not only did Grover Jameson attend the trial, he had actually seen Pete French and even talked with him. I doubt that there are five men remaining who can make that claim.

Mr. Jameson was ecstatic in his praise of Pete French. His cheeks glowed with a pink tinge of pride and excitement and the flow of his words quickened. Leaning forward to emphasize the thrust of his conviction, Mr. Jameson recalled: "He was a fine-*lookin'* man. He was a small fella, yeah, real small, but he was a fine fella. And how we kids remembered him so well and liked him so well, every time he'd come to town, he'd drive into the livery stable here on Main Street, and count we kids how many there were of us, might be ten or fifteen, not over twenty, he'd count us all, and say, 'Now you boys stay right here, I'll be back in just five minutes,' see, and he'd go across to the saloon and if there were twenty kids there he'd get twenty silver dollars and come over and give each kid a silver dollar a-piece. Well naturally, when Pete French come to town it was Fourth of July with we kids."

He returned to physical description, saying French was dark-complexioned, wiry and "a real light fella. I don't think he weighed over 135 or 140 pounds."

French was a very generous man—to people who didn't crowd him; and he was a popular boss, Mr. Jameson stated. "If you went to work for French once, and was a good cow man, why you stayed as long as you wanted to. Because he didn't jump around and hire Tom, Dick and Harry to replace a good man. He kept his crew, which was indicative of bein' a pretty nice feller to work for."

French was also a very courageous man, Mr. Jameson avowed. "He showed his courage in a good many instances during the Indian battles here. Take this battle of McCoy Creek Gorge. There were two rimrocks, and there was a pass between 'em, and French started to lead his men out when these Indians came. They were shootin' at him all the time, and French was the only cow man that had a gun. One man was shot off his horse down on the hillside and French, he rode back down that hill, and picked that man up, and put him on his horse, and took him to the P-Ranch, that was fifteen, sixteen miles away."

As late as his boyhood years, said Mr. Jameson, Indians and whites were firing at each other.

"Right here in Burns the Indians went around with guns, plenty of them," he declared. "I slept under the bed many a night, when I was a kid here. They'd walk around the house, y'know, and look in the windows, y'know. My oldest sister, she'd also guard the house at night by walking around the house with a rifle. She could shoot like a man, she was my dad's boy at that time.

"The Indians were dressed mostly in buckskin in those days. That's all they had. They'd come through here, the Umatilla Indians, they'd be two or three hundred in a bunch, and they'd go down to the Steens Mountains, and kill some deer. Well, there were a lot of deer in the country at that time, and they'd come back maybe in a month or six weeks and they'd have a hundred ponies all loaded with deer pelts and dried meat, see?

"Those Indians, you know, if they got a little whiskey, well, they were quite a bother, I'll tell you. That is, they'd scare people, y'know. Well, the man would be off there working or doing something, why they'd be walkin' around your house, lookin' in the window, y'know. If you had whiskey or coffee, why, you were all right. Give 'em a little coffee or a little whiskey and they'd take off, and leave y'alone."

Grover Jameson was born in Burns on January 22, 1886. There wasn't much to the town then—a saloon or two, blacksmith shop, two livery stables, dry goods store, grocery, barber shop, small hotel, and a motley collection of houses and shacks. There was also a newspaper, founded the year before.

The first high school didn't open in Burns until about 1905, Mr. Jameson said, so children his age didn't get to go to high school unless they left home, which very few did.

Burns was pretty isolated when Grover Jameson was a boy. The nearest railroad was at Ontario and it took the stage two days and a night to travel there. Newspapers coming into Burns, by stage from Canyon City, were a week old when they arrived. Today everybody has television and what was filmed yesterday in Asia or Africa is flashed into almost every Burns living room today.

Mr. Jameson had watched Burns grow for eight decades. He had taken everything in stride. Talking about the heyday of the cowpuncher, he said: "Well, Burns was pretty wild at times. Buckaroos come to town, get drunk, play a little poker, lose some money, shoot the lights out of the saloon, and so forth and so on, but then that was just things that happen in any frontier town. We thought nothing of it."

And he saw the homesteaders flood the sage like an unrelenting tide, and then after a few years dribble away, leaving behind sagging shacks that fell prey to the banshee winds.

"Here's what went wrong with the homesteaders," explained Mr. Jameson. "They had no transportation out. If they raised anything, they couldn't sell it. And the country isn't, wasn't at that time, suitable for farming. They didn't have the proper machinery to clear the land, cultivate the soil, and this is a semiarid country, and about all they could raise was a little rye hay which wouldn't support a family."

So the years went by, one after the other, like fenceposts on a rocky road. A heap of years, jumbled and sprawled. Grover Jameson was a big man in the cattle business at one time, being in charge of one of the largest cattle companies in the Pacific Northwest. Then he retired and turned to real estate.

A life filled with many faces and events, and yet one face and one event stand out. The face belongs to Pete French, the event was the trial of his killer.

Why are the face and the trial so important to him, we ask. Grover Jameson ponders. In a moment he shakes his head, as though the question needs no pondering. It can be answered directly.

"Pete French was a mighty important man around here," he replies.

A thought flickers across his eyes and he adds, with a soft smile: "And I was a boy, of course. And that sunk deep in me."

Prince Helfrich

The Lost Hunter

Some years ago I met Prince Helfrich on the streets of downtown Eugene and we had a brief and interesting conversation. What he said almost threw me for a loop, him being such a famous guide and finder of lost persons and such. It took me a while to savor the humor of that chat.

First, though, before I repeat our exchange of words, which were so startling that I wrote them down that evening,

I ought to tell you a little about Prince, which is his real given name.

He lives, as he did then, at the Rail Creek Ranch, just outside Vida, which is almost easier to find on the map than on the highway. In summer, whatever there is of Vida is quite lively, it being on the recreational McKenzie River, but the rest of the year things are sort of slow and lonesome.

Prince and his wife reside, as they have for many years, in a rambling ranch home back of a split rail fence. There Prince pores over maps, burrows himself in books on the Mountain Men of yore, and runs his outfitting and guide business, assisted by his three sons, now fully grown men with families of their own.

That day we bumped into each other on Willamette Street, in Eugene, Prince was, as he still is, one of the most famous boatmen in all the West. He had rowed at least 40,000 miles of turbulent Western streams. He was the first to run the Deschutes, the first to go down British Columbia's Clearwater and one of the first to boat the Rogue, the Owyhee, the Blitzen and the lower stretches of the John Day. Every year for 17 years he had run the fabled "River of No Return," the Middle Fork of the Salmon.

About six months before we met that day in Eugene, I had interviewed Helfrich for a magazine article and asked him to name the rivers he had boated. "Well, let's see now," he started. And the names fell from his lips like Stephen Vincent Benet's beautiful poem, *American Names*. The McKenzie, Willamette, Santiam, Metolius, John Day and Owyhee of Oregon; the Toutle, Cowlitz and Chehalis of Washington; the Madison and Big Hole of Montana.

"Let's see now." And he named off more rivers until it seemed as though there could be no more in the Northwest; then he took a breath and started again.

He was always seeking another stream—some new river, where you don't know what's around the bend, and the water is exciting-strange to you and there's the gladness of discovery; a river joyous-fresh, where Canadian honkers fill the low green islands and red-winged blackbirds and Western tanagers whoosh startled into the sky.

Prince never felt out of place on a river and he was

equally at home in the mountains. He had spent winters in the high hills, some of them alone, snowshoeing along his trap line, and returning each spring with the skins of marten, weasel and red fox.

At that time, the period when we spied each other near the corner of Willamette and Broadway, Prince was writing a weekly column, "Around the Campfire," for the Eugene *Register-Guard*. One of his columns described his experiences as a trapper:

"A man who traps alone in the snow combats a number of unseen enemies. Therefore he must have unusual ability along many lines. He must be able to take care of himself in a sudden storm, be able to find shelter and make a fire under adverse conditions. He must know where to find dry wood when the forests are dripping with moisture, and how to orient himself if he becomes lost. He should be rugged and healthy and able to live on scant rations if necessary. He must have coolness and strength as well as complete confidence in his ability to survive under conditions very unfriendly to men.

"The occupation also calls for a high degree of skill in trapping animals and a complete knowledge of the habits and ways of the animals in order to make this a profitable business.

"The final quality which a man must have is perhaps the most important of all. This is the ability to live alone in the wilderness. The solitude and loneliness become overpowering for some people, and they become victims of a queer ailment. One day while examining a trap a man may have the feeling that he is being watched. A quick look assures him that no one is about. He goes on with the business at hand. The feeling persists, and again he turns unexpectedly, only to confront a snow-covered scene. When he goes back to his cabin he travels a little faster than usual, his enthusiasm for his work is gone and the peacefulness and beauty have been ruined for him."

Prince's column was often touched with sensitivity and humor. In it he described such things as the lonely vigil a little Western harlequin, injured in Bear Creek Rapids and unable to migrate with the rest of his family, is keeping for their return; the association between different species ("Only a very few of the wild birds or animals want to live entirely alone"); the plight of small animals in a flood (". . . probably praying in their own little way that their improvised boat won't tip over"); the ferocity of the weasel; the miracle of a spring morning in the mountain meadows; the frantic flight of a China rooster from a golden eagle; getting caught in a mountain blizzard; the terror and ravages of a forest fire; and a recipe for cooking porcupine: "Place the freshly skinned carcass in a big kettle along with two round smooth rocks. Bring to a slow boil and cook until you can stick a fork in the rocks. Throw meat away and eat rocks."

Every once in a while there'd be an article about Prince in the local paper; how he was the first to be called upon when someone was reported missing in the mountains; how he could tell by the subtle trace of twigs and grass and stones where the lost person had been and how long before; how, in the wilderness, without compass, he could unerringly find his way back, day or night, to camp or to town.

Well, now you know a little about Prince, so I'll tell you about our meeting and what happened that startled me.

He was loping down the street, in his familiar fringed and braided deerskin jacket and broad-rimmed hat, perched with flair atop his long, lean head, when our eyes nailed each other and stopped us short.

"Say, Ralph," said the famous mountain man and river guide, "where in heck do you live?"

I told him the address, a house on Second Street near the railroad tracks. He pulled a slip of paper out of his Pendleton shirt pocket. "That's what I've got," he declared, "but there must be some mistake."

"Why?" I asked.

"Well," he replied, "last week I spent two hours driving around trying to find you. I was willing to bet there was no such place. I got pretty upset about it, believe me."

"You could have asked someone," I suggested.

He thumbed up the rim of his western hat and scratched his forehead. "Never thought of that."

When we parted I was still reeling, wondering why this

great guide was stymied by a couple of streets running into blind alleys.

Some time after that I saw the humor of it and still later I could draw a moral: the city can be more of a jungle than the wilderness.

Chris Schneider

The Golden Dream Fades

Almost half of Oregon's gold came from the mines of Cornucopia, northeast of Baker. But Chris Schneider swears that only a small fraction of the rich veins deep in the dark maw of the undulating hills has been worked.

Chris ought to know. He came to Cornucopia as a lad of eleven in 1897 and except for short-term jobs in other mining camps his life has been closely intertwined with the history of the place.

Cornucopia, overlooking the flowing green meadows of Pine Valley from its perch on the pine-clad hem of the Wallowa range, was only 14 years old when Chris arrived. He went to work in the mines at 17 and remained a miner for 38 years. That's a lot of time underground, in a very dangerous occupation, but Chris was lucky. In all those years he was never once seriously hurt. But his father was killed and so was his wife's first husband.

While the mines ran, things were lively, though leisurely, in Cornucopia. Before the coming of the automobile, horse-drawn freight wagons carted goods from Baker, taking three days up, a day to change loads, and three days back. The cargo to Baker was gold shipped in brick form and sent parcel post, insured. There were no holdups, a matter which Chris never regretted. "Life in the mines was hectic enough," he recalled dryly.

Incorporated in 1914, Cornucopia in its prime boasted 700 persons, 300 of whom were miners on the company payroll. The town had a post office, two-room grade school, city hall and jail, the two-story Keller Hotel, two mercantile stores, two taverns, two dance halls, and several sundry establishments, such as a barber shop. Elected officials consisted of a mayor, seven councilmen and a constable.

Chris knows all about the mayor's job. He was elected to that post in 1922 and reelected nine consecutive times. He was in office when the town shut down.

"I never wanted the job," he told us. "Three or four times I campaigned for my opponent. Once I won by one vote and my opponent demanded a recount. I said he was right, that he had really won, but when they counted again I was still ahead by that one vote. I declined every nomination, but they kept on electing me. I even thought of stuffing the ballot box once, but somebody was watching."

In 1934 a long tunnel in the Union Companion mine was started. Completed in 1936, it was dug to one-and-one-quarter miles long and 2,200 feet from apex to bottom. Everyone predicted the town would skyrocket, with gold as plentiful as honey in the horn. But five years later the giddy predictions collapsed overnight.

On October 31, 1941, the mine was abruptly closed. Within 24 hours a mass exodus was under way. Without pausing to write their resignations the constable and seven councilmen pulled stakes, followed by the miners, the school teachers, the hotel proprietor, the barber, the merchants, the postmaster and the bartenders. Houses were hastily boarded up and shops, stripped of their goods, were completely abandoned. Cornucopia was dead.

Only Chris Schneider stayed on, as watchman. The following year he married Jessie Mires and the two settled down to keep the ghosts company.

We first met Chris some years back, when we drove to Cornucopia and spread our sleeping bags under a lacy pine tree on the banks of Pine Creek. The water was clear and swift, with a regular, cheerful beat which through the night formed a soothing rhythm.

Just before twilight we strolled around and peeked into some of the cabins we found among clumps of pines. You couldn't see some of them until you were almost at the doorstep.

The beauty of Cornucopia, we agreed, was that you could camp just about wherever you wished, with no danger that anybody would come along screaming that you were on private property, or that you had to have a permit, or that you had to pay a dollar or two to stay overnight. We could have chosen any cabin we wanted but most of those we saw seemed infested by pack rats. Anyway, it was much nicer sleeping under a pine tree, with the sky so close there appeared to be a star hanging from every branch.

Next morning, before we started looking for Chris Schneider, we spotted some men on tractors standing in front of a cabin squatted on a rise in a meadow. They informed us that a logging contractor had purchased a bunch of houses, at $300 each, and was moving them intact down to Pine Valley, where he was selling them to farmers for $900 apiece.

We found Chris and Jessie Schneider in a large, white frame building at the upper end of what was once Main Street. The house was well-furnished and adequately heated by wood. It had a piano, radio and telephone. Winter storms sometimes caused power failure but phone service was quickly restored. "I don't think we've spent more than a week at a time without telephone service," said Chris. He considered that pretty good.

The house also had running water, coming in through pipes from the "city water system," a tank on the hill. Keeping the water in the tank from freezing in the winter was somewhat of a problem but after so many years in Cornucopia there weren't many such problems Chris couldn't handle.

From late spring to early fall, Chris was kept busy by tourists, who wanted to know all about the olden days. He had given so many tours of the town he couldn't even approximate the number. He charged no fee and declined all monetary compensation. "Just drop me a postcard sometime," he'd say. And some people actually did.

After the last tourist and camper departed, Chris put on a feverish spurt of stocking up for winter. Once a week, through the long snow months, he strapped on his skis and glided down to Carson, six miles below, to pick up the mail and a few groceries. It took him 90 minutes to descend, three hours to return.

"I never worry about him," said his wife, as she sat at the sewing machine, working at garments for her grandchildren. "That man is capable, absolutely capable."

We followed Chris down Main Street, now a maimed jag of rocky road. The crude shops of yesteryear, ravaged by the elements, were eerie landmarks waiting for a banshee wind to claw them to splinters. The awkward lettering on the clapboard fronts and the rough, frontier style of the sagging structures showed plainly that Cornucopia never lacked in earthiness.

Chris was already 70 but he looked ten years younger and he walked erect, with a long, brisk stride that would have done honor to a man of forty. When he had something to show us he'd stop, push up the brim of his hat, fold his arms, and point with the tilt of his chin. He spoke slowly, sometimes with wit, and patiently answered all our questions.

He seemed to grow six inches taller in front of the Union Companion Mine. "Some day," he vowed, "she'll come back. I know she will. Why, she hardly been touched." But then his shoulders slouched and he added wistfully, "But I don't think I'll ever see the time. She'll come back, but I won't be around."

About nine months later I sent Chris a magazine article I had done on Cornucopia. He wrote back: "I sure enjoyed your words. I like phrases that catch the eye and sing in the ear and paint a living picture, and you have done that. I didn't have much schooling but I like to read a lot. Right now I'm reading Shakespeare again. He really opens your mind and fills your heart."

A few years later Chris and Jessie acknowledged they weren't as hardy as they used to be, so in the winter they moved down to Halfway, 12 miles below.

By now Chris was convinced he'd see no more gold come out of Cornucopia.

Herman Oliver

Every Man in Grant County . . .

The last time we saw Herman Oliver was in his beautiful brick house on a side street in John Day. He still looked every inch the cattleman, though he was retired, and though, being medium-size and stocky, he didn't at all fit the literary image of a tall, slim-hipped cattle boss.

Herman ("I hate to be called Mr. Oliver") had lived a long life in this John Day Valley. Talking of the old timers, he said: "We have grown up from being afoot or a-horseback, or a-buggy, to the automobiles, the airplanes, and the jet planes, and, well, it's been interesting, it's been exciting, to watch these developments throughout these years that I've been in this country."

Pausing, he looked square at me and asked: "You gettin' this right?"

"That magazine story I did on you about ten years ago was right, wasn't it?" I replied.

"Yep, that was quite an article," Herman said. "Every man in Grant County musta read it."

That sentence struck a familiar note. When I was interviewing Herman for that article he'd sometimes stop, point a blunt finger at me, and caution: "Now, we gotta be this and we want 'em to know the truth."

The day my wife and I left John Day, on that first visit, we were walking down the main drag when we spied Herman, garbed like an old ranch hand, sitting on the sidewalk and leaning against the Grant County Bank, which he just about owned.

Herman shuffled to his feet, spread an infectious grin across his leathered face, and drawled: "Say folks, I just remembered somethin'. Gotta couple more little things to put in that story. We want to make it just right, don't we? Every man in Grant County will see that piece o' writin'."

About two or three times more that morning, in front of the theater, or some other building Herman held title to, he'd catch up with us again and read us what he had scribbled on a piece of paper or on the back of an envelope. And he'd always end with the need to be downright correct because "Every man in Grant County . . ."

After John Day we headed for Walla Walla, taking it easy because we were gathering free-lance material. At every town we stopped for the night, it seemed, we'd get a telephone call from Herman Oliver, modifying a statement he had made, changing a date, or enlarging upon something. And always there was the admonition: "Every man . . ."

How Herman found us has always remained a mystery to us and when I did ask him about it, in our last conversation, he just smiled, a teasing grin that meant he was enjoying himself immensely.

In Walla Walla, where we stayed about two weeks, we received a call from Herman every two or three days. Each time there were additions, deletions, corrections and suggestions, on every occasion closing with the cautionary note, which now had become an edict, on what each adult male of Grant County was sure to do.

But you couldn't take Herman Oliver lightly. You had to appreciate his dead earnestness. He had an important story to tell and he wanted it told properly.

For many years Herman Oliver had been Oregon's "Mr. Cattleman." His life was a saga of the industry. For 72 years, until 1957, he lived on the ranch where he was born. There, as a stockman, he had earned a name for many innovations. He was the first in the John Day Valley to dehorn beef cattle, saving carcasses from being bruised en route to market; to begin winter lambing; to put on a bull-grading demonstration; to raise crossbred sheep; to cull sheep for uniformity of wool and carcass.

Herman got rid of his sheep in 1939. "Of all the livestock," he explained, "sheep are the biggest gamble. They can make you or break you quicker than any other livestock and require too much personal supervision. Sheep get every kind of disease. Here's what can happen: a ewe will lie down right in front of you and die before your eyes."

Herman's father came to the John Day country from the Azore Islands in 1866, his mother from Germany a few years later. His father started ranching in 1878 and seven years later Herman was born. At the age of three or four, no later than four, he was riding a horse. He entered the ranching business "as fast as I grew up."

You could scour the state from one end to the other and find few men with the love for Eastern Oregon history that was a fever in Herman Oliver. At the age of 80 he was as excited about the "olden days" as he had been half a century earlier.

A cogent reason for this enthusiasm was his own life; he felt, and rightly so, that he was an actor in the drama of Eastern Oregon. Another strong reason was his personal link to the earliest white man days of Grant County.

Herman was born only 23 years after gold was first discovered at nearby Canyon City. As a boy he knew Billy Aldred, the initial finder.

"He lived within a mile and a quarter of the ranch where my father started to develop, and he used to come to town, come down to the ranch on the occasions that he wanted to ride into town to buy his supplies, and he'd ride down with my father on the milk wagon," Herman recalled.

"Oh, he was a wonderful old man," Herman sighed, his eyes glowing. "I never did know his nationality or anything of that sort, but he was a wonderful feller. He was an old bachelor and he liked youngsters, and that was where I got most of my mining stories written in my book *Gold and Cattle Country.*"

Herman was one of the founders of the Grant County Historical Society and built it a museum building. People who know about such things say it is one of the finest county historical museums in all the United States.

What schooling Oliver received—three months in the fall and three months in the spring for eight years—was pale stuff compared to what he picked up outdoors. "I learned from the cowboys, the horses, the cattle and even the grass," he said proudly.

At ten, Herman had his first taste of ownership. His father gave the six Oliver children 100 head of heifer calves. When the girl and a half-brother moved away, they sold their interest to the others, who applied themselves with such zeal that by 1906 they owned half the Oliver family cattle.

For Herman Oliver, 1906 was the year of decision. His aging parents decided to sell the spread. A deal was made with an agent.

The night before closing the sale, 21-year-old Herman embarked full sail upon a course he was never to regret. He explained it this way:

"My parents were in bed when I got to their room. They were tired, but I asked them to listen to me. I have always believed that real opportunity, which can shape a man's destiny, comes once in a lifetime, and you have to reach out and grab it. I felt that my one great opportunity was calling to me, and I didn't want to let it go.

"I asked my folks to start a partnership, with them owning the real estate and us boys, me and my younger brother, owning the cattle. They weren't happy about it. My older brother and the half-brother who had stayed on the ranch died a little earlier, both within a week, and my folks were broken up. They wanted to get out and forget about cattle. But I could see opportunity standing there big as life before me, lookin' at me, wondering what I'd do about my big chance, and I couldn't let it go. I just couldn't. I talked to the folks until two in the morning, and finally persuaded them to give the partnership idea a try for a couple of years."

Herman had another motive. He had just married pretty Eliza Laurance of Canyon City, whom he had met three years earlier at a masquerade dance in a schoolhouse. A year later a daughter, Anna, was born to them.

In Eliza, Herman found his equal: a strong, patient person who could match him stride for stride through the turbulent years ahead, and do it uncomplainingly. With a stock-centered singlemindedness that often excluded domestic affairs, a stubbornness that brooked no resistance and an impatience that could express itself in thunder-like crackling, Herman might have driven a dainty city-bred girl home to mother. But Eliza was built of stronger stuff. She was John Day country through and through, riding the range, nursing calves and lambs, cooking for the ranch crew, keeping the books and records and attuning herself to every mood of her man. With all their responsibilities Eliza and Herman found time to rear two boys, left motherless. Both were grown with families of their own by the time we started working with Herman on the magazine article.

When J. C. Oliver & Sons was organized the operation consisted of 8,000 acres and 1,200 cattle. (When Herman counted cattle it was only those which he had raised, not bought, fattened and sold.)

With Herman managing and younger brother Frank assisting, they "kept expanding, buying more land, increasing cattle and sheep, improving quality, raising our standards, learning, learning, learning."

They built up a plant of 50,000 acres of deeded land, and the firm controlled 100,000 acres of Government land through permits. It ran 3,500 cattle and 7,000 sheep and was the biggest spread the John Day Valley ever knew. This was in the late 1920s, just before Wall Street came tumbling down, and the firm, after the death of their parents, was known as Oliver Brothers.

The big spread had 250 miles of rail and wire fence, and the cowpunchers, later known as ranch hands, because they did all kinds of work, didn't come home at night to their families. They ate from the chuckwagon, bedded down under the stars, and when the cattle were restless at night they rode around them, whistling softly or crooning soothing melodies about lonely cowpokes.

Herman Oliver credited "three keys" to his success: farsightedness, ambition and love for livestock. The first, he felt, permitted him to predict the depression, a forecast followed by a decision to reduce livestock holdings by 50 percent.

When the depression struck full force the Oliver Bros. ranch was solvent, and was put up as security to keep the Grant County Bank from going under. Herman and a few friends took over the threatened banks of the valley and reorganized the banking system. They transferred the Canyon

City bank holdings to John Day and made the Prairie City bank, 13 miles east, a branch of the Grant County Bank. Herman became president of this bank and chairman of its board.

A few years before the depression reached out to shake up Grant County, the gold dredge fever had hit the John Day Valley and Herman had a chance to sell his best bottom land for a fancy price. A good number of farmers had traded soil for cash, leaving the range for the giant dredgers to tear apart, extract the gold, and contemptuously spit back lumps of rocks.

When the dredger company men prospected the Oliver property they found it rich in gold and offered the brothers $500 an acre, from $150 to $200 more than it was worth on the real estate market. But Herman snubbed the lucrative offer, declaring: "I love this country and I honor its future too dearly. This land is meant to feed people. I'm a livestock man, and a good livestock and range man is a real conservationist."

Herman Oliver had been preaching conservation for more than 40 years when we first met him, in 1955. He had said this, or something like it, a thousand times:

"The land must be conserved. It's wrong to wear out the soil. The days of free grass are over, and livestock raising now requires privately owned lands which have become expensive and add to the cost of feed far greater than the early days. Since real estate and feed have become more expensive, it's necessary to have better stock. Our goal must be quality, not numbers.

"We can't have quality without conservation. We can't treat the range as though it's here forever, whatever we do with it. We can kill the land by overgrazing. We've got to leave a little foliage on the plant to feed the root system in the ground. The foliage retards erosion and you have good grass next year. But strip the plant and you've hurt the land, yourself and the country."

Along with his love for Eastern Oregon history, Oliver had a passion for the John Day Valley and all the people in it. Any man who recognized him as a friend was someone to be embraced. He was proud as a peacock when someone called him a good neighbor. He worked hard to earn these laurels. Once, when the winter was overlong and many ranchers were desperate for feed, he put up $20,000 to purchase feed outside the valley, then established distributing stations and invited the ranchers to take what they needed. They did, and in due time repaid him, without interest. During another critical feed shortage he sold his surplus hay for one-fourth the price the ranchers would have had to pay elsewhere. Letting a John Day livestock man down was about the most damning sin he could imagine.

He was anxious to be liked by the youth, too, and equally desirous of continuing a strong range tradition in Grant County. He helped develop a strong 4-H movement, sponsored history contests among the county schools, would accept an invitation to talk to an elementary class at the drop of his Stetson. The saddle horse breeding contest which he started was the first of the numerous saddle horse and cow cutting contests in the West.

No office boss, Herman rode the range as a cowpuncher, driving himself twice as hard as any man in his pay. He took many a fall from a horse and when he was 56 was gored by a bull, which caught him against a corral fence and hooked a horn through his body. He was back in the saddle long before his doctors recommended it, the second time he had turned his back on medical advice. A few years before, when he needed crutches to pull himself along the ground, he rode with his leg in a cast, a sight which dismayed the town physicians and surgeons.

He was 70 when I interviewed him for the magazine article. Each morning he was up at five and spent a few hours riding around his property, seeing that the day was planned and the morning chores done before he returned to the house for breakfast. Sometimes he rested a bit in the afternoon but he could still get by on only four or five hours sleep. I was more than 30 years younger, but just the hustle and bustle of his coming and going tired me.

Somehow he found time to serve a term or two on the State Board of Higher Education and the State Highway Commission. He'd show up for meetings if he had to drive all night, sometimes through blizzards or windstorms that would have kept lesser men, just a notch lesser, settling for the fireplace. He had such a fervent belief in his own capacities that obstacles did no more than provoke his impatience.

"Do you feel," I asked, the last time we saw him, "that cattle ranching gave you an opportunity to be more of an individualist?"

"Yessir," Herman replied. "The cow business, in fact, the cattleman, has always been classified as an independent breed, all by themselves. They thought different, they were independent, they'd go out here and get 'em a cow horse, a saddle horse, and a few head o' cattle, and maybe pick up a homestead or something like that, and, well, they were just independent. They didn't worry about what was going on in the world or anything of that kind. They grew their own garden stuff, and their own beef or mutton or vegetables, whatever you had, they didn't buy much stuff. About the only thing they bought in those days was tea and coffee and sugar and flour, but all the rest of the stuff they produced on the ranches."

"That's mighty interesting," I declared, scribbling away.

"Just get it right," Herman said. "Somethin' about a local man comes out, word gets around. Every man in Grant County will see it."

John Silvertooth

The Sage of Antelope

Long John Silvertooth, gnarled as an old desert juniper, poured a beer for a dusty traveler who had churned into Antelope from a backwoods bend, and casually reckoned as to how he might be of a mind to sell his Idle Hour Saloon and his museum, in the next room, all for $20,000.

The price seemed mighty reasonable to me, because I had

thought for years that Silvertooth had one of the finest private historical museums in Oregon. But since I didn't have $20,000, and didn't know anybody who was interested, I shrugged off the matter.

Long John scratched the stubble on his lean face, cocked an elbow on the bar, probably the oldest in the state— it had come 'round the Horn on a sailing ship more than a century ago—and continued on the subject with a voice that was pretty much like the lay of the land around Antelope, flat in spots and undulating in others.

"Couple come to look a while ago," said John, with the twang of rusty sage scraping through some of the weeds. "We talked, but they didn't say nothin'."

Most of the people who ventured into Antelope, which from a rise on the Shaniko road looked like a clump of houses caught in the branches of willow trees, were the handful of ranch families from the valley or from even smaller and more isolated Ashwood, a few delivery men and, during the summer, a trickle of tourists.

Few of the tourists did business at the small, neat grocery store, which also had a lunch counter (and operated the gas pump outside), or at the tiny post office, in the same building as the grocery. But hardly a newcomer passed by Silvertooth's saloon. There hadn't been much written publicity on it but word of mouth had made both the saloon, itself a museum piece, and its proprietor legendary in Oregon.

Somehow Long John, looking a little like a rangeland Ichabod Crane, had acquired a reputation as a great story teller. In reality, he told few tales, but he had the air of a man who had many yarns to spin, and the atmosphere of his old saloon, with its dim lighting, stuffed wildlife, beat-up chairs and tables, antique display cases, and clientele you would have sworn had been hired to give the place its rustic, leathery flavor, all—the man and the saloon—conspired to convey the impression that Antelope was one of the last places in Oregon to retain an authentic pioneer flavor and that John Silvertooth was a living history of the area.

I have met men and women who, at the pilot light of suggestion, quickly boiled with enthusiasm about Silver-

tooth's storytelling, but none could remember a single tale,
The fact is, Old John could chuckle a few times, toss off
a couple of colorful remarks, drawl a mundane sentence
with an aura of authority and mystery, and listen with a
gravity that always flattered. The sum of these, not so odd
as it might seem in cold print, left visitors with the feeling
that they had encountered a most gripping and loquacious
character.

Probably what gave John Silvertooth his state-wide reputation, apart from his wonderful name, was that Antelope
was so small and he had been there so long and the Idle
Hour was a musty page out of an early Oregon album.

John's father, Felix Silvertooth, was a pioneer stagecoach
driver on The Dalles-Canyon City toll road. His mother,
Ella Caleb, was, in John's words, "the first white girl born
in Wasco County, before Wasco was even a county." Her
father was an army officer sent "to quiet the Indians."

About 1880, Felix and Ella Silvertooth moved to Antelope, where Felix opened a saloon. Five years later John
was born. He had been in Antelope all his life, watching
the growth and decline of a typical central Oregon back-
country settlement.

Actually, there were many more businesses in Antelope
when he was born than there are now. Then, as he told
us, there was a saloon, stores, livery stable, feed lot "and
other places."

The town had been started, Silvertooth said, as a pro-
visioning point on one of the tributaries of the Oregon Trail.
"The immigrants used to come here first, ya know. It was
all the Old Oregon Trail, they call it, now.

"Then this was a stagecoach stop. Had a hotel, too. Right
on a main stage line. An' the town kept growing. They
was a lot of traffic then. 'Twas all free range out here, the
sheep men come in and run sheep, and then the homesteaders come in, and the crowd took the free range, and
that done away with the sheep business."

Antelope had its largest population—perhaps as many as
250 people—in the boom years of the homesteaders, 1906
to 1908. It had a newspaper once, too, Old John recalled, the Antelope *Herald*, and one of its editors was

H. L. Davis, who later achieved literary fame with his *Honey in the Horn,* a biting novel about the homesteading days.

Arid land, distant markets, lack of know-how and insufficient capital sent the homesteaders packing in defeat, and Antelope declined.

"Used to be 30 ranches close around here," Silvertooth declared with a trace of nostalgia, "and now there's twelve men owns all Antelope Valley," an area of about 35 square miles. The country was back to stock again, sheep and cattle.

"All Antelope has now," he added resignedly, "is about 33 people—women, children 'n' old folks."

The saloon Felix Silvertooth started about 1880 burned down in 1898, along with the rest of Antelope. The next year Felix rebuilt the saloon and installed a bar which had been one of the first in The Dalles.

John Silvertooth had been part of the Idle Hour since 1899. He hadn't added much to the saloon, but at one time he had a barber shop in an adjoining room—the only unlicensed barber shop in the state—and he also plied the watchmaker's trade, having the only unlicensed watchmaker's shop in Oregon. The old barber chair and his old watchmaking tools were on display in the museum, along with a sizable collection of other artifacts, some dating back to the covered wagon days.

"Someday it'll probably be sold," John said with a dry sigh. "Probably when the old St. Peter calls me." And he turned to pour a beer for a new customer, a rancher who had joggled down from Ashwood, which has only about a dozen people, to see more of the world. He was the second customer in two hours. At that rate Silvertooth wasn't making much money, but keeping the saloon was more interesting than retiring. In Antelope there wasn't much to retire to. Anyway, it was easier to sell a place when it was open and its blood was circulating.

As we left, we told John we'd be back next year. "Oh," he replied cheerfully, with a big wave of his hand, "I'll be here. Me and the old saloon. We're too darn cussed to die. But say, if you know anybody's interested in buying it, tell 'em to look me up. They's a lot o' good stuff here, goin' back a hundred years and more. There's some stuff here nobody else has got. Buyer leaves it here or takes it away—same difference to me."

The next year we returned to Antelope. John Silvertooth was there but the Idle Hour was not. No one had bought it; it had burned to the ground some months before. Everything in it and the museum had been destroyed. All that remained was a sodden mound of debris.

John Silvertooth had opened another saloon in a shack across the street and up the road a bit from where the Idle Hour had been. It was one of the empty structures, houses and shacks, that had lined the lower part of Antelope the first time we had been there. Year by year one or two of the ghostly structures had been removed for one reason or another. Only a few were left, and John Silvertooth was doing business in a smaller one.

Not much of a business. Just a few cases of beer, it seemed to us at a quick glance. We didn't have the heart to go inside. Long John was sitting out front, bent and gaunt, gazing straight ahead while trading small talk with a stockman.

I told him I had written a book on Oregon.

"I heard," he said.

The book had something in it about Antelope, I continued.

"I heard," he repeated.

I tried to think of other things to say but couldn't. We started for our car. Before I opened a door I thought of one last thing: "Do you think you'll ever get out of Antelope?"

"I dunno," Long John said tiredly. "I get out once in a while. We got family in Portland, ya know. But we always come back. This is our home—for better or for worse." And for the first time since we were there he looked in the direction of the ruins.

George Milligan

The Man from Mercy

George Milligan was one of the few newsworthy people I have met who was absolutely indifferent to personal publicity. Any stories about him, he felt, were nothing but a waste of space. Once, to test his sincerity, I agreed. "You're right," I said, "you're really not the story." He smiled in relief. "I'm glad you see it that way. Now we can talk about the really important thing."

The "really important thing," which really owed so much of its being and success to George Milligan, was Medford's Mercy Flights, the first community-plan air ambulance service in all the United States.

There were then other air ambulance services in the country. But all were operated by Government agency or profit-making firm or under a group underwriting expenses. "Only in Medford," as the local *Mail Tribune* aptly put it, "is there an ambulance service which is not in business to make money, which is completely independent, which exists only to serve the sick and injured and which is operated by a few dedicated souls whose only reward is the feeling of satisfaction they get by knowing they are performing a vital and important service to their fellow human beings."

Our first meeting with George Milligan, who had reluctantly agreed to talk with us, took place inside Mercy's hangar at the Medford Airport in the autumn of 1955. He was a solid-built, balding man, in his mid-thirties, with an open face and a casual but polite manner. When he spoke he measured his words carefully and when he could not find the word he wanted he tugged a bit on the brim of the baseball cap he was wearing.

He divulged little of himself, treating every personal question as a road mine which had to be cautiously detoured.

He would talk about Mercy Flights but only as something he knew but was not an intimate part of, and any attempt to place him in a leading role was dodged by reference to what someone else had done. Eventually, with all of us sweating, through the probing and the yielding, we garnered sufficient information to tell us something of Mercy Flights and Milligan's part in it. This information was considerably expanded through interviews with more than 30 Medford people in the next two days.

Mercy Flights began in 1949, in the mind of George Milligan, a control tower operator for the CAA, at the Medford Airport, a position he still holds. The idea grew out of an incident. Archie Weintrout, a prominent automobile dealer, was stricken with polio and was taken to Portland by ambulance, a trip which over the then narrow and winding roads took 15 hours and four stops at hospitals for treatments. Four days later Weintrout died.

This gave 29-year-old Milligan pause. Medford then had a shortage of specialists, and some patients had to be taken elsewhere for treatment. But travel by auto was slow and torturous.

"Why not an airplane ambulance?" Milligan asked. He put this idea before Mayor Diamond Allen, who referred him to Eric Allen of the *Mail Tribune*. Allen suggested George feel out health officers and doctors. To test community sentiment, Allen wrote an article in his paper. Piloted by Milligan, a group formed a non-profit organization to raise $3,000 to buy a plane.

The money didn't come easily, but it came. Kids gave dimes; groups held rummage sales, square dances and benefit parties; businessmen contributed dollars, advertising and time.

Mercy Flight's first plane was a twin-engine Cessna, Air Force surplus, which somehow was put into the air, though there were times when no one knew where its next gallon of gas was coming from. If people couldn't pay they were carried anyway. Mercy Flights went steadily into debt.

After 18 months someone suggested the subscription idea —$2 a year per family. Immediately 1,100 subscribers signed up and debts were paid off. Another plane, a single-engine Stinson Reliant, was purchased.

"We needed it," recalled Milligan. "In 1953 Jackson County was hit hard with polio. Inside of two weeks, we took 23 cases to Eugene and Portland. On one trip I had a partial power failure and had to return. But I borrowed a plane and we continued full operations."

The turning point that comes to all struggling organizations that survive came to Mercy Flights in the autumn of 1952. Kentucky-style Col. Joe Burns, an angular auctioneer with a woodsman's gait and a hill preacher's tongue of fire, took up the cause. In three months he enrolled 4,000 new subscribers and gave Mercy Flights $8,000.

The corporation sold its old two-engine plane and purchased a specially equipped one. Later, it replaced its original plane and in 1955, when we first talked to Milligan, it had added two more planes to the fleet—twin-engine Beeches obatined from the Air Force. Worth $20,000, they were obtained by a special Act of Congress.

Milligan, who is the chief pilot, has had some interesting experiences over the years.

Flying back to Medford on a chill October afternoon in 1954, he heard the Medford tower radio: "Emergency flight waiting. Phone Dr. Cartwright in Gold Beach immediately."

After landing, Milligan learned that Dennis Winn, a Gold Beach logger, had cracked up his jeep in the woods, impaling himself on a gear shift.

"I asked for you," said Dr. Cartwright. "This man has got to be taken to Eugene for immediate surgery. There's a specialist there who may be able to save him."

Milligan asked Dick Foy, another pilot, to come along and they took off in a twin-engine Cessna.

En route to Gold Beach there was snow and ice and Milligan knew the route to Eugene was even more hazardous. "Let me take Winn back to Medford," he pleaded with Dr. Cartwright. "Sorry," replied the doctor. "He needs a specialist." Milligan and Foy tried to change the physician's mind. He remained firm. "It's Eugene or the man's a goner."

Winn was loaded into the plane on a stretcher, delirious

and losing blood rapidly. His wife came along. An oxygen mask was placed over his face.

The rain was torrential and Milligan followed the shore line, staying low to help Winn's breathing. They ran into so much rain they couldn't see. They rose over the Coast Range to 7,000 feet. The pilots flew blind in a mass of snow, sleet and icy rain.

Winn's wife yelled, "He's stopped breathing! He's dead! He's dead!" Foy bolted back, felt Winn's pulse, and shouted to Milligan, "We'd better drop some." The air pressure was too great for the injured logger. Milligan was forced to descend into even worse weather.

The crest of the Coast Range is 4,700 feet. Milligan went down to 5,000 feet. Winn started breathing again. With half vision they wound low through valleys, at last finding Mahlon Sweet Airport in Eugene. An ambulance was waiting and Winn was rushed to the operating room. Two hours later came the welcome word: Winn would live.

Again Milligan had proved the worthiness of his brain child.

"Once," Milligan recalled for us, after we had been at him for about two hours, "we carried a young Irish giant, fresh from the 'ould sod,' who got himself hurt and was bleeding badly. He was put in the plane and given a blood transfusion. Halfway to Medford he went wild, busting through the web belts, popping the needles out of his arm and slapping the plasma aside. I rushed back, pushed him down and sat on his legs. The nurse, who couldn't have been 90 pounds wringing wet, jumped on his chest. I put two web bands on each wrist. When he kept threshing, I put my face close to his and said, 'Listen, lad, if you don't stay quiet you'll have another Irishman to contend with.'"

Another flight gave Milligan as full a dose of the jitters as he ever hopes to get. Carrying a heart case and the man's wife, George suddenly felt a breeze up front. Looking back, he saw the door flung open and the woman half out of the plane. Without thinking, she had opened the door to empty her husband's burp pan.

Once George carried a pack of dogs—also on a mission of mercy. When Norman Wilson flew up from Los Gatos, Calif. to hunt for the Zeiszler family, lost in Fanno Mountain, his pilot, lacking experience and equipment, couldn't get over the gloomy, rain-pelted hills north of Medford. George took Wilson and Norman's three bloodhounds to Springfield, where another pilot and plane completed the journey. "We didn't have time to go farther," explained George. "We were pretty busy then."

There must be great satisfaction in your work, we said to Milligan.

"Yes," he replied, in his crisp but quiet and firmly controlled voice, "but they're little things, personal things. And everyone involved with Mercy Flights has had the same gratification. So it's not personal. It's many people."

Well, we asked, can you think of one flight—one you can recall immediately—that gave you a specially good feeling?

"Anytime you help save a life or decrease agony you have to feel good," he replied. "But if you want . . . well, just for example, there was six-year-old Ruth Alexander, of Dunsmuir, on the other side of the Siskiyou Mountains, in California."

We had read the story in the *Mail Tribune*. Bumping heads with a playmate, Ruth suffered a brain injury. Dunsmuir doctors knew she needed specialized facilities but were afraid that an ambulance ride over the 110 miles of mountain road was too risky. Within an hour little Ruth was on her way via Mercy Flights to a Medford hospital, where she recovered.

"When she was unloaded from the plane," remembered George, speaking so softly we could scarcely hear him, "she took my hand and whispered, 'Thanks'."

He stopped, feeling he had said enough. We gathered he had felt more honored by that single word of love than if he had been cited by the president of the United States before a national television audience.

As I was working on this book, I phoned Milligan and he brought me up to date on Mercy Flights. It now has three modern planes, including a super-cruiser Piper for landing on a mountain strip, 16 pilots, six co-pilots, and a corps of nurses. Some of these people receive money for their services. "It isn't much," said Milligan, "in fact it's darn little, but at least the time away from their jobs isn't a total loss."

Mercy's membership is about 5,500 families (or about 20,000 people) who reside in a 150-air-mile radius of Medford. Each family pays $6 per year for coverage, which extends 400-air-miles from Medford. There is no limit upon use. Renewals remain very high: about 95 per cent. "Only those who move out of our range drop," said Milligan.

There was a time when Mercy planes carried some of the sick and injured to San Francisco, with commercial hourly rates applied beyond the 400-air-mile radius, but today practically all patients are brought to Medford, which has grown into one of the largest hospital centers in Oregon.

Since 1950, when Mercy carried only 13 passengers, traffic has risen steadily. 1966 was the busiest year. In the first seven months, Mercy Flights averaged one trip a day.

"I don't know why this is so," said Milligan. "Maybe too many people on the road. We're involved with more automobile accidents than ever. It looks like the years ahead will be even bigger."

"That's quite a load on you folks," I noted.

"I'm glad we can help somebody," he replied.

As a last word, I declared: "George, you promised to take me on a flight, but there's never been an opportunity."

He laughed. "Tell you what," he said, "next time you come down here we'll take you up. If there's no case, we'll knock somebody over the head so we'll have an excuse to go up.

"One thing more," he added. "There's a lot of nice people who've done a lot for Mercy Flights. I'd like you to meet them, so come on down."

Effie Mae Williams

Sparrow in the Hills

We had come back to Fossil with Jack Steiwer, the town's mayor, from a day of banging around the back-country of Wheeler County and were ready to transfer our camera gear and tape recorder to our own car and head for Portland when Jack suggested we first pay a visit to Frank and Effie Mae Williams.

"I think you'll enjoy what they've done with rocks," said Jack, who is never given to overstatement.

He was right. The couple had built at the edge of Fossil a rock complex that was one of the most beautiful we had ever seen. A house, museum, fences, walks, fountains, benches, wishing well—all of cut rock.

Frank was a quiet man with a knack of turning people over to his wife, a sparrow of a woman with a nimble mind and birdlike gestures. She turned out to be even more interesting than the varied, many-colored rocks.

Effie Mae Williams and her husband, a retired carpenter, had tramped over a thousand hills, in Eastern Oregon, Arizona, Wyoming, Utah and Montana, in search of odd and attractive rocks. In the last few years, because of Carl's health, Effie had done most of the hiking.

"I only carry a rock pick," she said. "If I find larger rock, I go back to the car or pickup and get the men and larger tools."

A salty, spirited woman, wind-scoured and sun-baked by dozens of long open summers, Effie Mae Williams comprised an incredible and delightful combination of the human spirit. She was one of the most independent and self-reliant women we had ever encountered, yet it was clearly evident that her bond with her husband was very strong. Although she was in her mid-fifties, she had the elfin laugh of a rural maid. She looked tough enough to live with scorpions and gentle enough to be a tender nurse. She was not at all the conventional female type but she revealed at unexpected moments very feminine and sentimental touches. As unadorned as a bleached bone in her frankness, she could be very tactful and gracious. She loved to wage duels of wits with people whose minds she respected but it was obvious she relied more on oversimplifications to score points than on broad knowledge or depth.

I am terribly sorry that we did not tape record her or that I did not make notes then or immediately thereafter, for much of what she told us about her rock-collecting experiences was precious.

She was never really afraid of being lost, I remember her saying, but sometimes she wandered too far from her base and then had to establish points of identification. Once, she related, as I recall, she had run out of marking devices and so began using her clothes. "I was down to my panties and bra and wondered which one I'd take off next when I saw the car," she narrated, in describing one of her expeditions.

Who could forget a remarkable quote like that! Later I wrote her, asking her to detail the particular circumstances which prompted such a dilemma—panties or bra—and she replied in two words: "Arizona desert." I am still mystified.

The more she spoke of being out in the hills to collect rocks the more it was apparent that something else was involved: wandering in the hills, far from people, gave her a spiritual satisfaction she could find nowhere else. I asked her if she counted as lost those days in which she did not find interesting rocks and she replied: "Oh no! It's just nice being out there."

Perhaps she felt that I was asking too many questions, for she suddenly exclaimed: "Want to know my motto?"

I nodded. "Dear God," she said, "Please keep me from sticking my nose into other people's business."

"That would put us reporters out of work," I replied.

She laughed saucily and pointed at the hills: "Who needs them up there?" she asked.

George Boone

"Everything's All Different"

Trow Long, then Chamber of Commerce manager at Lakeview, wouldn't let us leave town until we talked to George Boone, a venerable old timer who had been in Lake County since 1892, when he was seven years old.

Mr. Boone, a crusty, forthright soul, allowed as to how his memory wasn't very good for dates, but he did recall being born down in Cedarville, which is in the Surprise Valley of Modoc County, Calif.

In all his meanderings, mostly in Lake County, Mr. Boone hadn't worked more than 50 miles from Lakeview. Fact of the matter is, Cedarville isn't much farther than that from Lakeview so, geographically speaking, George Boone hadn't cut a wide swath in his life.

When he was a boy, living with his family on a ranch in Warner Valley, which is east of Lakeview, the folks in the valley would get their supplies at Fort Bidwell, in the upper part of Surprise Valley. Fort Bidwell had started as an army post in 1866 and by the time the horse troopers held their last parade, in 1892, Fort Bidwell was a settlement, too, with several stores, which served a large area. People up in Warner Valley would hitch a team of horses to a wagon and drive maybe 40 miles to Fort Bidwell. And when a doctor was needed, in the days when George Boone was a boy, somebody would ride hard down to Fort Bidwell to fetch one.

"When I first went out to work for wages, I rode for Pete French out to Steens Mountain," Mr. Boone recalled. But before he could see French, the cattle baron was gunned down by a homesteader.

It occurred to me later that in the year Pete French was killed George Boone was only 12 years of age. Either some boys started doing men's work very early in life then or expanded their memories as they grew old.

Cowboys didn't own the horses they rode, Mr. Boone remembered. The horses were company property. Each buckaroo had his own saddle, however. The one Boone had cost him $60, which was two months' wages.

Each ranch included a bunkhouse, but like as not the cowboys slept in the sagebrush. "Too far to go back and too early to get up," Mr. Boone explained.

A bath was where you found one, generally in a river. "Whenever you got to a place where you could take a bath, why, you pulled your clothes off and jumped in." Once in a while you went in with your clothes on—but that was accidental. "Sometimes your horse dumped ya."

When there was time the buckaroos washed their clothes. They'd "just get an old can and get some water and put it on the fire and get it hot and start washin'."

Everything the cowboy thought he'd need out in the open he'd throw into his bedroll, which was carried in the chuckwagon. Those who shaved took out their razor and soap about once a week to scrape their faces. Mr. Boone didn't shave when he rode the range. It was less bother that way, and nobody minded, because so many of the other fellows also let their whiskers grow. When a cowpoke wanted a smoke he'd roll his own. "There was no tailor-made cigarettes then," Mr. Boone commented with a chuckle. Once in a while there was fighting. "Some guy'd get too much to drink and got smart and somebody'd knock the devil out of him."

When folks in Lakeview wanted to visit Alturas, Calif. they'd take the stage. The route was 60 miles and the trip would require all day. There was a noonday stop for lunch at Davis Creek, a roadhouse. Lunch was waiting and passengers ate family style. For 50 cents they'd have a "nice meal, nothin' fancy about it. You got good meat, potatoes, home-made bread, gravy, home-made pie or cake or somethin'." Coffee? "I guess, if you'd use it."

The trip from Lakeview to Klamath Falls required two days, with an overnight stop at Bly. A room rented for about $1.50.

The coach to Klamath Falls was drawn by two horses; the Alturas stage usually used four horses. "There was more traffic that-a-way, and more load, and they had a bigger outfit."

Nobody on the stage rode shotgun and on occasion the stage was stuck up. But the sheriff never gathered a posse to hunt down the culprit. He'd just gallop off by himself and after a spell he'd come back with the varmint. There were probably almost as many informers around then, on a per ratio population basis, as there are now.

Generally, though, there wasn't anything exciting about the stage coach ride. "Just a bumpy old road," Mr. Boone said flatly. Passengers inside chatted with each other—"that's all there was to do, talked a blue streak"—and those riding the top of the stage carried on conversations with the driver, who liked company, to while away the tedious hours. If a person had a sudden need to relieve himself—or herself— a shout to the driver and the reins would be drawn. The passenger would dismount and go off into the brush while the others discreetly ignored the incident.

Once, when he was a lad, George Boone saw a body hung from a bannister in the building that houses the local court. The man had been executed during the night, just a few hours before George Boone spied the limp form early in the morning, while helping his father deliver milk in Lakeview. The boy didn't wait around to investigate. "I went home, yellin', if you want to know," Mr. Boone declared in no uncertain terms.

Did he have any idea who had hanged the man? Mr. Boone was silent for quite a while. Finally, he half-whispered through taut lips: "Well, I can't say . . ." I had the feeling that if he knew he wouldn't have told. Old timers, as I have learned, are very reluctant to dredge up the sins of the past. Perhaps it is a code of honor, perhaps they feel that nothing can be gained by it, that the dark deeds of the fathers should not becloud the lives of their children and grandchildren.

George Boone saw his first automobile in 1905. It was a big attraction in Lakeview. "Everybody walkin' up and down the street lookin' at the thing."

A few weeks later he had his first automobile ride, and it shook him up a bit. "Well, it felt like it went one hundred miles an hour, you know, I wasn't used to that kind of stuff." Actually, he explained with a grin spread across his broad, sun-tanned face that eight decades of life had not treated badly, the car wasn't going any faster than perhaps 25 miles an hour.

The automobile changed everything, Mr. Boone said ruefully, and then a bit angrily. "Everything's all different. Everything's just rushin' through life. Just go, go, go! Used to, you took time to get someplace, you had to go either afoot or wagon or horseback. Nowadays just jump on the automobile, and there they go."

Whenever you meet an old timer he tells you how friendly were the days of his youth. George Boone was no exception. He spoke more about the differences in hospitality than about anything else. He said:

"You wanted to go someplace, why you could go, and when you got to a man's ranch or his home, you could stop and eat and sleep and go on and it'd never cost you nothin'. These people, these sheep men, one time there were three hundred thousand sheep here in Lake County, you'd go out here ridin' on the desert, and they had stuff stored out there, in their camps, you could go out there, and eat, and wash your dishes, and go on, nobody'd say a word, perfectly all right. Now you can't even leave the camp all day, somebody'd steal somethin'. People didn't take anything—unless they were a bandit or something like that; people didn't take anything that didn't *belong* to them. They took something that they needed, why, they told the people where they got it, and whose it was, and all about it.

"Anytime somebody was sick, somebody took 'em to the doctor. Lots of times I made trips from Plush over here with sick people. Many trips over here to send a doctor over there. There was no telephone, or anything, you know. Get a horse in the evening and go over to Lakeview and get a doctor and he'd take off for Plush or Adel or whatever it was. That's the way they done it."

He seemed sad and bitter after he had said this. He bit his lip and looked at the floor, then at the lawn through the open window. In a moment or two he lifted his head, mopped his brow, and looked at us, as though to declare: Well, the past is gone, what now?

How much of a mail delivery was there between Plush and Lakeview about 60 years ago, we asked.

"Three times a week," he replied. "Come over one day and come back the next."

And how much mail service is there now between Plush and Lakeview?

"Three times a week," he responded quickly.

His chin shot up, in revelation, and a laugh geysered out of his thinly wrinkled throat.

"Well," he observed with a wry grin, "I guess everything hasn't changed."

George McUne

A Mulish Endeavor

When Fibber and Molly pass away, one of these days, George McUne would like to have them mounted and attached to the covered wagon they pulled two-thirds across the country.

Fibber and Molly are white mules McUne bought in Independence, Missouri in April, 1959, for the westward trek to publicize Oregon's centennial exposition.

George McUne has had this dream of mounting Fibber and Molly since 1960 but each year the dream grows dimmer. In 1962 he figure it would take about $2,000— "I haven't got anything like that;" in 1967 he described the cost as "prohibitive to me at this time."

So while George McUne wasn't getting any richer his mules were getting older, and as they headed for the sunset hills of their lives McUne's worries increased. His fondness for his mules had turned into an obsession for their preservation by proxy.

McUne, a lanky, rawhide, long-striding man, isn't quite sure how old Fibber and Molly are. At least I don't think he is. In 1962 he told me: "Could be 15, could be 17. Folks I bought them from didn't know which." In 1967 he wrote me: "Fibber is about 20 years old now and Molly probably about 30." I can see where his guessing about Fibber is consistent but if Molly was 17 in 1962 simple arithmetic would dictate that she be no more than 22 in 1967. But I did not challenge McUne. It really wasn't that important.

A year after the long haul of 1959 pitched its final encampment at Independence, Oregon, McUne hitched his mules to the same covered wagon and took off on a jaunt into Canada. Altogether, the mules pulled the covered wagon across nine states, crossing three states twice, and British Columbia.

Today, as they have been for some years, Fibber and Molly are at home in McUne's Pioneer Village, a stockade-enclosed replica of an early frontier town at the eastern edge of Jacksonville.

For several summers McUne hitched Fibber and Molly to a Concord stagecoach, carrying tourists on a 20-minute "historic tour of Jacksonville." Sometimes the mules pulled haywagons, also for tourist benefit, into the undulating Applegate Valley and the soft sloping hills that look down upon the creeks once streaked with gold.

McUne was still driving the mules in parades as late as 1967 but "for the most part" Molly had retired. Fibber, however, was still earning his keep with the tourist trade. Both mules looked hale and hearty but it was evident that Molly was more interested in munching and dozing than plodding round and round the stockade. One doesn't have to be a mule to know when a mule thinks she's had it.

The rugged, steel-eyed, intense McUne has a strong affection for his mules, whom he regards as the paragons of gentleness, consistency and fidelity.

"They never did balk on me," he said once, his face softening.

"I could drive them over a cliff. They gave me their best and I took care of them. Their legs got stiff on the Oregon

Trail and I used bottle after bottle of liniment on their legs. Legs get stiff on pavement.

"A few times they've tried to run off. They took off at the same time, as though they got the message together. I was at the reins so I could stop them after a while. But if someone else was at the reins they'd have been long gone for sure. But there never was any hard feelings between us."

A meticulous man, McUne painstakingly developed some statistics on his mules in the westward trek across the Oregon Trail. Fibber and Molly took 1,750 steps to the mile, or about 3,692,500 steps between the starting and stopping points named Independence.

"And they can go six miles an hour," he added.

In 1967 McUne was becoming almost desperate about having his mules mounted. "I have given some thought," he wrote me, "to donating them to the Oregon Historical Society if there was no other way."

And I remembered then what he once told me, putting his hand on mine for emphasis: "I want to give them the best tribute a man could give to mules—to put them where they belong in history, hitched to a covered wagon, headed west. I want to see them as they were in the greatest days of our lives."

Then, brushing his eyes, he quickly arose and strode away.

Nellie Hartness

"Last of the Old Time Feather Makers"

"Last of the Old Time Feather Makers" was what octogenarian Nellie Hartness called herself—and she was probably right.

"Actually," she explained in her rich and witty Scottish tongue, which six decades of life in the United States had fortunately not distorted, "I'm a *plumacier*, but Lord, lad, how many people would know what I'm talking about?"

I found the bent but spry Mrs. Hartness in an old pile of a third-rate rundown building in downtown Portland. The dim corridors were lined with small offices, studios and workshops, inhabited by ghostly men sagged behind desks heaped over their heads with every bit of mail they had ever received, tailors who needled the droning hours away in their pincushion cubbyholes, salesmen and insurance agents who hadn't picked up a new client in years, and voice studios where gusty ladies who sounded like thin winds scampering about in a cave dreamed of singing to audiences more prestigious than the East Gresham Cultural Society.

Sometime in the summer of 1960 I first met Nellie Hartness, simply by coming to her shop. She did not think it odd than anyone should want to write an article on her; she had lived a long and fascinating life, she felt, and what she had seen would fill a book. "If properly told, of course."

The long career of this short, gentle, merry-eyed craftswoman had its seed when she was a four-year-old tot in a village outside Edinburgh. "My mother taught me how to make clever things out of chicken feathers, and after that I didn't want toys, I just wanted feathers."

But her real feather story started in 1904, in a cleaning and dyeing shop owned by her late husband. When no one else could be found to dye feathers, she took on the work, and mastered it.

Since then, through good days and bad, she had watched the feather business move through several phases.

"It was comparable to the fur business in amount of money involved before federal law prohibited importation of feathers," she said. "Why, Birds of Paradise feathers sold for $175 to $350 a fin."

When I appeared a bit puzzled she hastily explained that Birds of Paradise feathers came from New Guinea, "you know," and that a fin is a plume, "of course."

The vogue in the last seven years before 1960 had been "fancy things made of domestic feathers"—pompoms, pads, bands and whole hats.

When I knew her she was making and dyeing hats from

"hunted bird feathers." Pheasant was most popular. "Most people bring in their own after hunting season." One hat she had made recently had feathers of pheasant, goose, mallard duck and turkey.

In 1960, about half of her business came from cleaning and replacing Knight Templars (Masons) plumes, which were sent to her from all parts of Oregon and Washington.

Twice she had seen feathers go completely out of style. Then she had to turn to making cloth flowers. "Don't like them," she snapped, her eyes sizzling. And, in sad explanation, she added: "Aye, lad, it's a wearying task for the few pennies."

A moment later, staring backward into time gone by, she continued, "What a big difference to the costly things I made." The most expensive was a dress of coque—tail feathers off the rooster—for a female impersonator. It sold for $780—"but took two weeks, day and night, to make, and the feathers cost a lot."

Some of her customers had "a dandering" for peacock feathers, which are body feathers off the peacock, but they were difficult to obtain since imports were halted, and the price was a steep five dollars an ounce.

"A few people around here raise peacocks and I try to coax them to pick up the body feathers off the ground—but there's not much enthusiasm," she sighed. "One peacock owner found that rats were picking up the feathers and making nests out of them."

Most of her feathers came from New York when I knew her. "There are no feather dealers on the Pacific Coast," Mrs. Hartness observed gloomily. "Such a shame, what with all the industrious people out here."

Between 1905 and 1915 willow plumes were the rage, especially among the telephone operators, who regarded hats of willow plumes as the height of status. But ostrich made the biggest cackle—before it suddenly laid an egg.

In 1931, said Mrs. Hartness, ostrich feathers soared into popularity, due to some fancy teamwork between the British royal family, which was heavily involved in South African ostrich raising, and French milliners. Between July and

October, hats with ostrich feathers dyed black were the craze, and Mrs. Hartness was weeks behind in orders.

Then, as she told it: "A single man in London practically controlled the ostrich market, and he kept raising the price until it was too high to be practical, so the millinery industry planned the hats for the October tenth opening with no ostrich, and that finished the ostrich fad. After October 10, 1931, you couldn't sell or give away an ostrich plume for a long time. The depression helped, too, of course."

Ostrich did find a limited market, for unconventional purposes, but in the fashion sense it was dead as the dodo. However, after a lapse of almost three decades, ostrich was regaining favor, especially for evening wear. "We feather makers," said Mrs. Hartness, "just live in hope that this seeming revival of ostrich will gain strength, but so few know how to handle them now in America that it leaves the industry to France and England."

Taking the long look, the philosophical Mrs. Hartness, who read Tolstoi and Walt Whitman and revered her fellow Scotsman, Robbie Burns, said frankly: "As you stay in business, fashion changes. As styles change, you come into contact with different customers. Theatrical trade always used feathers in their work. It was natural for fan dancers to come to me."

Mrs. Hartness made fans for 20 years. Female impersonators were the largest users of ostrich feathers but some of the nation's best-known fan dancers also called upon the Portland specialist. Sally Rand, remembered as "a nice, friendly lady," paid $150 for one feather fan. Each of her performing clients gave her free tickets to the theater, which Mrs. Hartness never turned down.

And what did she think of the fan dancers? "Beautiful feathers," she replied, quite seriously. "They were a delight to behold."

Since 1920, Mrs. Hartness had filled orders for Indian headdresses used in theatrical work, and had—as a commentary on "progress"—dyed feathers for Northwest Indian tribes. In the 1950s a San Francisco producer wired an order for six full-length Indian headdresses, to be delivered in a week. Mrs. Hartness' helpers—her employees had numbered from one to 50, depending on the state of her business—were then on vacation. "I couldn't turn that order down," she recalled, "so I fell to it myself, and by sleeping in the shop, getting about two hours sleep a night, the order was filled on time."

When Mrs. Hartness had to make her own dyes—when I knew her she had turned to buying them in drug stores and supermarkets, the same as other women—she often worked until three or four a.m. Much of her work in 1960 was still in dyeing. "Whatever the customer brings in to match, I match. On one hat I did six dye jobs."

All her life Mrs. Hartness had shown an ambivalence about feathers. They were her joy and her passion but it sorely grieved her to read of birds slaughtered for feathers. "Do you know," she said, her voice rising, "that between 1880 and 1890 more than a million white herons in the Klamath marshes were killed during breeding season by plume hunters from Europe and the United States. When the birds were down to a few hundred, that good-hearted, great Oregon naturalist William Finley successfully fought for legislation establishing the Klamath marshes as a wild life sanctuary. I hope they never change it."

A few weeks before I first met her, Mrs. Hartness had moved her feather business out of her small southwest side home—it took up three of the four rooms—into the downtown building.

"I have to be closer to the trade," she explained. "You can't fall behind, not a wee bit. Feathers have been my first love, and, anyway, lad, it's all I know how to do, and I'm not for the poorhouse yet."

John A. Zehntbauer

The Red Diving Girl

One of the most famous trademarks in the United States is Jantzen's diving girl in the red swim suit, sometimes called the red diving girl.

I had heard many stories of how this symbol became famous and since no two of them matched I thought I would put the question to the one person who ought to know, John A. Zehntbauer, the founder of Jantzen.

"Could you tell us once and for all and definitively about this red diving girl?" I asked.

"Yes, I can," replied Mr. Zehntbauer, with a broad grin that dropped beams of light into the furrowed face of this still erect octogenarian. "But what I will tell you," he added, "won't be agreed to by everyone who does know something about it."

So we sat back, letting the tape recorder do the work for us, while we listened to Mr. Zehntbauer tell the story about the way the trademark became famous. It happened about 1915, though he couldn't be sure, and the name of the firm then was Portland Knitting Company.

"We had a retail store—that's the way we started our business—at 150 Third Avenue," Mr. Zehntbauer began.

"We had a catalog printed with a red diving girl on the outside of the catalog. Some folks had cut this red diving girl out as a nice figure and pasted it on the windshield of their automobile or the back glass. One day a country boy came in and asked the man in charge of our store—Mr. Otto Matthes—for twenty catalogs. And Otto said: 'Well, what would you do with twenty of our catalogs?' 'We cut the diving girl out, to stick it on our windshields,' the boy replied.

" 'Well,' Otto said, 'these things are expensive. I can't

give you twenty of our catalogs just to cut out the diving girl off the front page. I'll give you one catalog.'

"Well, the boy was glad to take the one catalog, but that just spoiled his scheme, to get a lot of these diving girls to stick on the windshields of his group. We thought if youngsters liked these so, perhaps we could some way provide diving girls for stickers to put on cars. And a way came soon because our advertising agent suggested we print some of these stickers to use for window trims. For Jantzen Week—our suits were called Jantzen—or whatever you want, and in the window we'd put a lot of diving girls. String 'em across the window and put 'em on everywhere, and that'd be an advertisement, a trademark. We did that. So we had diving girls to give away. They weren't glued, you had to stick 'em on with tape, on the windows.

"Then Mr. Gerber, our advertising agent, suggested that we print them on glued paper, so that they could be stuck on the windshield or wherever you wanted them. And we did that. Then the kids, who came in and asked for diving girls—and they soon learned to do that—we'd give them one or two or half-a-dozen or how many they wanted and that grew to be a very big thing, and in three years we printed ten million diving girl stickers and gave them away. I saw these things on automobiles in New Zealand, Australia and South America as I traveled. American people traveling, and they'd take the car along, and there'd be a diving girl sticker on the windshield or on the back glass. I remember Mrs. Zehntbauer and I were getting off the boat at Wellington, New Zealand, and here came on the sling where they were unloading cars, first one unloaded with a diving girl sticker right across the windshield. First time I'd seen one outside of this country. And pretty soon before the ship was unloaded there was another one, so there were two diving girl stickers on automobile windshields on that ship that was unloading.

"The diving girl was copied. We had it carried in all of our advertising. And one time going east on the train, I picked up a copy of *The Oregonian* and it had a red diving girl across the page, clear across the page, wasn't much more in it, except that the paper was claiming that Oregon was where this diving girl originated. That's about all they said down below. That was a great free ad, because the diving girl had become so popular.

"And I remember," he continued, with a burst of laughter, "a banker once said to me, he'd just been down to the beach, 'John, what have you done to us here, sticking red diving girl stickers all over automobiles, because I don't think that from here to Seaside I saw an automobile without one of those red diving girl stickers on it.' I said, 'Sure, if we missed one, why it was a mistake.'"

And Mr. Zehntbauer chuckled, remembering the old days.

There was something else we wanted to know about the famous emblem: who was the person who thought up the trademark and was the red diving girl a model or just a figure out of someone's mind?

"It came out of an artist's mind," explained Mr. Zehntbauer. "We asked for it—we wanted a diving girl, and the artist provided one. It's been refined a little from time to time. I think an artist by the name of Clark, who worked for Botsford, Constantine and Tyler, has credit for it, because he finally developed it into the one that we used. I think, however, Mr. Gerber told me, that he had a woman on his staff who made the original.

"Mr. Gerber was in the printing business and he did our first advertising. He had a little print shop across the street from us on Alder Street, where we began our business, and he did printing for us, and then also wrote some advertising copy for us."

Mr. Zehntbauer, a fine build of a man, with a full shock of gray hair that curled like a stand of wheat on a breezy day, had come a long way from his birthplace, a log cabin outside Purdin, Missouri, a town that numbered 150 people—if you counted all the farmers who traded there.

"My dad had a cooper shop, made barrels for apples, and whiskey, and cider, and what not," Mr. Zehntbauer recalled. "I learned to do everything in the shop. Mechanically inclined, and I actually made a barrel when I was quite young—oh, twelve-thirteen years old. I think that helped me because I was the oldest youngster in the family. Dad was away in his cooper shop while we were on the little country place nearby, on the farm, and I was the man of the house then and we had to learn a lot of things that youngsters wouldn't ordinarily do. Dad was away, and if something went wrong I had to learn how to fix it, which I did."

At the age of 15 he left Missouri and after eight months in Denver came to Portland and "went out to find a job right away.

"There was," he recounted with a long chuckle, "a sign in the window on Third Street—boy wanted—so I went in. 'Here I am.' And Mr. Luke, the owner, said, 'Well, what I want is some boy who would learn to run a knitting machine.' I said I was the boy. 'Come to work in the morning,' Mr. Luke said. Which I did. I think it was seven-thirty I was supposed to be there. I learned how to knit and I found, after I'd been there a little while, there were three boys Mr. Luke had hired. He intended to keep only one. But he had to try 'em out and see who could learn to knit. And I learned to knit quicker, so he gave me the job. And the other two boys weren't there the next Monday morning. That's how I got into the knitting business. With Mr. Luke I learned how to wait on trade, and to clean the cuspidors, and sweep the floors, and whatever was to be done, and then I used to also be sent to the whole-sale house to buy whatever was needed, socks and under-wear and the other things that were carried in Mr. Luke's store. After I was there about two years I felt that I had learned about all I could in that business."

So he quit Mr. Luke and went to work for the whole-sale house of Fleischner-Mayer Company, in its day the best known dry goods house west of the Missouri.

"My schooling was neglected," said Mr. Zehntbauer, "be-cause, in a country school where you have one teacher and about fifty youngsters in one room and teach all grades, to get an education you have to do it yourself. But I was a good student and I studied and I was good at my studies, and I was persuaded, or it was suggested to me, that I join the YMCA and go to school at night. Which is Multno-mah College now. Well, that just suited me, and which I did. Joined it and went to school at night, went four nights a week for six years. Missed only two nights, because of a cold or something else."

After some years at Fleischner-Mayer, Mr. Zehntbauer's health was beginning to suffer from overwork. His doctor suggested he take a vacation, which he did, and in six weeks gained 25 pounds, while living with friends at Hood River. As soon as he returned to work, however, his weight fell again—"the routine of the studying, the working, and the long hours." This time his doctor recommended he take a year off. John Zehntbauer went back to Hood River and worked outdoors. When he came back to Portland he turned down his old job at Fleischner-Mayer and started selling real estate. In the process, he acquired ten acres of land near Gresham. Then, he "got a price" from his first employer, Mr. Luke, to buy out the knitting business, which would leave Mr. Luke his store to run.

A loan was needed, and what followed almost led to disaster. But all's well that ends well, and the empire that became Jantzen was born. Hear it from Mr. Zehntbauer in his own words:

"I went down to the bank, which was at that time Portland Trust Company, and the head of it was Mr. Cohen. I told him I wanted to borrow some money—five thousand dollars—and I had this real estate that I wanted to put up for collateral. He looked it over and he talked with me, and he said, 'Well, you know, that isn't the best bankable proposition, that real estate that you own, and all,' and he said, 'I couldn't loan it to you on that. But,' he said, 'I've heard about you, and I'm going to loan you the money on you, see?'

"Mr. Cohen then went up to Victoria, on a vacation, played golf, and dropped dead on the golf course. I had nothing—well, I had his word and then I had also drawn fifteen hundred dollars of the five thousand. When I went back to get more money, which I'd already obligated myself for, no Mr. Cohen there, but a new man. When I came in, I think he called me in, he said that he wanted me to pay off, pay that money back, and I said, 'Well, I made arrangements to get five thousand dollars.' 'Well,' he said, 'I couldn't do that. I want you to pay this off. Fifteen hundred.' I said, 'Now don't you want to know the circumstances, what I'm doing, and what I borrowed the money for, don't you want to know anything about it?' 'No,' he said, 'I don't want to have anything to do with it.'

"So there I was in a pickle. I couldn't pay the money back. I had ninety-day notes, those were. So, on the suggestion of a friend, I went to see a banker, George W. Bates, and I told him the whole story, and he says, 'I'll loan you that five thousand dollars and you go pay them off. I'll deposit here and you go give them a check and pay him off and the thirty-five hundred we'll take care of.' And I had obligated myself, you know, I bought merchandise, we had rented a store, we were all ready to start in and got the machinery down there, and we had to have the money. And that's the way we got started in the knitting business."

When Mr. Zehntbauer spoke of "we" he meant his brother, Roy, and Carl Jantzen, who had been a Hood River orchardist. Both were with him from the beginning.

John Zehntbauer and Carl Jantzen were on a hunting and fishing trip at Lost Lake, near Mt. Hood, when they decided to become partners. Out of personal incidents such as this were present-day great companies founded even in the first decade of the twentieth century.

"We were on the left end of the lake and we had a raft we'd built and we stuck up our coats and one thing and another on poles and the wind was blowing, to take us across the lake on this raft," Mr. Zehntbauer narrated as the reels on our tape recorder spun quietly.

"As we were about to land, I said, 'Well now, Carl, when I land over here it'll be a long time before I can do this again. I'm just making arrangements to buy out the old man I used to work for, Mr. Luke.' He said: 'Well, I wish I could sell this orchard and get into something like that.' I said: 'Well, I'm gonna have to have some more money and I'm going to take in a partner.' He said: 'I'd just like to sell my place here and go in with you.' I said: 'Well, you go ahead, I'm gonna have to have a partner.'"

Mr. Jantzen sold his ten acres of orchard and with his wife and baby moved to Portland.

Looking down at his still strong hands, the hands of a handyman mechanic, John Zehntbauer studied them as though they were pages chronicling the past. And he spoke of his partner, who had years ago passed away:

"I liked Mr. Jantzen for the reason that he was good company, and he was artistic, he could just take his pencil or pen and draw any kind of pictures you wanted, and he was just nice to go hunting and fishing with, and also good company, and he was intelligent. So I really liked him."

Mr. Zehntbauer looked up, his bright, searching eyes probing ours, perhaps to see if we were paying attention, and continued:

"Well, we started in. My sister, she knew how to finish this toe of the stocking, and we had a knitter who did the knitting of the sweaters and sock and I knew how to show 'em. The first day we opened for business, this was at two-thirty-one Alder, in the summer of nineteen-nine, my sister was in the store, and she sold one pair of thirty-five cent gardening gloves; that was the day's sale. In the two years we had this store going on Alder Street, before we bought the Luke store and everything else there on Third Street, we lost money and didn't have much capital left. But we had friends and relatives and we sold them some stock so we could pay our bills, and also enough money to buy out Mr. Luke's store, which gave us a new location on a going business, because he was making money. After we moved to Third Street we made a little profit, enough so we could pay our salaries, which were—well, I got seventy-five dollars a month and Mr. Jantzen seventy-five dollars and I don't remember what we paid my sister but it wasn't that much." And he chuckled again. His sister couldn't have gotten very much.

Four years later, when it was still the Portland Knitting Company, an event, or series of events, took place which radically changed the character of the firm and revolutionized the swimsuit industry.

As legend has it, I said to Mr. Zehntbauer, the turning point of your company came when you began to manufacture swim suits. Wasn't there an incident that led to this, something involving the Multnomah Athletic Club?

"You don't have it quite right," replied Mr. Zehntbauer, "but you're on the track, I'd say. We carried swim suits at our store. We called them bathing suits then. And we had, I think, as nice a business in bathing suits as anyone in the city. It was quite a good part of the business.

"I belonged to the rowing club because I liked water and liked to swim, and row, and one day a man came in who belonged to the rowing club—he was a fellow member—he came up to me and he says, 'John,' he says, 'I almost freeze to death when I go down to the coast and go swimming. My wife can stand that water but I just can't stand it.' "

Mr. Zehntbauer stopped abruptly and stared at us. "That's wrong, I'm ahead of the story, I want to get something in ahead of that. What'll I do now?"

Start from the beginning, we suggested.

"All right," he agreed. "He came in and said, 'Can you make a pair of trunks with a sweater cuff?' 'That stitch?' I said. 'Sure we can.' He says, 'I think a rib stitch like that would make a trunk that would fit close, keep you warmer, and you wouldn't have to have such a tight drawstring to hold them up, and it would be a better pair of trunks made with that rib stitch.' I said, 'So do I.' And he said: 'I wish you'd make a pair for me.' And I did. And I of course soon made a pair for myself, too, because I liked them well. And that trunk soon became so popular everybody at the rowing club had them, wanted a pair like it.

"This same man came in later—and now I'm going to hook up with this other—'I'm going down to the coast, I'm on vacation,' and he said, 'Can't you make me a bathing suit of this same stitch as these trunks?' I said, 'Ye-e-s, but if we make a suit for you like that, with the upper and trunks and all and that heavy yarn, that'll be heavy, I don't think you could swim hardly with it,' and I talked him out of it.

"Well, he came back a little later, and he said, 'Well, I can see that'd be heavy when it's wet but that's all right. Let it be heavy. It'll be warm. Will you go ahead? Will you make a suit for me?' And you know, those were the days when they had little sleeves, and they had stripes, stripes across the chest, stripes on the bottom of the skirt, stripes on the legs, and they came down to your knees, and it was quite a garment, with a lot of wool in it. So we made it. He came back, and I can see him yet, when he came in and he was grinning from ear to ear, and he says, 'You know, that was the greatest thing in the world.' He says, 'I could stand in the water as long as my wife could stay in it. That just keeps you warm because it doesn't let the air in it between the suit and the body, and it's a warm suit.' And that was fine. We were all happy. He liked it and that's all there was to it.

"I then thought, well, that's really an idea. That would be a warm suit. But it doesn't have to be that heavy. We must make that of tight rib stitch and a thin one and it'll give you the warmth and the comfort of a snug fitting and it won't be so heavy and it won't hold so much water."

The kind of yarn that had to be made was unique, one that would hold its shape and elasticity. New machinery was ordered, new techniques devised. Finally, after much experimentation with the yarn—"a certain kind of long, staple wool" and with dyes and with stitching methods, several suits were made for members and friends of the firm. "They were just everything we wanted," said Mr. Zehntbauer. "They fitted closely, they were warm, and they dried quickly, and you could swim with them because they didn't have heavy resistance, and they weren't bad looking. Of course, in those days men's suits had stripes and everything. They would look funny now."

The best suit on the market made by standard knitting companies then sold for $4.50. The Portland Knitting suit, because of the yarn and the way it had to be knitted, was twice as expensive. Every member of the Multnomah Athletic Club wanted a suit, and when some suits were put on display in the store they were also sold. But still there was pessimism, the lack of confidence rooted in the price.

"We thought it would be so high that people wouldn't buy them, but they did," remembered Mr. Zehntbauer, "and we soon had this machine that we had snowed under. We couldn't make enough. We kept it running day and night, Sundays, holidays, we couldn't make enough for the store. We ordered another machine. It hadn't arrived yet when Miss Kitchen, a buyer for Meier and Frank, came down, and she said: 'John, you're just really in the bathing suit business here, with this blame ribstitch thing. Everybody wants them. I want to buy some.'" And Mr. Zehntbauer laughed appreciatively.

More orders meant more equipment was needed. Which meant more money had to be borrowed. For a time, the bank had more money in the company than did the stockholders.

In the midst of heavy borrowing, difficulties developed. The suit was popular in the Portland area but it was unknown elsewhere. Mr. Zehntbauer took to the road. So did a bright young salesman, Mitchell Heinemann, who eventually became an executive vice-president.

Mr. Zehntbauer related with relish an ingenious maneuver Mitch Heinemann used in the Emporium, in San Francisco, to obtain an order.

"The buyer there said, 'I couldn't sell that suit, that small suit, people wouldn't buy that for a 40 size, and it's an odd thing,' and he didn't want it, so Mitchell said, 'Well, they're made that way for a purpose.' And he pulled off his coat and he took one of his samples and he put the suit right on over his clothes. And demonstrated that it would stretch and fit a man that would take a 40 or a 38 or whatever it was. And the fellow says: 'Well, it looks like they will go on.' So he bought a few. And that's the way it had to be sold. It was hard selling to start with."

The company was now drifting into the great swimwear firm it was to become. As soon as it started advertising its suits, which it did early but modestly, the Jantzen name was applied to them.

A few years later the name of the company was changed to Jantzen, following a suggestion by advertising man Joe Gerber. He argued that Portland Knitting Company, or the PK brand that the firm had, were not potent advertising titles. Gerber urged that the John Zehntbauer name be used, but his advice was rejected.

"I told him," Mr. Zehntbauer said, "my name is too hard to spell, and it's just not a good name. I'd rather have—why don't we use Mr. Jantzen's name? 'Well,' he said, 'Why don't you use a combination, Jan-Zen?' 'That doesn't sound as good to me,' I said. 'Jantzen is a name known in Europe, it's a common name amongst Germans, a lot of people know it—Jantzen's easy, and it looks good, the scroll is good, and I'm not interested in my name being connected with it, I want the business to succeed, and I don't care, I'm not interested in getting credit.' He still argued that it should have been some other name except Jantzen, it should have been something connected with me. Well, Jantzen proved to be a very good trademark, we got an artist, I had a young artist come up, and I said I would like for you to make an artist's scroll of Jantzen, a scroll, and we'll make a plate, and that's what we're gonna use as our trademark. We were still Portland Knitting Company but we used Jantzen as a trademark. When we got under way with that, and with a little advertising in our catalog, other places, we called it Jantzen sweaters, Jantzen swim suits, but it was Portland Knitting Company down at the bottom. People wouldn't pay any attention to Portland Knitting Company, they'd write in to Jantzen. And that was the scroll, and that was the trademark. So I said to Gerber and Carl: 'Why waste space with Portland Knitting Company? People already know it as Jantzen. Let's change the name to Jantzen.' Which we did, I think, in nineteen-eighteen."

The long interview was coming to a close. One question was left: Looking back over the years, what are you most proud of and what would you like to be remembered for?

He shifted his shoulders, still square and firm, from side to side, and peered at the table through his thick lenses.

"Well," he said, "you're asking me about something that I've not found time to give much thought to. I don't think you can give much thought to that and do the job the way you ought to do it. I would say, now that you asked me, my ability to build an organization is, I think, my greatest asset. Greatest contribution. To make friends and get people to join the organization and feel a part of it.

"If you can build an organization, I think that's the most valuable. So I say that anything that I've done that's been worth anything, that's been outstanding, is my success in building an organization. So I didn't do the work. I just got people who could do the work, y'see."

Jim O'Donahue

The Odd Hunter

Jim O'Donahue, of Klamath Falls, was surely one of the nation's most unusual hunters.

While other men roamed the plains, marshes, woods and hills of southeastern Oregon with rifles and shotguns, O'Donahue and his Labrador retriever, King, searched for wounded animals and birds. Especially birds. By the time I met him he had for more than 20 years saved the lives of better than 100 birds a year.

Most of the birds were crippled ducks and geese but he had also been the salvation of the California house fink, eagles, falcons and other species.

In addition, the grain-feeding program he maintained had helped thousands of birds survive bitter winters.

Bringing in the birds from fields and water to the half-acre lot O'Donahue had fenced in with wire four feet high back of his home was only the first step in his hospital conservation program. Together with his wife, Helen, he ascertained the injuries of the feathered casualties. If the birds were strong enough to be let loose in the half-acre pen to convalesce, a wing was first clipped.

"I do it," explained the silver-haired, soft-voiced O'Donahue, "so the birds can't leave us until they've either regained their strength or I feel they're permanent cripples."

Birds requiring more treatment were kept in one of the smaller pens O'Donahue had in his back yard and they were nursed to the point where they, too, could have a wing clipped and be placed in the larger enclosure.

The birds remained in the half-acre "sanitarium" until they had remolted and repaired the clipped wing. In late spring and summer, after six or seven months of convalescing, the healed birds flew away. The permanent cripples were given to Pacific Northwest zoos, where they were placed in enclosures built so they could leave if they ever recovered.

O'Donahue's wildlife interest started more than a quarter of a century before I met him, when his health broke down and he was required to move to the southwestern desert. For two years he lived alone in a small, isolated cabin on the lonely wasteland east of Banning, California and there, "through sheer necessity," made the acquaintance of "everything that moved."

"It didn't take me long to realize," recalled O'Donahue, "that the occasional birds, insects and reptiles were great companions for breaking the monotony."

His desert living gave O'Donahue a sympathy for the rattlesnakes, whom he adjudged "the most misrepresented creatures on earth.

"If people knew them like I do they wouldn't hate them," he declared firmly.

After O'Donahue left the desert he moved to the mountainous region near Butte Falls, Oregon, where he developed mining property. While there, and still living alone, he studied other forms of wildlife. In 1937, after a stay at Medford, he put down stakes at Klamath Falls, where he began his rescue operations.

"I was fortunate in having a wonderful opportunity to study nature and to learn to appreciate the value of conservation," he told me as we strolled in front of his home, at the edge of Klamath Falls. "I now have a thoroughly satisfying time working with the homeless and injured wild birds and animals."

With a twinkle in his soft brown eyes, O'Donahue remarked that business was "only fair" during his first years in Klamath Falls. But ten years after his arrival volume picked up considerably because of botulism. "I must have worked with more than five or six hundred sick birds during each of the bad years," he recalled.

His efforts in that trying period attracted widespread attention around Klamath Falls. Conservation-minded people, from state policemen to ranchers, brought him helpless birds and animals found throughout the county.

Inhabitants of the half-acre field included, in addition to birds, fawns considered lost by naive hunters, crippled does and bucks, half-starved coyotes, beavers and skunks.

In the beginning, all of the money for his convalescent and feeding program came out of his own pocket. Until the end he bore the brunt of the cost but during the last years was aided by several persons and agencies.

Although his spreading of grain had undoubtedly prevented starvation, perhaps on a large scale, during the worst of the hungry seasons, he was best known for his unique rescue operations. The genial samaritan made 15 to 20 trips yearly to the Tulelake Wildlife Refuge, the giant Labrador, King, at his side. Man and dog proceeded cautiously, fearful for their lives. "I won't go among hunters," said O'Donahue. "I stay clear of them, and out in the open. I don't want to be shot."

Years of searching for wounded birds had given O'Donahue rare insight into bird movement and psychology. He noted, as we sauntered up and down the street in our shirt sleeves, "Generally, when a bird is winged it may go a mile and a half or two miles before the wing collapses and the bird comes down. Until the wing collapses the bird never knows how bad off it is.

"Hunting for wounded birds becomes the easiest thing. Birds gather together when hurt—the same as humans. I've seen as many as forty-five geese in a single band, all crippled, on water, all unable to fly. In time, the wounded birds get together, finding each other from all the birds in the band. The misfit that can't fly wants company, and the birds gradually drift together. King can tell a crippled bird from a distance—must better than I can."

In his almost quarter century of caring for 5,000 birds and about 100 animals, O'Donahue had come to some definite opinions. On the subject of gratitude, he said: "I think birds vary just like humans, even in species. Some animals, I think, will show gratitude quicker than birds. There is a variation in temperament that is hard to explain. The white pelican is the one bird that shows immediately that he realizes he is being cared for."

Although O'Donahue loved all of the wildlife creatures he had handled, he was partial to hawks, owls and eagles. "They are the finest things outdoors," he declared. "Personally, I consider they are the most beneficial of all our birds. In the balance of nature they are the most valuable."

He had some ideas about conservation, too: "Habitat comes first. Conserve your land and water and you conserve your game. I'm not one who thinks just on conserving birds and tearing up land. That's pretty narrow. Conservation is a unified thing."

As we walked up and down the street, filling with houses, King followed O'Donahue, shuffling along lazily. Several times I called to the dog, but apart from a vacant glance out of the corner of his eye he ignored me. He sloughed off every attempt I made to photograph him, angling off as I focused my camera in his direction.

"King is indifferent to publicity," O'Donahue explained with a smile. "The people who invite me to talk to their groups always insist I take King along. Some of them treat him as the star attraction. But King just lies down and snoozes. There was a picture in *Life* magazine of both of us on a platform. I was talking and King was sound asleep."

However, with O'Donahue's hand on King's collar, the dog stood still. I took several photos. All but one showed King yawning.

O'Donahue's work excited me and I wanted to write an article that would bring him wider support than he had been receiving.

"Don't," he advised. "My work is through."

I was bewildered. "What do you mean?"

"Civilization is closing in on me," O'Donahue said in a very low voice. He spoke vaguely of what had happened. I gathered that the street he lived on was taking on the characteristics of suburbia and there had been objections from some people about all the birds and their noises. His neighbors didn't think it befitted a respectable middle class neighborhood.

"So I'm subdividing," O'Donahue said. "Selling land for homes."

"But you could move somewhere else, out in the country," I prodded.

O'Donahue sighed. "Too old." He patted King. "We've had it."

We walked silently to my car. "I feel very sad," I told him. "I really do."

"So do I," replied O'Donahue. "But you can't stand in the way of progress."

He said it grimly, I thought. Then he shook hands, his eyes past me, and turned for home, King nodding at his heels.

Don Kennedy

The Admirals Were Bug-Eyed

For years I had picked up bits of fascinating information on Don Kennedy, now executive vice-president of White Stag Manufacturing Company. The details—an item here and an item there, and some of them contradicting each other—had to do with a remarkable little tale of World War II; how young Don Kennedy had been named personal aide to Third Fleet Admiral William F. "'Bull" Halsey, the legendary sea dog of the Pacific.

One day it occurred to me that the simplest way to get the story full and straight was to ask Don Kennedy. He was delighted. "Tell you what," he offered, "I'll write it myself and send it to you. You'll have it in a week." Realizing how busy he was, probably spending more time in planes than in his office or home bed, I made a note to remind him in a month of his promise. But long before then the story was in my hands.

I have done very little editing. Some of the jargon will be familiar only to Navy people, but I don't think this hinders the flow of the story.

The tale that follows is told in Don Kennedy's words:

It all happened fast.

It was on a hot and humid day in April, 1944, in the radio shack of the headquarters of the Commander of the South Pacific (COMSOPAC). I had just finished a 6 a.m. to noon communications watch and decided to stick around and read some of the dispatches. It was a little cooler in the shack anyway. After turning the afternoon shift over to the new CWO (Communications Watch Officer) I went into the radio sending room to talk to the Chief.

From topside, the Admiral's office, came a "Top Secret —Urgent" dispatch marked *"O"*—meaning go-go-fast, and it was beamed to MacArthur as the action addressee.

I read the dispatch over the shoulder of the new watch officer and we smiled and both knew Halsey was *upset,* and told MacArthur so, concerning Halsey's plan to start island hopping toward the Philippines and thus save a lot of time, a lot of lives and a lot of ships which we did not want to lose. CINPAC (Commander in Chief of the Pacific) Nimitz's logistic department was dragging its feet. Halsey and Carney, his Chief of Staff, later Chief of Naval Operations in Washington, wanted MacArthur's support and usually got it. Halsey had not heard from the General by a previous priority dispatch and Halsey was puzzled. Obviously, MacArthur's staff was giving it some study. Halsey's "Urgent" was, as sometimes he was, a bit impatient. He was also sometimes inclined to write a little humor or "dig" into his dispatches. He had done it in this one!

The *"O* Urgent" was coded and run back for accuracy and the heading was applied and into the radio shack it went for urgent sending. We gulped and said: "Fireworks are about to start."

At that precise moment a radio man said 2TK is getting a priority from COMGENPAC MacArthur. Navy regulations won't let an *"O* Urgent" dispatch be delayed one second by anybody but the originator, so even as a priority came in, the "Urgent" had to go out. Who knows, I thought, they're probably on different subjects anyway.

As I was in charge of the Top Secret Codes and dispatches, I just happened to be familiar with the history of this island hopping plan.

I said to the CEVO: "We'd better read this Top Secret priority before we send the 'Urgent'." He said: "Do you want to get sent to Green Island?" (Green Island, a communications unit outpost, had a reputation as being the last place a communications officer wanted to go!) It was his watch shift, not mine, so theoretically I could have cared less. But somehow I did! I had a premonition! I grabbed the type-up as it came out and went over to the radio man who was starting to send the "Urgent" and I said, "This is Top Secret, hold that 'Urgent.' I take the responsibility for the delay." I knew that if I could break the MacArthur message the first time I put it through the coding machine not much time would be lost. The radio man gulped. He seemed stunned. But I knew him from some softball games we played, and he held up.

I was lucky. The long dispatch from MacArthur broke the first time. It was in no uncertain words, and opened with, "I agree with your plan, Halsey. If CINPAC won't go along I'll fly to Washington to see King and Roosevelt if necessary." (King was the top naval commander.) I came out of the code room on the double, tape flying behind me, and dashed into the radio room, calling, "Give me that 'Urgent', I'm going up to see Admiral Halsey. We have the answers and he won't want to send this now."

The radio man didn't say a word. He didn't hand it to me; I just took it and the CEVO on watch just nodded, and up the ladder (stairs) I flew. Halfway up I realized I had never met the Admiral before. Well—here goes.

I ran up to the guard on duty and exclaimed: "I must see the Admiral or his Chief of Staff (Rear Admiral Carney). Urgent!"

In the guard took me. Carney, a brilliant, wonderful man, looked up from behind his glasses as I saluted and announced, "Sir, Lieutenant Kennedy, CWO. I have a Top Secret tape from General MacArthur. I believe you will want to see it immediately. I have not taken the time to paste it up, I thought you would want to see it pronto."

Mick Carney called, "Admiral Bill, MacArthur finally replied!" and the Admiral came rushing in, all serious as get out. By this time I had gotten out of attention and was spreading the tape. They were bug-eyed!

The message had quite a few code words and the Admiral bellowed, "Get someone to bring up that new fancy Top Secret book with the Codes!" It just so happened that that fancy book was my innovation, but the Admiral didn't know it! He always liked the book and the way it was improved over the old folder pile of junk. I said: "Admiral, I know the codes, the book isn't necessary," and proceeded to tell him what they were. (Cactus stood for Guadalcanal, etc.) He sort of opened his eyes and said, "Okay, what the hell do they mean?" I told him and the message made sense. Halsey and Carney said at once, "Oh goddammit, we're in the soup again now by sending that damn 'Urgent' dispatch. Why the hell didn't we wait!" Halsey took the blame but Carney tried to lessen it by saying it was his idea.

I was a little white at this point. I didn't know whether I had done the right thing or would get shot. I said, screwing up my courage: "Admiral, sir, could I speak for a moment?" He turned and nodded. "Go ahead, young fellow." Very stern, but kindly. He was a man with a great heart and the most lovable, hard fighting person I ever knew. I got to know him like an Uncle Bill as time went on.

"Admiral, Sir, I was in the radio room just off watch; I hung around after my morning watch to check a few urgent Top Secrets. As I coded your 'Urgent' to MacArthur and was about to send it, this dispatch started coming in from the General. I just thought, Sir, it might be the answer to your first message," and holding up the "Urgent" dispatch, said: "Sir, I took the liberty of holding this 'Urgent' message. It has not been sent. I take the responsibility. Shall I send it now?" I knew he would answer "HELL NO!" and he did. Then they both just stared at me! It seemed a week but was only seconds. Admiral Carney then said: "Thank God— good thinking, young man—God damn good clear thinking." Halsey added: "Thank God someone thinks around here."

They laughed, ordered me some coffee, and kidded me a bit. They asked my name again, where I was from—and seemed really congenial. At least I wasn't to be sent to Green Island. Carney was scribbling out a dispatch reply and the first one was given the deep six (waste basket). He said, "Kennedy, get a coding officer up here." I replied: "I am one." He said, "Can you type?" I said yes, so he started to dictate. I wrote the message and he said, "This one you be sure you send and don't pull this one off the air. It's against Navy regulations. You want to live a long time." He was completely sober. Then he broke into a wide grin, put his arm around me, and said, "We appreciate your alertness, you saved us from a mess." I left—and away the happy reply went!

Next morning I had an early call that Admirals Halsey and Carney wanted to see me. I grabbed the Top Secret book and left on a dead run.

Into their office I marched and stood at attention. Admiral Halsey said, "I understand that book is your doing. I just want to tell you I like it, but how in hell did you know all those code names?" I replied, "I just memorized them, Sir. I just thought that sometime, because of security, we might get separated from the book." Halsey exclaimed: "That answers that! We want you here; I never could remember those code names anyhow."

Carney said, "I want to congratulate you on that total job you did yesterday. I've checked you out and we are having a desk moved into my office and you'll be my aide and assistant to the Chief of Staff and handle all Top Secrets—just like you apparently have been."

Three days later, Admiral Bill, Admiral Mick, Lt. Commander Harold Stassen, Lt. Bill Kitchell and I flew to San Francisco for a Top Secret meeting with Admiral King, Admiral Nimitz, Secretary of the Navy Forrestal, and the lot. I had been away from home for 16 months—and what a break! All because of one dispatch! And you know what? We spent three days in San Francisco.

My wife and two-year-old son were visiting in McCook Nebraska. If you will remember, in those days it took weeks to get an airline priority. Admiral Halsey asked me on the plane from the South Pacific to San Francisco, would I get to see my wife and kid. I told him of the problem. He said no more, but that evening he had me at Mills Field, with a Navy car picking them up. He flew them to me—what a guy!

My experience from this date as an aide to these two great leaders was the most rewarding and exciting of my life.

Bob Lee

What a Man Was Grandfather

Robert Ormond Lee, the Georgia-Pacific executive, has climbed and explored on six continents but he would rather talk about his forbears.

He has surmounted the Singalila Ridge in the Kanchenjunga area of Nepal, Sikkim and Tibet; conquered 18,700-foot Orizaba, in south-central Mexico; paddled a dugout up the ghostly Rio Para deep into the "Green Hell" of the Amazon; led an expedition across the jungle of Quintana Roo in Yucatan and, on the milder side, gone to the top of every snow peak in the Northwest.

You would think that Bob Lee's experiences would provide a fascinating story but Bob, an intense, introspective man with a quixotic streak sometimes protruding through an imperious layer of iron discipline, thinks otherwise.

"My ancestors were very interesting people. You should write about them," he quietly insists.

What he says of his lineage is undoubtedly true. You can find in his family tree a Chief of a Welsh clan, a bishop in the Church of England, a captain in the English Army who participated in the "Charge of the Light Brigade," cotton merchants trading with India and China, and a soprano soloist for Queen Victoria.

But the most absorbing, emphasizes Bob Lee, was his paternal grandfather, Robert Charlton Lee, who is still remembered in Eastern Oregon as a brimstone-and-fire preacher hell-bent on exiling vice from the provinces where he betook himself.

Let me tell you what I learned of Robert Charlton Lee and see if the old man is not worth a book.

At 14 he entered Owens College, in Manchester, England. At 16 he was enrolled at Christ Church College, Oxford where he studied natural sciences and physics under the great Sir Thomas Huxley. He was there also a pupil of the eminent art teacher, Professor Dow, and Grandfather Lee's water colors were exhibited at South Kensington Museum, London, and Agnew Galleries in Manchester and London. On the side, he took private piano lessons, which he had started when he was seven years old. And, with all this, he acquired mastery of seven languages.

At the age of 19 Robert Charlton Lee graduated with a degree in Theology. Two months later he was to have been ordained a priest, but a gypsy breeze in him was too restless. So he hied himself off to London where his father had him apprenticed to the Black Ball Line.

In three years he passed an examination and became a Third Mate. Ten months later he met the requirements for a Second Mate's papers. He was hardly 27 when he received his Master's certificate and his own ship. For 13 years he was a deep-sea salt. Then he ran up and down the Pacific Coast for several years, until he retired to go into the real estate business in Seattle.

The mariner Lee led no somnolent life. He shipped on all the seven seas, calling at any port where cargo was billed for unloading or might be obtainable. Seven times he rounded Cape Horn. He was First Mate on the sturdy *Dumbarton* that chased slave ships off the Mozambique River on the Zanzibar Coast. The Ashanti War came on and the English government offered a bounty of 5,000 pounds for the capture of any slave vessel and 500 pounds for the seizure of any slave dhow, a flat-bottomed boat that supplied the larger vessels. The *Dumbarton* captured several large ships and many dhows, and Lee shared in the rewards.

He was skipper of the coal-bearing *Memnon* when it ran from Cardiff to Callao, Iquiqui and Valparaiso on the west coast of South America. On one trip he was witness to the great earthquake and tidal wave at Iquiqui which took a toll of a thousand lives. About 60 vessels were waiting there for nitrates and many were swept onto the beaches. But the *Memnon,* lunging for the open sea, escaped the catastrophe.

The panic of 1893 ended his real estate career in Seattle and, at the suggestion of the presiding elder of the Methodist Church there, he embarked upon a career of preaching. His first pulpit was at Sequim; then he moved to Dungeness, where he built the first church in that crab village.

After a turn at South Bend, Lee went on to Marshfield, in 1900, and founded the first Methodist Church in Coos County.

By now he had a family and needed stronger financial plankings than the church could provide. So, together with a man named Charles Grissen, he opened a store stocked with musical instruments, chinaware and curios. But the pace was too slow to match his restless nature and his moral indignation. After four years he sold out and returned to Seattle. Henceforth his life was to be spent in the ministry.

It began, this second and final phase of his church career, with conducting evangelistic services, under Methodist auspices, in Portland, Walla Walla, Spokane and other cities. While at Portland, giving sermons at Epworth Church, he was asked to shift his base to Eastern Oregon. He complied and his parsonages thereafter were in the small, unvarnished rip-roaring railroad and mining towns of Huntington, Sumpter, Haines, Union, all in Oregon, and Weiser, Idaho. He spent ten years at Union, a long time for a man on the go, and is buried there, though he died, in 1948, at the ripe old age of 96, in the Pythian Home at Vancouver, Wash.

Grandfather Lee had a penchant for boldly confronting what he considered to be the cesspools of sin. In particular, he declared war upon the saloon and the dance hall. A typical campaign was fought out in Huntington, which then enjoyed the distinction of being "one of the most wide-open towns in the West, with gambling tables and dancing halls defying all civic law."

Soon after taking up his ministerial duties in Huntington, he commenced a series of sermons "with the object of destroying sin." His Sunday services brought out large audiences. His attacks were not personal, however, and on many occasions every saloon keeper was present in his congregation. When the collection plate was passed, these gentlemen proved to be the most liberal donors.

But there were men who resented Lee and surreptitiously fought back. They sent him anonymous letters, threatening violence, and they discharged giant firecrackers about his home at all hours of the night. Soon the faithful of the church became fearful of the safety of their pastor and his family.

One Sunday, when the tension had reached the near breaking point, a few of the faithful were ominously warned that trouble of a serious nature was due to develop in an hour, when the service was scheduled to begin. The word was out: have Lee cancel his sermon.

The admonition swept the town and crowded the church. Lee, who had received the dire message, entered the front door at the usual time for the Sunday evening service, strode down the aisle, mounted the platform, and laid a revolver on each side of the Bible.

"I have been informed," he declared in measured words, "that there might be trouble here this evening. All I desire is that in any case of any disturbance whatsoever, I do not want anyone to arise in their seat. You might be unintentionally injured."

According to the old and unspecified press dispatch, from which I have been quoting, "The sermon proceeded and the best of decorum prevailed."

Bob Lee has had this clipping for many years. It was given him by his grandfather. It tells, also, of the time the Huntington gamblers tried—vainly, of course—to bribe the preacher. Several hundred dollars would be delivered to him each month if he directed his "assault on other matters than the open saloons, gambling tables and dance halls."

"It proved," stated the reporter who penned the article, "that the enemy were becoming disturbed."

Now that the issue became personal the battle lines were joined—the forces of good versus the forces of bad. The choice was clear: destroy or be destroyed. The Day of Judgment was at hand and its outcome was detailed in the juiciest part of the dispatch.

Governor Oswald West, at Lee's invitation, came to Huntington to help the reverend clean up the town. West had offered the Oregon Militia but Lee countered that the presence of the governor himself would suffice. The article tells what happened:

"About 11 o'clock in the evening the two entered a dance hall when the music was at its heighth. Glasses were clicking at the bar, dancing girls were swinging their partners, unencumbered by long trailing skirts. The governor took possession and the activities ceased. Within a few minutes the Methodist minister found himself officially in charge of a dance hall with unlimited power, and the governor went to his hotel and retired. The unexpected transition of immediately being placed in charge of a dance hall was another chapter in a long life of varied experiences. His first act was to call the dancing women together and direct them to retire and appear later in proper dress. During this period he made up his mind that he was not going to take over the management of this dance hall, having neither the experience nor inclination, so when the women returned he informed them that he was not used to keeping late hours and that he would probably not get up the next morning until about nine o'clock, and remarked that between six and seven the next morning, passenger trains left the city of Huntington going either east or west, and upon his return in the morning he would have his plan worked out.

"Inquiry the next morning secured the information that all the women had purchased tickets for outside points and that the proprietor of the dance hall had placed a padlock on the establishment. Governor West returned to his official duties at Salem. The moral atmosphere in and about Huntington began to clarify and from that day to this Huntington has been a much better city in which to live."

The reverend must have looked like a little giant, five feet tall and stocky. Bob Lee described him as "A runt of a man but one of those iron men in wooden ships." My image of him was, physically and philosophically, that of a fire hydrant, ready to gush the cold water of wrath on the fire of evil. That is, evil as he saw it and wrath as he could get away with it in his time. Today, any minister barging into dance halls and taverns to drive out sin would be, at best, regarded as ludicrous. But Robert Charlton Lee lived in a different time and mood.

Bob Lee, a handsome man of 46 when I spoke to him in the early summer of 1967, was a native of Seattle and had lived in Oregon since 1955. But he felt that Grandfather gave him a slightly larger claim on the state. Also, on Bob's maternal side, a man named Rhodes came across the plains from the Deep South in the 1860s, piloting a Conestoga wagon clear to Tillamook County.

In several senses, Bob Lee is like his grandfather. He has the same wanderlust, the same physical drive, the same yearning to reduce life to neatly packaged abstractions.

"I am much happier out in the bush than I am downtown," Bob Lee mused, in his spacious, handsomely-furnished office. "And I am a more natural man out in the jungle or on a mountain than when I am exposed to a lot of people. Maybe this is because I am dealing with the public twenty-four hours a day and have to get away from people once in a while. I have a large ranch in the upper Hood River Valley where I enjoy going. I would like to be up there all the time. You might say I am introverted in that fashion. I like to get away from civilization. I like the animals. I know the animals. I like the native people, who are kind and simple. When I get away in the jungle I don't know what time of the day it is—or even what day of the week it is. Life is much simpler."

What do you think you would do if you were trapped in an elevator, I asked.

"I am sure I would get impatient." He frowned. "I am not a very patient man!" he stated emphatically.

Are you patient in the bush?

"Yes."

But you say you are not a very patient man.

He put his arm up, as a crutch, and rested his head in its palm. "You have a good point," he said indifferently.

Do you ever get afraid while driving down the highway?

"Yes, definitely."

Do you feel safer in the jungle than walking on the streets at night?

"I think that you probably are safer in the jungle than walking through many parts of big cities."

What is the one thing that you have most in common with your Grandfather Lee?

"Probably an inquisitive mind and spirit of adventure."

This provided Bob Lee with the opportunity to return to his grandfather, and he added quickly, and proudly, before another question could be launched: "As a small boy I used to go over to Union to visit him. I spent summers over there riding bareback with the Indian boys. He had a parrot named Billy. I also have a parrot. The parrot would say grace and the old man, too, would say grace."

Bob Lee sighed. "He was quite a man. I'm glad you came here, so I could tell you about him."

But I came to do a story on you, I reminded him.

"Sometimes," he said softly, with the first relaxed smile I had noted since I arrived, "a fellow finds better than he expected."

Dave Wilson

"Just to Do a Feller a Favor"

Dave Wilson didn't want to be mayor of Shaniko. "No sirree," he asserted doggedly. "I don't want no part of it."

Lanky and gnarled as a prairie rail that has withstood ages of sun and snow, Dave sat on an old-fashioned straight-back wooden chair set up against the weary hotel and swept his eyes past the ghost of Shaniko and up the vast naked tableland of the central Oregon plateau.

"No sirree," he repeated. "I don't want to be mayor. I wish somebody would tell me how I can get out of this job."

A breeze drifted off the shorn grainfields, whistled thinly as it wriggled through the sage tufting between the ancient livery stables and the deserted warehouses, swept up some dirt and pebbles as it crossed the street, and rose to nudge the hotel sign reading: Family style meals. Adults $1. Children 50 cents.

"I tried to resign but they won't let me," Dave said, fisting up the brim of his old hat and thumbing through a patch of white stubble that curved around his head. On top he was gleaming bald.

"The Wasco County district attorney came up here once and I asked him what to do," he went on. "He said I couldn't do anything until the town gets another mayor. But nobody wants the job."

Dave Wilson, 77, rubbed tobacco into his pipe, lighted up, put the pipe aside, and talked about his troubles.

"I became mayor just to do a feller a favor. He wanted to quit. I said I'd be mayor one year. The year's up. I resigned, but nobody wants to accept it. It's been mighty tough trying to quit, I tell you.

"There's only thirty-nine people in Shaniko," Wilson continued, pondering through a frown. "No judge, no policeman, no school. The only paid official is the city recorder, the man who runs the gas station. He gets ten dollars a month, being recorder.

"The city gets its money from the water system. The mayor is supposed to tend the water system, but I don't know anything about running that. Service station feller takes care of it.

"We're incorporated. Have been for a long time. The charter calls for city council of five, but we have only three —two women and a man. Women run this town."

There ought to have been some honor in being mayor of Shaniko, Oregon's most picturesque "ghost town." Sixty years before old Dave had been saddled with the job of mayor, like a retired plow horse being taken out of pasture to haul a milk wagon, which it had never done before, Shaniko was the greatest wool-shipping center in the world. It boasted a population of more than 1,000—a sizable number in that part of the state in those days—with drug stores, livery stables, a department store, two hotels and nine saloons. And it was the terminus of the only railroad into "interior" Oregon.

Cow hands and sheep herders whooped it up in the saloons, with red eye a dime a toss and black eyes free for the asking. Freight wagons, drawn by six- and eight-horse teams, cluttered the streets. And Indians, who named the town, pronouncing best as they could the cumbrous last name of pioneer settler August Schernackau, serpentined through the hurly-burly streets to the prairie, to dig for camas roots.

Dave Wilson homesteaded near Shaniko in 1908, two years before a bigger railroad came up the Deschutes canyon, bypassing the town. Thereafter, wool, cattle and grain went down the other line. Shaniko faded and in 1925, when a highway was built through central Oregon, its mirage-dream of revival was put to sleep for good.

The highway—U.S. 97—zipped past the outskirts of Shaniko, and not one in a thousand tourist cars paused to see the once proud, brawling town that had become a ghostly piece of history.

The Shaniko Hotel, built in 1902 as the Columbia Southern, "Queen of the Hostelries," was still open, but the scarecrow-looking city hall had been boarded up for years.

Dave Wilson denied Shaniko was a ghost town. "We've got people here," he insisted stubbornly. "We're still incorporated. But," he added, his voice trailing off, "there's not enough here to do anything."

He tamped his pipe and gave it fire again.

"I wish somebody would tell me how I can resign," he muttered plaintively, kicking a pebble in the direction of the water trough that drowsed in front of the hotel. "I just became mayor to do a feller a favor. I'm not cut out to be a politician."

John Crow

One Fall Too Many

At the age of 61 John Crow fell off a horse and broke his back. It wasn't the first time he had fallen off a horse but it was the first time he had broken his back and it put an end to his cowpunching career.

A year after the bad spill we found Johnny Crow and his wife in a small frame house on a gravel side street in Burns. Johnny was getting around, all right, but in a stiffish sort of way. By and by he'd make a fine pedestrian. He and his missus didn't have very much to do except chat with folks who came by, drive downtown now and then, or watch television. They could sit in their little living room watching television for hours on end, but one kind of program they shunned was the Western. "Too phoney," said Johnny simply.

John Crow was a man who could tell you a thing or two about cowpunchers and cattle drives. His father had been a *vaquero* for the legendary Pete French, and when French was slain, Johnny's father, Dave, rode from Sod House clear to Winnemucca, Nevada, the nearest telegraph office, to send the news of French's killing to the Glenn family, Pete's partner. Johnny's father, Dave Crow, changed horses nine times before he reached Winnemucca.

When Johnny was three his father lifted him up and set him down in a saddle buckled over a placid pony and taught him how to ride and after that he trailed his dad around the Crow homestead, 80 miles south of Burns.

Johnny was in the middle of his teens when he became a full-fledged cowpuncher. He was still going strong 45 years later when that nasty fall put him out of commission.

What was an ordinary day like for a buckaroo when

you were young, I asked. What did you do from the time you awoke until you went to bed?

His cheeks, which still bore traces of youth, kneaded under a stroke of laughter. "*If* you went to bed! Sometimes we didn't, you know. Well, when we was at the P-Ranch, we had breakfast about five-thirty, go out and work cattle till about two or three o'clock usually, and come in and the cook would fix us a lunch. Then we might rest the rest of the day."

What did he mean by working cattle? He shook his lean, graying head a bit sadly. What a dude, he must have thought. Actually, I have been around cattle ranches long enough to know what the term means, but I figured that maybe some of our readers might be greenhorns, and I wanted to get the explanation straight from the horseman's mouth.

He shrugged his shoulders, as though he might as well get this chore over with, and ambled into explanation. "They might have a lot of cattle on hay and part of them would be poor. We'd go out and work out the thin ones, and put 'em on better feed. And we'd wean the calves away from their mothers, at weaning time. Around December, January."

When roundup time arrived, Johnny and the other cowpunchers took to the hills where the cattle were. "We used to go with the wagon. The buckaroo wagon. We stayed wherever we was camped. Then we'd move the wagon from one range to another. We'd sleep in tents, and around the wagons sometimes without any tents."

He had settled his spare frame snugly in an old upholstered chair but when I asked him if he had ever been caught in a stampede he lurched forward and snorted: "Never saw one but we couldn't stop 'em. That stuff on television, they goose the cattle and start 'em runnin'."

Was life pretty exciting as a cowpuncher or was it generally pretty much of a work-a-day existence?

"Well," said Johnny thoughtfully, "it was exciting at times. Part of the boys rode broncos and sometimes they'd get bucked off. Horse get away from 'em. We'd have to catch 'em, and bring 'em back. It was exciting at times, but at times it was just everyday work.

"We worked every day. Oh, sometimes we'd go to dances at Diamond, the Narrows and Catlow Valley."

I hear some of the dances lasted all night, I commented.

"Oh, yeah, and half the next day sometimes," and threw his head back and laughed.

He added that the dances sometimes got a little rough— "a few fights now and then," but it wasn't often that anyone started shooting, and for some reason he laughed again. Then he said quietly: "I never saw much shooting. That wasn't an every day deal. The outfits I worked for never carried guns."

Most literature dealing with the interesting occupations of people, including those as supposedly romantic as cowboys, neglect to mention details of living which I believe would add more substance to the literary accounts. Food, for example. I asked Johnny what he normally ate at the P-Ranch.

"Just an ordinary breakfast," he replied. "Usually beef steak, potatoes and hot cakes, eggs, sometimes biscuits, gravy." For lunch—"just something plain," usually meat and bread. And a "light" supper—beans, potatoes, meat and bread.

The longest drive Johnny was on ran from Sod House to Klamath Marsh. Or maybe, he guessed, from Burns to the other side of Lakeview. The drive was interesting but it could get tiring, he declared. You rode all day, eating your share of dust, and after you bedded the cattle down you'd grab some shuteye, but not too much. Part of the crew would guard in the forepart of the night and at midnight there would be a change of shifts.

A famous old cowboy, the late Charlie Demick, of Alturas, California, whom every old-time cowpoke in the Western cattle country had at least heard about, once told me that his buckaroos never sang around the cattle at night because it made them nervous. I asked Johnny about this and he replied: "Well, that'd depend on how you felt." It was a hazy answer and I tried the question another way but the reply was just as vague. What I gathered he meant was that some cowboys sang around the cattle but if they sounded nervous the cattle got jittery.

The buckaroo of 40 and 50 years ago didn't get into

town often, Johnny said. "Maybe once 'n two or three months." But wherever he went, "everyone was friendly. We never had any enemies, you might say, much. You was welcome at pretty near every house. The latch string was always out."

Johnny Crow's wages at the P-Ranch were $30 a month and board. It was enough to keep him going, and if he had to live life over again he didn't think he would do it much differently.

"I might make a few short cuts here and there," he reckoned. And one thing he would never do, if he had his way, was to fall off a horse at the age of 61 and break his back. Because a buckaroo who can't ride isn't much good around cattle, and cow-punching was Johnny Crow's life.

When Dave Crow, John's father, was an old man, he dictated to John's wife an account of what he called the "Pete French Shooting." John Crow and his wife made us a copy of the original transcript. With very minor editing, it is fully presented.

"We moved from Buena Vista to Sod House on Christmas Day, 1897. The next morning, December 26, we rode to Rockyford Lane to move 2,000 head of cows and calves into the Wright Field. Pete French rode ahead of the cows to open the gate into the Wright Field. Oliver met him at the gate. After an apparent exchange of words, Pete returned to the cows. Oliver shot him behind the right ear and left by way of the west side of Sagebrush Field.

"Emanuel Clark was the first [of the seven men riding with Pete French that day] to reach French, who had been fatally shot. Bert French, Pete's brother, was second to get to him. I rode up as Pete died. Bert, by his side, was trying to get him to speak, but it was too late. This happened at 2 p.m., on December 26, 1897.

"I rode from the scene to the P-Ranch and on to Winnemucca, Nevada to take the message of Pete's death. I was to send a telegram to the Glenn Boys in Chico, California. (At this time there were no telephones in the area. The nearest, at Canyon City, was connected to the telegraph at

Baker, Oregon. A man was sent each way to be sure one would get word to the Glenns.)

"I changed horses at P-Ranch and rode to Roaring Springs Ranch in Catlow Valley. A change of horses there took me on to Spangleburger Ranch. Here I slept two-and-a-half hours, then went to Field Station. Another change of horses and I headed out for Colony. On my way I met Melvin Doan, Sam Hall and Bill Goar. Because this last horse only wanted to buck and not travel, I traded with Melvin Doan. I rode this horse to Denio. Here Ed Bell gave me a horse to ride to Quinn River Crossing. The next stop was a place called Sodhouse. Here I again slept for two-and-a-half hours. I changed horses and rode off for Paradise Hill.

"When I rode into a dark barn at Paradise Hill I stepped off my horse onto an old sow with little pigs. She had covered herself with hay and did not take kindly to being roused. It did not take long to get into the manger. The only fresh horse here was a small Indian pony hitched to a horse power water pump. This pony carried me into Winnemucca just at 2 p.m., 48 hours after the shooting. I sent a wire to the Glenns, at Chico.

"Bert French went to Burns, where he hired a man to go to Canyon City, 70 miles away. At Canyon City they telephoned to Baker, and from Baker a telegram was sent to Chico. Though the distance I rode was much longer, my wire was received only an hour later than the one from Baker."

Index

MOONTRAP
Don Berry

A haunting novel of the Willamette Valley and the mountain men who came down to settle there.

"a tough, stark story; The whole book is rich with history glancingly told, vivid frontier lore, alive with the look and feel and smell of the wilderness. Characters are splendidly drawn . . . honest, vital and true."

—Hal Borland
New York Times

$1.25

A COMSTOCK EDITION

To order by mail, send price of book plus 10¢ for handling to Dept. CS, Ballantine Books, 36 West 20th Street, New York, N.Y. 10003.

The Western Frontier
1822-1834

A MAJORITY OF SCOUNDRELS

Don Berry

The authentic and provocative story of the legendary trader-trappers of the Rocky Mountain Fur Company. Based on the journals and letters of the participants, A MAJORITY OF SCOUNDRELS is an epic of discovery, yarn-spinning and intrigue told with strength, directness, and a sparkling sense of humor.

$1.25

A COMSTOCK EDITION

To order by mail, send price of book plus 10¢ for handling to Dept. CS, Ballantine Books, 36 West 20th Street, New York, N.Y. 10003.